*Twayne's English Authors Series*

EDITOR OF THIS VOLUME

Kinley E. Roby
*Northeastern University*

*Jean Rhys*

TEAS 294

# JEAN RHYS

### By PETER WOLFE
*University of Missouri, St. Louis*

**TWAYNE PUBLISHERS**
A DIVISION OF G. K. HALL & CO., BOSTON

Published in 1980 by Twayne Publishers,
A Division of G. K. Hall & Co.
All Rights Reserved

Printed on permanent/durable acid-free paper and bound
in the United States of America

*First Printing*

Frontispiece photo of Jean Rhys © by Fay Godwin, London

**Library of Congress Cataloging in Publication Data**

Wolfe, Peter, 1933–
Jean Rhys.

(Twayne's English authors series; TEAS 294)
Bibliography: p. 182–83
Includes index.
1. Rhys, Jean
Criticism and interpretation.
PR6035.H96Z94      823'.912      79–27739
ISBN 0-8057-6698-7

To
James S. Davis
Pfc., U.S. Army (4th Ordnance Company), Miesau, Germany, 1958–
59("Who's Domizia?")
His fame was born 6 km. from Breda

# Contents

# *About the Author*

Born in New York City, Peter Wolfe received his B.A. from the City College of New York, his M.A. from Lehigh University, and his Ph.D. from the University of Wisconsin. In 1967, after teaching for three years at the University of Nebraska-Lincoln, he joined the English faculty of the University of Missouri-St. Louis. Since that time, he has held guest professorships at the University of Windsor (Ontario), UCLA, and the University of Waikato (New Zealand). In 1971, he chaired the Modern Literature section of the MLA, and in 1975, he won a grant from the National Endowment for the Humanities. Besides reviewing for *Saturday Review, New Republic,* and *New York Times Book Review,* Wolfe has published books on Iris Murdoch (1966), Mary Renault (1969), Rebecca West (1971), Graham Greene (1972), John Fowles (1976), Ross Macdonald (1977), and Dashiell Hammett (1980). He is now writing a book on Patrick White.

# *Preface*

Jean Rhys's work developed considerably in the course of a publishing career spanning some fifty years. Miss Rhys also wrote in a variety of voices and evolved a variety of narrative techniques. At the same time, her novels and short stories cohere powerfully when treated as a whole. The critical aim of this book is threefold: to seek the unity of individual works, to define her artistry through her whole development, and to compare this development to that of other women fiction writers of our century.

Writing the book taught me several things: which elements unify the Rhys canon; what impulses prompted the canon's composition; why, after years of neglect, she has emerged, especially in feminist circles, as an admired novelist; how her remarkable novels and stories are best read; finally, where this work stands relative to that of other British women who produce fiction. Fortunately, her small output enables us both to drive into the text in order to analyze structure, symbolism, and style, and to let the text stir the soul. We can honor both inner light and details of formal composition in her seven short books.

Each one of these books disturbs as it rouses. Jean Rhys has performed in her fiction the rare feat of writing good books about dull characters trapped in numbing routines. Her main contribution to modern literature consists of the shrewd yet sympathetic look she takes at a character type heretofore ignored, patronized, or used merely to flesh out a social category—the dispossessed urban spinster. No liberal-humanist heroine, the archetypal Rhys figure lacks ideas, job, and man.

I have tried to work out her importance by exploring both her character and her changing relationship to an indifferent or hostile society. These concerns are both familiar and strange to the average reader. They are familiar because Jean Rhys records the thoughts, trials, and emotions of the inner life with almost shocking accuracy and honesty. Strangeness comes from the distance dividing the heroines from habitual patterns of familial and social behavior; like its main figures, Jean Rhys's work stands apart from the secular tradition of social or journalistic realism. Along with other writers of

her day, she has helped evolve a feminine counterpart to realistic fiction, that by-product of the male secularism that has ruled Western culture since the Victorian age. My last chapter shows how she and these others have advanced novelistic frontiers. The New Zealander Katherine Mansfield, the English native Dorothy Richardson, the Persian-born and Southern Rhodesia-reared Doris Lessing, and the West Indian creole of Welsh ancestry, Jean Rhys, all write from a female standpoint. All write with a civilizing purpose, as well, which shows in their psychological accuracy and the concern they share in improving the man-woman relationship.

The straight chronological approach I have adopted to study the Rhys canon lends this civilizing purpose some coherence and direction. As several critics have said, all the Rhys novels center on the same woman at different times in her life. Thus my approach allows for a developing character study with the appropriate foreshadowings, reverberations, and connections. There is more to the novels than their heroines. Most confessional writing—writing in which the narrating self and the experiencing self tend to merge—has trouble maintaining balance: a passionately engaged narrator will overshadow a supporting cast of cardboard cutouts. Jean Rhys is too much the artist to make this mistake. And artistry of any worth demands organization and control. In relating the Rhys heroine to her background, therefore, my study also surveys narrative technique. Once again, the chronological approach reaps gains, fulfilling the aim of revealing Jean Rhys as a developing artist. The technical mastery of her maturity has its roots in early books like *Quartet* (1928) and *After Leaving Mr. Mackenzie* (1930). What distinguishes these works from their more polished successors is, chiefly, grip. The technical control of Jean Rhys's later phase strengthens her vision while sharpening her narrative economy. I have tried to convey this blend of form and content by comparing the novels structurally, by showing how each novel uses the city, and by explaining how the manipulation of point of view helps express Jean Rhys's attitudes more clearly and fully as the canon builds.

The time and energy of several people besides me went into the writing of this book. Special thanks are owing to Jean Rhys's step-daughter, my fellow St. Louisan Phyllis Smyser, for supplying rich background data; to Barbara Bullock, for typing and proofreading the manuscript; to Elgin Mellown, for important bibliographical help; and to the University of Missouri–St. Louis Graduate College for grants to cover expenses connected with the manuscript's preparation.

*Preface*

Author and publisher join hands in expressing their thanks for permission to quote copyrighted passages to the following: from *Quartet, After Leaving Mr. Mackenzie, Good Morning, Midnight, Tigers Are Better-looking,* and *Sleep It Off, Lady,* by permission of Harper and Row, Publishers; from *Voyage in the Dark* and *Wide Sargasso Sea,* by permission of W. W. Norton and Company, Publishers.

The combined help of the following people amounts to a major contribution: Gertrude Iwamoto, Gini Stevens, Max Kolsky, Roland Champagne, Syl Pegram, Eugene Hammond, Miguel Tafoya, Bob Hamilton, Howard Schwartz, and Kitt Pledger.

PETER WOLFE

*University of Missouri, St. Louis*

# Chronology

1894 Jean Williams born 24 August in Roseau, Dominica, the West Indies; one of five children born to Dr. William Rhys and Minna (née Lockhart) Williams.

1910 Emigrates to England to study acting at the Royal Academy of Dramatic Art.

1919 Marries French-Dutch songwriter and journalist Jean Langlet and goes to live on the Continent.

1922 Daughter, Maryvonne, born in Brussels.

1927 Divorces Langlet; returns to England; publication of *The Left Bank and Other Stories*.

1928 *Quartet*; entitled *Postures* in the United Kingdom.

1930 *After Leaving Mr. Mackenzie*.

1934 *Voyage in the Dark*.

1938 Marries Leslie Tilden-Smith, a publisher's reader, and settles in Cornwall.

1939 *Good Morning, Midnight*.

1945 Death of Tilden-Smith.

1946 Marries poet and retired naval officer Max Hamer.

1958 BBC dramatizes *Good Morning, Midnight*.

1961 Moves from Cornwall to Devon.

1966 *Wide Sargasso Sea*; elected a Fellow of the Royal Society of Literature.

1967 Wins the W. H. Smith £1,000 literary award and the Arts Council of Great Britain Award for Writers, both for *Wide Sargasso Sea*; American publication of *Wide Sargasso Sea*.

1968 *Tigers Are Better-looking*.

1974 American publication of *Tigers Are Better-looking*.

1976 *Sleep It Off Lady*.

1979 Dies, 14 May, at Exeter Hospital, near her Devonshire cottage.

# Down and Out in London and Paris

CRITICS since 1970 or so have been heralding the rediscovery of Jean Rhys. Rediscovery? Although the five books Jean Rhys published between 1927 and 1939 were well received, they also had a small readership. Near-obscurity followed. The books dropped from print during the Second War, and neither they nor their author came to the fore again until 1958. The much heralded Jean Rhys revival is no revival at all, but a long-overdue recognition. Nor has the recognition been that widespread. Lionel Stevenson ignores her in his forty-one-page chapter, "A Group of Able Dames" (Chapter 6), in *The History of the English Novel: Yesterday and After,* XI (New York: Barnes & Noble, 1967). Somewhat more surprisingly, considering her insight into women, she also goes unmentioned in Sydney Janet Kaplan's *Feminine Consciousness in the Modern British Novel* (Urbana: University of Illinois, 1975).

Reviewers have pondered Jean Rhys's failure to win readers. Paul Theroux, an expatriate himself, ascribes her long-standing neglect to her "placelessness": "Writers of nationalities usually get a more sympathetic reaction. Hemingway was a great traveler, but always an American, and Joyce was never thought to be anything but Irish; what about [the Caribbean-born] Miss Rhys? Welsh? West Indian? English?" Other explanations for her longstanding neglect, besides the traditional English obsession with period and place, come to mind. Bypassing issues raised by birth and citizenship, some critics have found her too astringent. In a 1967 review called "A Stark Reserve," Francis Wyndham refers both to her "shattering honesty" and "the uncomfortable truth of her personal vision." Shirley Hazzard follows the same line of thinking; it doesn't make sense to look for sorrow and frustration:

The art of Jean Rhys derives from an acute, even morbid, sensibility and perception.... Her heroines (there are no heroes) embody not so much a

capacity for suffering as a thwarted capacity for joy. . . . These attributes . . .
evoke uneasiness and hostility in contemporary critics.[1]

Advances in women's rights have taught the critics to bite back their
malaise. Before coping with a problem, one must state it correctly;
few writers in English before Jean Rhys have looked so steadily at the
jobless single woman in today's urban society. Jean Rhys wrote about
women before the revolution in birth control gave them freedoms
they had never before enjoyed; her latest short stories home in on
spinsters both unemployable and beyond child-bearing. Yet she has
been taken up as a founding mother of feminism. At the same time,
she transcends women's movements. Her timeliness does not detract
from her artistry. That her understanding of women is more
novelistic than political shows in the praise she has won in literary
circles. The literary establishment slowly made her its darling.
From 1967, she has won the Heinemann Award of the Royal Society
of Literature, the £1,000 W. H. Smith Literary Award, and the £1,200
Council of Great Britain Award for Writers; all her books are back in
print, both in the United Kingdom and the United States; figures like
Shirley Hazzard, V. S. Naipaul, and A. Alvarez have saluted her; she
has been interviewed in the *Guardian*, the *Sunday Observer*, and
*Mademoiselle*; her picture appeared on the cover of the 3 June 1974
number of the *New Review*; her stories are being translated into
French.[2]

But the questions remain as to who she is, what her beliefs are, and
why she writes. Paul Theroux's remark about her mixed heritage
points the way to dovetailing her life and thought. She was born 24
August 1894 in Roseau, Dominica, one of the Leeward Islands in the
Antilles. Her father, William Rhys Williams, a Welsh doctor, had
migrated to the West Indies. Her mother (née Minna Lockhart) came
from a Creole family, i.e., a family that had settled many years before
in the British-owned islands. In 1910, after attending a convent
school in Roseau, Jean went to London with an aunt (the model for
Anna Morgan's rasping Aunt Hester in *Voyage in the Dark* [1934]?)
to study acting at the Royal Academy of Dramatic Arts. But her
father's death the next year, cutting off her allowance, ended her
schooling. It also gave her a firsthand knowledge of transience. Adrift
in a cold northern city and an alien culture, she toured the English
provinces as a chorus girl and then worked as a model before
becoming a writer. She left England in 1919 with her new husband,
Jean Langlet, a Dutch-French songwriter and journalist. Roaming

the Continent, the ill-fated couple lived impecuniously in Paris, Vienna, and Budapest. This vagrant period also saw Jean Rhys's first publication—a ghost-written book about eighteenth-century furniture. The failure of her marriage led to an affair with Ford Madox Ford, who also sponsored her first work of fiction, a short-story collection called *The Left Bank* (1927). Although artistically fertile, her haphazard expatriate years were full of stress. The same sorrows riding the marooned characters of *The Left Bank* also rode their creator. Stella Bowen, Ford's common-law Australian wife, called her "a doomed soul, violent and demoralized," living "in an underworld of darkness and disorder."[3] If the description speaks home, then Ford must have cast her off with great relief.

She returned to England in 1927 both seasoned and saddened, a wrecked marriage, a sad affair, and a book of short stories behind her. She continued to write, publishing novels in 1928, 1930, 1934, and 1939. She and her second husband, Leslie Tilden-Smith, a publisher's reader for Hamish Hamilton Ltd., lived in Cornwall until the latter's death in 1945. In 1946 she married her second husband's cousin, poet and retired naval officer Max Hamer. The Hamers moved in 1961 from Cornwall to Devon, where Jean Rhys spent her last, widowed years. A heart attack she suffered after Max Hamer's death made it advisable for her to spend some months in a London nursing home; and, because of her great age, she would winter in a London retirement center. Her only child, a married daughter, Maryvonne Moermann (b. 1922), lives in the Netherlands.

The combination of World War II and the failure to win readers silenced her pen in the 1940s and 1950s. Ending her quiet retirement in the country was a decision of the BBC's Third Programme to dramatize *Good Morning, Midnight* in 1958. Although the BBC did adapt and then produce Jean Rhys's 1939 novel, they did not know where to send the royalty check. The writer replied to a request for information about her whereabouts in the *New Statesman* and, heartened by her newly won acclaim, wrote several short stories later printed in the *London Magazine* and *Art and Literature*. More acclaim followed, encouraging her to move ahead with her novel-in-progress about Edward Rochester's mad West Indian wife in Charlotte Brontë's *Jane Eyre* (1847). After considerable reworking, the book came out in 1966 as *Wide Sargasso Sea*. Critics have lauded Jean Rhys's fifth and last novel not only as the writer's best but also as one of the best English novels of the 1960s.

Both *Sargasso* and its predecessors take root in Jean Rhys's private

experience. Disguised and rearranged, the materials of her life pulse through the novels. Nor does she deny this strong autobiographical thrust. In 1968 she told a Manchester *Guardian* interviewer, "If you want to write the truth . . . you must write from yourself. It must go out from yourself. I don't see what else you can do. I am the only real truth I know."[4] Thus she shares many of her heroine's experiences: Anna Morgan's letdown in first coming to London from the West Indies and then her short turn as a chorus girl in *Voyage in the Dark*; Marya Zelli's marriage to a threadbare continental in *Quartet* (1928); Sasha Jansen's brief modeling career in *Good Morning, Midnight*; and Julia Martin's lonely exile in *After Leaving Mr. Mackenzie* (1930). Sadness runs through both her work and her life. Happiness flickers but briefly, and with good reason. It must be enjoyed before it fades: "When one is happy one is completely absorbed in it," she told Hannah Carter in 1968. Sorrow needn't engulf, she continued: "You can write-out a sadness and then it isn't so bad. It is the only lucky thing about being a writer."[5] Depression ignites bursts of literary activity. As she says, she can write out her pain through her fiction. But before it leaves her, it has stirred her imagination, gained new shape as fictional art, and strengthened her coping power. The world has gained a bargain. The process by which grief nourishes creativity is noted by a woman in one of the sketches comprising *Left Bank*: "For the first time she had dimly realized that only the hopeless are starkly sincere and that only the unhappy can either give or take sympathy" (pp. 120–21). Dorothy Dufreyne's ability to pluck profit from her stony-broke, haphazard life extends the writer's argument. Success and happiness both harden hearts. Sorrow humanizes; in in failure come insight and compassion. Ironically, Jean Rhys's heroines—outcasts and discards all—have nobody with whom to share their vision. Does the vision deepen, darken, or even paralyze for want of outlets?

## I   *The Uses of Privation*

Rosalind Miles's *The Fiction of Sex* (1974) explains Jean Rhys as the enemy of the middle-class male sexist establishment:

It is her recurrent, almost obsessive theme, that women are perpetual victims of masculine society. . . . Jean Rhys is thus one of the few women writers to make explicit the link between the sex war and the class struggle. To be female is to inhabit, without hope of escape, the lowest class of all in a sexist society.[6]

Opposing this view, A. Alvarez says she is "absolutely nonintellec-
tual" with "no axe to grind, no ideas to tout."[7] This reading of Jean
Rhys carves out an artistic context for her values and commitments.
Jean Rhys's heroines *do* lack the security of job and family; their
welfare *does* ride on the ability to rouse and then hold a man; since
their identity is largely sexual, they lead shadow-lives after age thirty-
five. But Jean Rhys's treatment of her subject isn't frenzied or
feverish. No matter how impassioned her motives, she keeps the
narratives low-keyed. Neither ideological nor self-pitying, she shuns
sensational effects. No stridency mars the pace, vigor, or deft
organization of the fiction. Hers is the art of the unstated and the
implied. Now good writing entails knowing what to leave out as much
as knowing what to put in. Alvarez's belief that Jean Rhys is the best
living English novelist rests partly on her selectivity: "Although her
range is narrow, sometimes to the point of obsession, there is no one
else now writing who combines such emotional penetration and
formal artistry or approaches her unemphatic, unblinking truthfulness." Robert Nye also commends her avoidance of the high-pitched
and the shrill; her "dry-eyed understanding" of "woman's experience
of the male" lifts her artistically above Colette for Nye.[8]

Control is the key; there is no substitute for stylistic restraint in any
art. Though Jean Rhys speaks for all those who pass through life
without having a life, she does not shout. Her short, well-built
declarative sentences glitter without blinding. Their spareness helps
control our responses. Because of it, her rare figures of speech leap
out; because of it, she commits us imaginatively to her characters and
their problems. Nobody better understands the differences between
art and propaganda than Jean Rhys. Very few practice a more severe
economy of means. Her pared-down vocabulary and muted sentence
rhythms have won Shirley Hazzard's highest praise—the comparing
of her prose to great poetry: "For me her power lies in the very
transformation of self-pity into literature—a feat of artistic strength
seldom managed even by poets."[9]

Poetic undertones in Jean Rhys stem from narrative strategy.
Predicament all but replaces plot in her novels. Instead of telling a
story, she places and then develops a situation. The basic one—that
of the single city woman who has nothing and fits nowhere—had not
been treated seriously before. Elgin W. Mellown rightly calls Jean
Rhys's major accomplishment "the portrayal of a psychological type
never before so accurately described."[10] This claim can be supported.
Henry James's tragic heiresses cling to the consolations of wealth
and/or renunciation; Molly Bloom, Joyce's Everywoman in *Ulysses*,

has a singing career, a daughter, a lover, and a husband who brings her breakfast in bed; Moll Flanders rarely goes long without a man, a hot meal, or a mug of beer. The lot of the Rhys heroine is to do nothing and to do it alone. Several critics have noted that the heroines of the first four novels are the same woman given different names and viewed at different stages in life. The novels *do* have a similar impulse and do reach into each other as an extended character study. Disliking the literature of ideas, Jean Rhys studies human psychology. She treats, in particular, the female psyche when it has begun to droop or panic from neglect. Although ignorant of her plight, the Rhys heroine must grow up or die. This is the heart of the problem—nobody has taught her how to grow up; nobody gives her any room to grow into. The predicament is stated most directly in *Midnight*. Even when they can get jobs, women in business earn less and risk more than men:

Well, let's argue this out, Mr. Blank. You, who represent Society, have the right to pay me four hundred francs a month. That's my market value, for I am an inefficient member of Society, slow on the uptake, uncertain, slightly damaged in the fray, there's no denying it. So you have the right to pay me four hundred francs a month, to lodge me in a small, dark room, to clothe me shabbily, to harass me with worry and monotony and unsatisfied longings till you get me to the point when I blush at a look, cry at a word. (p. 29)

The novels begin like epilogues or postscripts to conventional love stories where boy gets girl and embarks with her on a life of happiness on the last page. The girl in Jean Rhys does not get the boy. The novels specialize in the loser, the discard, the also-ran. But not the dropout: the Rhys heroine does not invite aloneness. At the start of *Mr. Mackenzie*, Julia Martin goes underground—typically, in a cheap Parisian hotel—after being cast off by her lover. But going underground, or dropping out, for her means dropping in. She faces squarely the monotony and squalor that befall women without jobs, men, or inheritance. Character exists before action in the novels. Rather than enriching or refining the self, the heroines fight to keep the self together. The most they hope for is a stalemate. No Cinderellas or Sleeping Beauties people the novels.

The sealing-off of outlets for growth blocks character development in the usual sense. It promotes negation elsewhere, as well. The breakdown and withdrawal described in *Midnight* and *Sargasso* stem logically from what precedes. To exist sexually, as the Rhys heroine

does, is to court ruin: hopelessness is a natural condition of sex, and deprival is a natural corollary of life in these curiously sex-free novels. "There is never an escape for the Rhys heroine," says Mellown; "happiness is always followed by sadness, and her last state is always worse than her first."[11] Marya Zelli of *Quartet* supports Mellown's argument. By Chapter 3, her husband, a shady dealer, has been jailed; the police refuse to tell her anything about him; her only friend is out of town; she has no money or job. Then the novel's main conflict arises, making things worse for Marya.

All of Jean Rhys's critics have noted the dispossession and denial stalking the heroines. Alvarez names the three constants of her world, "fear, loneliness, and the lack of money." He may be right; any one of these states leads quickly to the other two. V. S. Naipaul, following his grim logic, sees the Rhys heroine as a victim of exile and financial dependence: "The society is closed; the isolation of the expatriate, the woman, the outsider, is complete; she exists in a void."[12] The fiction's investigation of homelessness includes a look at what the homeless substitute for security, comfort, and love. Antoinette Cosway of *Sargasso* tells a friend, "I often wonder who I am and where is my country and where do I belong and why was I ever born at all" (p. 102).

These are hard questions. And they lead to others, equally hard. Why is the Rhys woman an exile on native grounds? Or an invalid who must nurse herself through each day, as Rosalind Miles believes?[13] Which forces hold her down and sap her vim? These turn out to be both intrinsic and imposed. Jean Rhys states the case of the have-not in the urbanized, technocratic West—the unmarried, untrained woman who owns no property and has no money. Not-having entails heavy penalties. Many of the stories and novels begin with the main character moving in or out of cheap lodgings. She will probably move again before the action ends. Having learned no skill, she cannot earn anything and she lacks bargaining power. The men she leans on do not ask much. But since they want her to be available on short notice, they block outlets for self-expression. This blockage has spread into the business world. Selina Davis, the black West Indian immigrant-ingenue of "Let Them Call It Jazz" (1962), has a skill—sewing. But England's garment trade prizes speed over crafts-manship: "They tell me all this fine handsewing take too long," notes Selina. "Waste of time—too slow. They want somebody to work quick and to hell with the small stitches" (p. 54). Denied creativity, woman is forced to react or adapt to standards set by men.

Her adaptation carries the sanction of tradition. Her centuries-long identification with the moon shows that woman has always lived in a borrowed light. Her reality depends on what she borrows or reflects: mistreat her and she sinks—in Jean Rhys, to a sullen drunkenness; love her and she will glow. Names like Selina Davis, Petronella Grey ("Till September Petronella" [1960]), Inez Best ("Outside the Machine" [1960]), and Lotus Heath ("The Lotus" [1967]) express this potential. Whereas the last names of these women spell out their drab legacy, a yearning for magic and wonder comes through in their exotic first names. Born in the lush Antilles of a Creole mother, Jean Rhys writes about women who combine the romantic with the matter-of-fact. These women aspire, but settle. And settle they must. Their looks, not their hearts or minds, shape their lives. Looking pretty means garnering jewels, fine clothes, elegant dinners, and perhaps a protector. But beauty is more of a curse than a gift. Few women can resist the temptation of trading on their looks: "My life from seventeen to twenty-two is responsible for my damned weakness" (p. 221), complains a woman who never learned self-respect in "Vienne" (1927).

Had this woman and her counterparts looked plain, they would have worked in factories or offices near their parents' homes and then married neighborhood boys. But their good looks won them jobs as models, chorus girls, and actresses, sometimes taking them to Mayfair and Paris. This glimpse of high, or at least fast, society taught them to revere the fashionable ("chic" and "smart" are their favorite terms of approbation). It has also made them unfit for ordinary work. The ones who stay single pass from man to man, sometimes drifting into the street or jail. Where else can they go? The way is always down. As the book's title implies, the key event of Julia Martin's adult life in *After Leaving Mr. Mackenzie* is being cast off:

I was all right till I met that swine Mackenzie. But he sort of—I don't know—he sort of smashed me up. Before that I'd always been pretty sure that things would turn out all right for me, but afterwards I didn't believe in myself any more. I only wanted to go away and hide. (p. 49)

She has no money, plans, or family who will help her to her feet. Her thin supply of cash will only last three or four days. She has to beg. But begging from ex-lovers and, sometimes, righteous relatives does not teach the middle-class virtues of thrift and practicality. Neither moral reform nor moral aspiration exists for her. She spends

whatever money she gets immediately, mostly on clothes. Unaccustomed to happiness, she must enjoy it before it goes away. Perhaps she even wants to drive it out. Antoinette Cosway defines the attitude in *Sargasso* when she says, "I am not used to happiness. . . . It makes me afraid" (p. 92). Julia Martin says of a £10 gift, "I'll spend the whole lot. . . . It seems a mad thing to do, but I don't care" (p. 182).

Her rashness is typical. The Rhys heroine lacks the self-respect to believe she deserves riches or joy. She has already been condemned to the desolation of apartness before we meet her. She has been dropped by her married friends, who fear their husbands' possibly roving eyes; also by other single women, who fear her as competition. The family whose middle-class values she snubbed in favor of glamor has deeper motives for keeping her away. Not only do they despise her failure to live glamorously; they also enjoy the bittersweet satisfaction of seeing her proud hope of rising above them go flat. Last, they ignore her— even to the point of resisting the temptation to sermonize—for fear of being asked for money.

Thus hamstrung, why should she hurt her chances still more by incompetence and recklessness? Curiously, cynicism and the will to violence and madness protect her. Disparaging a goal draws the sting of failing to gain it. Indifference and fatalism ward off gloom, stilling the threat of denial. Marya Zelli of *Quartet* asks herself, "What's the use of worrying about things . . . ? I don't care. I'm sick of being sad" (p. 47). Sasha Jansen of *Midnight* rates indifference as life's greatest good: "People talk about the happy life, but that's the happy life when you don't care any longer if you live or die" (p. 91). Living near the edge fosters boldness as well as fear and moral exhaustion. Howard Moss explains the humiliation dogging the Rhys woman as psychological stress: "To hate the respectable world and to be dependent on it, to be rebellious and helpless at the same time, produces resignation and rage; there are no more uncomfortable bedfellows."[14] To release these bottled-up impulses, she squanders money; the fact of ruin ends the dread of impending ruin. Hitting rock bottom brings relief; you can relax when you know that your predicament cannot worsen. Though denied free-standing identity, the Rhys heroine refuses to wilt or blench. A hidden spring will snap, and she will be rude and outrageous. Often, she will outrage somebody with power over her. Marya Zelli slaps her protector's face; Anna Morgan stubs her cigarette on *her* protector's hand in *Voyage*; Selina Davis of "Let Them Call It Jazz" throws a rock through the stained-glass window of a London neighbor who had had her arrested the previous month.

The premonition of failure blocks the drive to passion and power. And just as well: tragedy calls for free-standing characters. Women prized for their ability to produce pleasant physical sensations lack this force. Men want nothing essential in women. Though prizing female chastity, they also want to violate it. Thus they never give women the self-respect that makes *them* prize chastity. Men solve the problem by dividing women into nice girls and tarts. Women fail to solve it at all. They lack the intellectual or sensory energy to fight back. Nor are they taught positive values; nothing men gives them lasts long. No wonder they drift into prostitution. Anna Morgan is speaking candidly in *Voyage* when she says of a friend, "Why shouldn't she be a tart? It's just as good as anything else, as far as I can see" (p. 127). Earlier in the book somebody asked, "Have you ever thought that a girl's clothes cost more than the girl inside them?" (p. 45). The question shows that Jean Rhys's dispossessed urban women, rather than existing in the public sphere, live below history and below society.

Their casual attitude toward sex and their readiness to lean on men also limit their private domains. The neo-romantic urge to connect found in E. M. Forster and Virginia Woolf invites attention in Jean Rhys because of its absence. She does not connect the female principle with serenity, comfort, and healing-power. The most basic ties—the parental and the sexual—barely exist. Marriage never lasts. And, as Mellown shows, neither does motherhood or its fulfillments:

These tortured women cannot reach maturity by giving birth to a child which, depending on them, will force them into adulthood. . . . If they do give birth . . . then they are unable to keep the child alive. Woman as creator and sustainer of life has no part in the archetypal figure.[15]

Though rarely a wife or a mother, the archetypal figure gives men the central place in her life. She has no identity deeper and more important than that found in a relationship with a man. In a 1974 interview for *Mademoiselle*, Jean Rhys said, "I'm perfectly sure women need men."[16] The canon vindicates this judgment. The sky crashes down on women without men all through the fiction. A wife in "Vienne" warns her despairing bankrupt husband, "If you kill yourself you know what will happen to me" (p. 226). Marya Zelli of *Quartet* sells her dresses and grows feverish within a week of her husband's arrest. Quite simply, men stand between women and destitution. The Rhys heroine does not fight for the right to live her

own way. Rebellion and moral self-examination never happen. The
self-questioning that does occur goes on at a lower intellectual level
than in Doris Lessing and at a lower psychic level than in Sylvia
Plath. The Jean Rhys heroine will sleep with a man she does not care
about rather than go hungry. But her readiness to subjugate herself
has a by-product: it perpetuates male tyranny. Although she gets
little, she asks for little. Nothing exists for her beyond the moment.
Lacking ideas about independence and identity, she needs a protector
to survive. Being dropped by Mackenzie dulls Julia Martin: "Nowa-
days something had happened to her; she was tired. She hardly ever
thought of men, or of love" (p. 12). What follows is a long, gloomy
round of solitary eating and drinking.

Life leaks away by degrees. As Julia Martin shows, being discarded
speeds the process. In either event, women have acres of time to fill
while waiting for a man to call or write. And time always whittles
them down. *Quartet* flashes before us "a pale, long-faced girl in front
of an untouched drink, watching the door. She was waiting for the
gentleman with whom she had spent the preceding night to come
along and pay for it, and naturally she was waiting in vain" (pp.
33–34). Having their minds ignored and their bodies used as barter
for a free dinner and some new togs makes time drag. The Rhys
heroine has not learned to be good company for herself. Mistrusting
her powers, she probably dislikes herself as well. She reveals herself in
passivity. What she hates most, being alone, is also what she does
most. The future darkens her fears, forcing her to draw on her
diminishing resources. As her wardrobe goes out of style, as her
figure sags, and as her face seams, she can no longer attract men. She
loses her social identity. The fiction portrays women separated from
their society even while within it. A character in "Temps Perdi" (1967)
who wants to play "Time on My Hands" on the piano has chosen the
theme song of her sisterhood. For the dispossessed urban woman,
solitude always slides into apartness and then isolation.

A masseuse of forty in *Voyage* shrills, "D'you know how old I
am . . . ? If I can't get hold of some money in the next few years,
what's going to become of me?" (p. 146). Sasha Jansen of *Midnight*,
who is several years older, confirms the masseuse's fears. The passage
of the years has meant fewer friends, cheaper lodgings, and worse
neighborhoods. And she knows that the years have not finished
wringing her. To protect herself, she has lapsed into a mechanical
routine. With the positive goal of happiness out of reach, all she can
do is dull herself to the cruelties of time. She has learned to sleep

fifteen hours a day, and she spends her meager waking hours numbed
by alcohol. As the closing words of Part 3 of the book imply, time is
always an enemy. Past the age where she can win a man, she must
manage on her own. Her survival depends on eradicating the normal
passage of time: "Tomorrow I'll go to the Galeries Lafayette. . . .
And when I have had a couple of drinks I shan't know whether it's
yesterday, today or tomorrow" (p. 145). Starved of a sexual
existence, she sees no reason for existing at all.

## II    *The Underdog Dogged*

Life never offers the Rhys heroine much. If the lack of a man
shrinks her, the presence of one makes her a victim. Either men are
brutes or their blatantly sexual goals corrupt them. Alvarez calls Jean
Rhys's Englishmen "stone cold and destructive"; John Hall, writing
in the *Guardian* in 1972, interprets "her perennial theme" in lean,
hard terms: "life is cruel, and men are dreary swine."[17] The canon
contains supporting evidence for these views. The end of an affair
relieves men but, depriving them of their chief source of food,
clothing and shelter, saddens women. Somebody in "Till September
Petronella" reads a book about the biological inferiority of women;
somebody else calls England "a country where females are only
tolerated at best" (p. 17). The judgment need not be restricted either
to England or to our century. Though Jean Rhys dramatizes the
problem of being a woman in between-wars London and Paris, her
portrayal of the nineteenth-century Creole, Antoinette Cosway, in
*Sargasso*, shows women to have been mistreated and exiled in the last
century as well.

But Jean Rhys does not study the dynamics of dominance and
dependence. Her male characters do not crave control, power, or
strength; these advantages come to them naturally. Nor do they
usually cheat women. In the first three novels, they give their
mistresses a great deal of money, perhaps more than they can afford;
and they keep paying after they break relations. Here is the moral
issue coloring sexual relationships in Jean Rhys: Sex is a battlefield
where only one rule of warfare applies—the double standard of
morality. Like every other war, the battle of the sexes produces
casualties. These are mostly women, the weaponless. The Freudian
sexual pairings noted by Mellown suggest other reasons for womanly
woe. The much-older male lovers in the canon stand for the cruel
paternal society that exacts strict obedience. Men can no more escape

this determinism than can women. Walter Jeffries, Anna Morgan's first lover in *Voyage*, is, as Mellown says, "old enough to be her father"; after calling Stephan Zelli of *Quartet* Marya's "older lover-husband," Mellown says that Marya's lover, Hugh Heidler, is "as always, older and, as always, a brute."[18] The father who works his will without checks cannot help causing distress.

The Oedipal materials infusing the work spread the distress. A staple of the canon is the absentee father. Antoinette Cosway comes closest to having a father of any Rhys heroine. But her father dies before the time of the novel, and her eccentric stepfather is rejected and rejecting, in turn. Ironically, his crowning act of fatherly love, his willing her half his large fortune, leads to her greatest sadness—her marriage to Edward Rochester of *Jane Eyre*. Rochester's cruelty to Antoinette traces an Elektral curve. The couple enjoy their best times together in the days following their marriage—as young newlyweds. Rochester's cheating her out of her inheritance and his emotional rejection of her push them symbolically from the realm of husband and wife into that of father and daughter. Their new relationship fits Jean Rhys's paradigm of the received construct. As interacting adults, the newlyweds thrive; lapsing into the parent-child relationship grieves both. Rochester, as the stern father, withholds both his love and his presence from his daughter-wife, further punishing her alleged mischief by stowing her in a remote part of the house. This relationship saddens everybody. The ordeal in the West Indies leading to Antoinette's virtual house-arrest ages Rochester beyond his years and robs Antoinette of a controlled adult life. At the end, she needs a full-time governess-nurse to help her manage the trivialities of her dwarfed existence.

Other uses of the construct are more pointed. "La Grosse Fifi" (1927) tells of a twenty-four-year-old Frenchman who killed a lover exactly twice his age when she threatened to blind him, and *Mackenzie* (whose title character is also forty-eight) mentions a girl who prayed that her lover would go blind. Oedipus's self-punishment emerges again in *Voyage*. After her first sexual experience, typically with a much-older man, Anna Morgan mutters, "'I must go. . . . Where's the door. . . .' It was as if I were blind" (pp. 36–7). Later, during a sexually troubled time, she asks, "Who said, 'O Lord, let me see'? I would rather say, 'O Lord, keep me blind'" (p. 110). Finally, Antoinette Cosway says of her mother in *Sargasso*, "She was my father's second wife, far too young for him" (p. 17). None of these Freudian allusions convert to textbook theory. Eschewing systems,

Jean Rhys commits herself morally and poetically to her themes. The Freudian-Sophoclean materials in her fiction, besides supplying an intellectual frame, prefigure the sexual calamity befalling her heroines. Even as a raw physical act, sex means little, bringing neither joy nor agony. The implied comparison between Oedipus's tragic passion and the nasty, guttering affairs of today mocks our unheroic age. None of Jean Rhys's people loves madly or dangerously; none except Antoinette and the heroine of "La Grosse Fifi" would blast his or her eyes out of guilt or grief. Sexual ties begin and end quickly in Jean Rhys's novels, their sudden finales leaving the lovers numb or indifferent, not pained.

Their free participation in these empty relationships uncovers a self-destructive streak in the women. Jean Rhys rates the female instinct for survival low: "My women are so much lacking in common sense," she said in 1974; Rosaline Miles grumbles about "the inability of women to offer even the most elementary support for one another" in the 1966 story, "I Spy a Stranger"; and, in a January 1976 article in *Ms.*, Judith Thurman claims that Jean Rhys "perceives women as even more treacherous than men."[19] Women do little to guard against male exploitation. But they are not always passive. Sometimes the danger they do each other outpaces that inflicted by men. A character in "Till September Petronella" says, "The other day I spent a long time trying to decide which are worse—men or women" (p. 15). The matter cannot be decided quickly. Lois Heidler's complicity in her husband's affair with Marya Zelli in *Quartet* hurts Marya more than the husband's cruelties; Julia Martin of *Mackenzie* is driven from her mother's house by a woman; women of all ages and backgrounds fleece nineteen-year-old Anna Morgan in *Voyage*. An artist, Jean Rhys assigns neither blame nor guilt. Nor does she take sides in the battle of the sexes. In fact, her male characters, no flashy villains, slide progressively into the shadows. Messrs. Mackenzie and Horsfield, Julia Martin's lovers, have little of the vividness of Hugh Heidler of *Quartet*. The men in Sasha Jansen's life in *Midnight* often lack names; sometimes they are not even described. This waning of interest in her heroines' lovers reflects a shift in both Jean Rhys's focus and strategy. The moral and aesthetic purposes of her later work favor sketches over portraits. Because her outcast heroines exist outside society, she gives the dreary monotony of the solitary precedence over fleshed-out characters. Dramatic encounters between round characters could even distract from her intent. As has been said, the lot of the Rhys woman is loneliness. Jean Rhys's

cutting back and forth between images of blocked desire and moral depression unites the images in a disturbing, but artistic, whole, the absence of character interplay spelling out the doom of the doomed.

This fate rarely touches our hearts. That the Rhys heroine neither asks for nor gives much rules out sentiment. Quite simply, like Tennessee Williams's Blanche du Bois of *A Streetcar Named Desire* (*Sargasso* has a character named Dubois), she depends on the kindness of strangers. Dependence and submissiveness come easily to her. She does not complain about needing men. Nor does she pretend that love will fulfill, enrich, or gladden her. The dark, wordless erotic bonds found in D. H. Lawrence occur nowhere in Jean Rhys; nobody loves wildly, nobody except Antoinette in *Sargasso* and Fifi in "La Grosse Fifi" is destroyed by passion. As has been seen, the archetypal figure wants a man to pay her rent, stand her dinners, and keep her looking stylish. The identity of the man hardly matters. Anna Morgan's wants are simple: "I . . . like going fast in a car and eating and drinking and hot baths" (p. 142). Thrills and creature comforts: such goals, held down by motives of self-preservation, keep the novels small-scale.

But why write about slack, self-indulgent women who practice no skill and throw away money on clothes and drink? In his preface to *The Left Bank*, Jean Rhys's first critic, Ford Madox Ford, cites "a terrific—an almost lurid!—passion for stating the case of the underdog."[20] Women who have sex with men they dislike and for prizes that will not last become underdogs quickly. But they also practice a magic. Jean Rhys's best critic, Elgin Mellown, has shown her heroines surviving by mocking or ignoring the chief realities of their lives. This mental sleight-of-hand takes the self-detachment of the creative artist or the mystic. To know that one's identity rests on sex and money and to shrug off the knowledge approaches self-transcendence. But, while helping survival, the knowledge also stresses denial—even if the denial is denied. The Rhys heroine cannot escape negation:

These women are forever alone outside the realm of everyday society and cut off from the ordinary patterns of life. . . . They know that they are alive because they suffer and because money passes through their hands. . . . In this understanding of life lies the origin of one of Rhys's most important themes, that personal identity is determined by economic wealth. . . . The Rhys woman reasons that, since her physical existence depends on money, everything else does too—character, morals, ethics, even religious values.

And . . . she knows too that money is merely an artificial thing, that which men give to women when they make love to them, or when they send them away. . . . These women find their identity and a truth for themselves by flaunting their disdain for . . . money.[21]

The passion for the underdog that Ford saluted in 1927 has survived. The canon contains no upperdogs; even oppressors like Heidler and Mackenzie invite sympathy. *The Left Bank* includes exiles from Holland, England, the Antilles, Japan, and America. "Vienne," the last story in the book, treats frayed exiles scraping along in a fading, desperate city. "Hunger" records the progressive giddiness of a starving English woman in Paris; the self-styled citizen of the land of Lost Causes who tells the story lists the effects of going without food for each of five days. An Arab prisoner is clubbed to death in "The Sidi." Prisons also promote inhumanity in "From a French Prison" and *Quartet*. Distrusting public institutions, Jean Rhys equates hospitals with prisons in both these works as well as in "Let Them Call It Jazz" (1962) and "Out of the Machine" (1960). But one need not be institutionalized; jails and hospitals cast long shadows, the outsider quickly learns. Acting out the city-as-maze metaphor of Baudelaire and T. S. Eliot, Jean Rhys's Caribbeans cannot cope with the European city. Judith Thurman notes "a yearning . . . for a lost warmth"[22] in these islanders. They yearn with good reason. Paris and London are murky, Philistine places. Their drizzling, sunless pavements dishearten after the rich green luxuriance and tropical ease of the islands. The dishwater drabness of the European city drowns color and cheer. Anna Morgan cannot believe that London's thin, sad sunlight is the same that warms her island home. The dark, frowning houses and dim streets of provincial England stretch out in an expanse of gray:

The towns we went to always looked so exactly alike. You were perpetually moving to another place which was perpetually the same. There was always a little grey street leading to the stage-door of the theatre and another little grey street where your lodgings were . . . and a grey stone promenade running hard, naked and straight by the side of the grey-brown or grey-green sea. (p. 8)

Other groups besides Caribbean exiles marked down for grief include old people and intellectuals. A lady writer in "The Lotus" goes mad because her neighbors mock her. "Cracky ideas" help send Laura of "I Spy a Stranger" (1966) to a mental home; what defeats her

aren't her ideas but the fact that she, a foreigner at that, should even have them. The years have heightened Jean Rhys's sympathy with the aged. The 1974 story, "Sleep It Off Lady," shows an elderly spinster left to die amid a scatter of rubbish as a neighbor's daughter ignores her call for help. "A Solid House" (1963) homes in on the aging residents of a London rooming house during the Blitz. A *Times* featurette Jean Rhys wrote for the International Woman's Year series in May 1975, "Whatever Became of Old Mrs. Pearce?" (an Olly Pearce appears in "A Solid House"), states the case for the old:

Old people, especially women living alone, are very vulnerable. Some are protected by money (up to a point), some by friends or relatives (perhaps, perhaps). But some are not. And the older and frailer they grow, the weaker their position, the greater their dread of being interfered with.[23]

Like the women in the novels, the old people in Jean Rhys's late stories have nothing but hopelessness in store. The defenseless are still natural victims. The onset of years may have made Jean Rhys more aware of the problems of aging; she admitted to Judith Thurman that old age "is as terrible as she always knew it would be."[24] But her imagination has always converted the faded and the rundown into art. She judges nobody; as has been seen, she even sympathizes with oppressors. Rather than dogmatizing, she mines obscure seams for literary ore. The lode she extracts is all the more precious for its obscure origins. The heroines in Jane Austen, Henry James, and Elizabeth Bowen all belong in the liberal-humanist tradition. Jean Rhys's culture-starved women are harder to write about. Yet there are fifty Julia Martins walking our sidewalks for every Elizabeth Bennett or Isabel Archer. We see them every day and barely notice them. By presenting them honestly and by withholding judgment, Jean Rhys has sharpened our understanding of daily reality.

CHAPTER 2

# *The Short Fiction*

JEAN Rhys's short stories fit into two chronological groups—the ones written in the 1920s and included in *The Left Bank* and those of the 1960s and 1970s. The late fiction does not outrank the earlier work. The stories in *Left Bank* contain different materials from the late fiction and use the materials differently. Aiming at different goals, as well, they achieve them with the same economy and precision of their later counterparts. Jean Rhys does not develop as a short-story writer; shifting interests and techniques, she puts the genre to different uses at different times in her career. Distinguishing the two groups of stories is technique. In fiction, logical plotting can offset almost any fault. But plotting is not everything. The stories in *Left Bank* do not need a hard logical structure. Instead of developing a plot, they focus on a neighborhood—usually Paris's Montparnasse, a local type, or a condition expressive of the locale. As with Katherine Mansfield's early (1911) book of stories, *In a German Pension*, their effect is cumulative. Not designed to stand on their own, they give the pulse of the city through mood, texture, and speech rhythms. Many of them—brushstrokes of local color—extend less than five pages.

The later work, drawing character and incident more closely, observes the rules governing most good storytelling. Their rigging is tight and trim; they follow through smoothly; they can stand on their own. But they are not written to formula; Jean Rhys does not peddle mechanical contrivances. Coming from her maturity, these stories include humane insights which warm their technical dazzle. Lapses and blemishes? If these occur more often in the late work than in *Left Bank,* they spread themselves over a much-broadened canvas; to attempt more is to risk more. The late stories run longer than those in *Left Bank* and contain more complicated actions. Having published no short work from 1927 to 1960 and no novels from 1939 to 1966, Jean Rhys practically had to relearn fictional technique in her late years. Her dedication lends the recent stories a mellowness that

complements the lyricism of *Left Bank*. This mirroring relationship is important. The two sets of tales, with their different aims and techniques, show between them that, though usually disregarded as a short-story writer, Jean Rhys has met most of the challenges posed by the genre.

## I The Left Bank

A gathering of twenty-two stories, *Left Bank* (1927) fits as comfortably into the category of *belles lettres* as into that of fiction. These soft-focus monologues, character studies, and urban cameos often resemble tone poems or sketches for longer works. Infusing all is an attitude implicit in the book's title. Now the Left Bank (Paris's XIIIe Arrondisement) is nearly a city itself, including the Luxemburg Gardens, the stylish Boulevards Montparnasse and St. Michel, and the Sorbonne, or University of Paris, center of the town's artistic and intellectual life. Famous literary expatriates like Gertrude Stein and Ernest Hemingway lived on Paris's Left Bank in the 1920s, when the stories in the book take place; and Jean Rhys features artists of different nationalities to capture the mood of creativity and exile. Her close rendering of the spirit of place has struck different readers. Ford Madox Ford's praise of her "profound knowledge of the Left Bank" (p. 23) in his long preface reechoes in an analysis of the book's title in the *New York Times Book Review* of 11 December 1927. The title, *The Left Bank*, says the anonymous reviewer, "symbolizes the material with which Miss Rhys has worked, the people, the situations, the life in general. . . . The spirit these stories show of undisciplined and unconventional youth, of hardship, of disillusion, of loose and nervous and artificial existences, is expressively brought out by the term 'left bank.'"[1] Following suit, Rosalind Miles, writing in 1974, interprets the Left Bank as "that shabby fringe of society" peopled by "the sinister, the frightening, the out of order."[2]

Both critics are right. Most of the stories depict crises, reverse normal expectations, or, most often, enact a failure to communicate or connect. The characters are confused, tricked, despairing; living alone in sordid digs, they have nobody to turn to. But this negation strikes obliquely. Howard Moss is mistaken to dismiss these early stories as "dated and trifling,"[3] for they give the human problems they depict the proper rhetorical emphasis. Craftsmanship both tempers and focuses subject matter in *Left Bank*. Even as a beginner, Jean Rhys knew that suffering must be portrayed carefully in order to keep

it from sliding into moral preachment and sentimentality. "Her very remarkable technical gifts" (p. 23), said Ford, include selection, economy, and distancing: "These sketches begin exactly where they should and end exactly when their job is done" (p. 25). Taking his cue from Ford, the *New York Times Book Review* reviewer saw Jean Rhys practicing indirection to tease out essences and to uncover indwelling truths:

She gains her effects as much by what she omits as by what she includes; and she omits a great deal. Yet one is sometimes able, so strong is Miss Rhys's gift of connotation, to grasp in a moment all that is behind the situation and inherent in the character.[4]

Often the underlying truth will either stay hidden until the very end or emerge piecemeal. Jean Rhys avoids overstatement, direct appeals to both our feeling or our moral sense, and fully developed themes. Her indirection, a system of hints and images, finds its appropriate symbol in a white marble block that appears in "A Spiritualist," the second story in *Left Bank*. Untouched by any sculptor's chisel, the cube houses potential beauty. Accordingly she carves meaning and beauty out of the chunks of experience recounted in *Left Bank*. She also shapes her data by grouping some of the stories thematically. The book has a flow or curve, if not a linear structure. First meetings hold sway in Stories VII and VIII (Jean Rhys's numbering), "In the Luxemburg Gardens" and "Tea with an Artist"; Stories IX–XI, "Trio," "Mixing Cocktails," and "Again the Antilles," make up a West Indian group; the last three stories all take place away from Paris—"At the Villa D'Or" and "La Grosse Fifi" occur on the French Riviera and "Vienne" slews east from Vienna to Budapest and Prague. Sometimes an idea or character type from an earlier story will reemerge in different form later in the book. Thus Miss Bruce, an English portrait painter in "Illusion," the first story, resembles an old Flemish artist in the eighth, "Tea with an Artist," in their preference for the simple, the unpretentious, and the orderly over the wild and exotic. The ordinariness of the painter mistaken for a dope fiend in Story V, "Tout Montparnasse and a Lady," shows in his name—Guy; he could be anybody. The simile embedded in the only sentence he utters, "I'm as happy as a sandboy" (p. 58), spells out his commonness. What is more coarse and common than sand?

Sometimes, a story will send out reverberations that echo in different parts of the book. If "Illusion" prefigures "Tea with an

Artist" in its main character, its main idea knits with that of its immediate successor, "A Spiritualist." Both stories play off appearance against reality in order to show the extraordinary nature of the ordinary. To symbolize the strangeness that lurks beneath plain surfaces, both show the routine inspection of a wardrobe emitting shock. Accompanying the shock in each case is the blasting of an illusion. The illusion of the Commandant, the main character of "A Spiritualist," is that love can be safe and rational. At the story's climax, the spirit of the only woman he found submissive enough to make him happy drops a large marble block near the Commandant with a crash. Sometimes contrast joins the sketches. Story III, "From a French Prison," moves from illusion to stark reality. The story's brutal, sordid setting and the cruelty of a guard prove that ugliness can exist alongside the gauze and tinsel usually associated with Paris of the 1920s.

Another group of tales, XII–XV, shows, from different angles, the deprivation of deprived women. The most striking of these, "Discourse of a Lady Standing a Dinner to a Down-and-out Friend," has some of the sting and technical brilliance of another very short work, Strindberg's "The Stronger." Like this mini-play, the still shorter "Discourse" consists of a one-sided dialogue in which the nonspeaking part becomes as real as the speaker. The story opens as well as any other in the canon, setting forth character, mood, and idea in its opening paragraph: "Darling, I think you are simply wonderful. I always say, if I were in your place I'd go crazy. . . . Have some more soup. . . . Soup is *so* nourishing" (p. 105). These silky patronizing phrases lead to the revelation that the down-and-out friend is not abject enough for the lady-speaker, whose asking price for the dinner is her friend's moral and financial ruin: "It is all very well, but she has not forgotten to rouge her lips" (p. 105). This statement, like all the others relating the lady's thoughts, appears between parentheses. Asides like this resonate ironically with the spoken passages. Primarily, they express the lady's resentment over the friend's failure to gush gratitude with every mouthful, over her ability to hold a style, and, in spite of being poor, both her attractiveness to men and her ladylike restraint: "There is that man opposite making eyes at her. Quite a good-looking man. Well, if she is that sort. . . . Well, why *doesn't* she?" (p. 107). By the end, the lady is fuming because she cannot find a reason to despise the friend.

The next story, "A Night," depicts a black moment in the life of a down-and-outer like the dinner guest of "Discourse." Psychological,

it traces the random thoughts of a lonely woman flirting with suicide. "In the Rue de l'Arrivée," which follows "A Night," another English woman stranded in Paris gives rein to depression. Yet both stories move to happiness and self-acceptance, as does the next one, "Learning to be a Mother," which features a new mother who surprises herself by suddenly loving her baby boy.

This affirmation occurs rarely in *Left Bank*. The irony informing the book's cosmopolitanism makes itself felt in the main character of "Illusion," the opening story. At odds with her environment, Miss Bruce (no first name) has lived in Montparnasse for seven years. No starving Bohemian, she lives comfortably on a "respectably large" (p. 152) private income and has even sold a painting. The practicality implied by her Scots name tallies with her sober, steady life style; she lives alone, keeps to herself, and follows a regular routine. In one of the world's most ribald, romantic cities, she brims with health, good sense, and diligence:

One thought of her as a shining example of what character and training— British character and training—can do. After seven years in Paris she appeared utterly untouched ... by anything hectic, slightly exotic or unwholesome. Going on all the time round her were the cult of beauty and the worship of physical love: she just looked at her surroundings in her healthy, sensible way, and then dismissed them from her thoughts. (p. 151)

"Illusion" gets its bite from what it leaves out. When an appendicitis attack sends Miss Bruce to the hospital (appropriately, in view of the British distrust of foreigners, to the English Hospital), the narrator, her casual friend, goes to the artist's flat to collect some clothes. She finds, to her amazement, "a glow of color, a riot of soft silks ... everything that one did not expect" (p. 153) from Miss Bruce, a wearer of plain, serviceable clothes.

The discovery of the finery is the story's climax. The square solid wardrobe holding the flowing, rustling high-fashion frocks symbolizes the plain fronts which hide the strange and the beautiful everywhere. Like any good symbol, it raises questions. Why did Miss Bruce buy the dresses? Does she wear them in private? for somebody else? does she dress a friend in them? She cannot hide her womanliness from herself. Despite her brisk facade, she possesses "the perpetual hunger to be beautiful and that thirst to be loved which is the real curse of Eve" (p. 154). What is more, she has an artist's passion for beauty and the truth of the imagination, which she indulges everyday in her work.

But this passion must stay hidden. Meeting the narrator a week after the wardrobe incident, Miss Bruce, breezily denying that she wears the frocks, claims to be only a collector. Herein lies the significance of the title. The illusion refers both to Miss Bruce's low profile and to the narrator's mistaken belief that she understands her friend. No ironic distance divides the narrating self from the experiencing self. Nor do we know Miss Bruce any better than the puzzled friend does. Helped by her throwaway tone, she maintains her facade to the end. (Appropriately, one of the dresses hidden in her wardrobe, a carnival costume, came "complete with a mask" [p. 153].)

"Tea with an Artist," the companion piece to "Illusion," also takes place in the Latin Quarter and highlights a painter with no first name. These similarities notwithstanding, Jean Rhys is too much the artist to repeat herself. Miss Bruce is a woman, the Flemish painter Verhausen, a man. If she wears a mask in public, he has outgrown the need for one. The first paragraph of "Tea" shows the reputedly mad artist from the land of Hieronymus Bosch and Jan Breughel relaxing with his pipe. Like that of Miss Bruce, his ordinariness jars us at first. Making no concessions to Bohemian flourishes, he practices orderly work habits and keeps his studio clean. The woman he lives with, no young siren, is a middle-aged matron with a sturdy peasant build. Her longstanding love and loyalty find ironic expression in a ditty played on a gramophone across the street from Verhausen's studio:

*Souvent femme varie*
*Bien fol est qui s'y fie!*

This song about female inconstancy (to trust fickle woman is folly) runs counter to the main action. A Brechtian fillip that precedes Brecht, it throws back at us our distorted romantic ideas both about Flemish artists and the Latin Quarter. Verhausen's one eccentricity is his refusal to show or sell his paintings. But the eccentricity bespeaks confidence. Verhausen has the craftsmanly pride and self-esteem both to paint for himself and to live as he pleases. His choice of a frump for a lover bears out his independence; the love she shows him bears out his integrity. Verhausen has all he needs for happiness within arm's reach. Why should he care what other people think?

"In a Café," which falls midway between "Tea" and "Illusion" on the Table of Contents page, also joins the drab and the lyrical. Again, reversals come in pairs; again, too, the scene is Paris's Left Bank. The

cabaret music billed as "the best in the Quarter" (p. 49) is as prosaic as both its setting and nondescript middle-aged players; competence rather than inspiration rules in the "respectably full" (p. 49) cabaret where the story takes place. The staid mood is broken by a stout singer in evening dress. The loud applause greeting his song, "*Les Grues de Paris*," shatters the decorum of the quiet bourgeois audience. But no sooner does the natty singer acknowledge the cheers than he starts peddling copies of his song for a franc apiece. Wonder has flickered but briefly, the flashing magic of the song subsiding into the profit motive. The singer has sung his rousing song for money.

But for a while he soared. "In a Café" belongs in a group of stories that stress the power of art; in all the stories, the artistry of the artist reflects a carefully developed life-mode. The portrait-painters of "Illusion" and "Tea" have their counterpart in the singer-composer of "In a Café." These artists have all evolved a personal style that rivals their artistry both in power and in cunning. Yet, as has been seen, a motif in one story can echo in several others. Thus the story that follows "Café," "Tout Montparnasse and a Lady," also takes place in a cabaret. Like "Illusion" before it and "Tea" after it, "Montparnasse" gives the lie to the fiction that all Paris glitters with gaiety and recklessness. An American fashion artist addicted to lemonade builds a romantic background for a local portrait painter. The painter's regular habits prove again that romantic Paris gets much of its pulse and vigor from middle-class steadiness.

The merchant-artist who sang for money in "Café" invokes two counterparts in Story XX, "At the Villa D'Or." This work not only includes a Russian gardener who earns extra money by singing in a casino; it also has in its cast a Belgian artist about whom it is said, "He's a great artist. His name on a picture means something—means dollars" (p. 162). What price greatness? The painter, who has "somewhat pathetic eyes" (p. 161), seems unhappy. Except for Verhausen, artists in *Left Bank* perform for money. But they forestall our contempt. If they commercialize art, they also depend on art to survive. The Belgian painter of "Villa D'Or," though saddened by the need to market his wares, will live to paint more pictures. When somebody follows the credo of art for art's sake—as in XIX, "The Sidi"—he comes to grief. "The Sidi" carries forward the penalties of failing to communicate or connect, a subject first broached in another prison story, "From a French Prison," where a blind old man who speaks no French goes to a prison every week on visiting day. Though

the failure to communicate with the prison authorities confuses and pains him, it kills the main character of "The Sidi."

Much of the tale's action reaches us directly. One of the convicts, known only as No. 54, tries to guess the identity of the new prisoner in the next cell. But nearly every guess he makes about his Moroccan neighbor is wrong. No "ragged, verminous" (p. 147) Arab, the prisoner is "quite a young man and beautiful as some savage Christ" (p. 148). Yet Jean Rhys smudges the bright lyricism of her description of the Moroccan, or Sidi, which includes "a head sharply cut, as it were, out of ivory and ebony, very black eyes under long eyelashes, a red-lipped mouth with teeth marvellously white and even" (p. 148), by making his first words a grunt, "You—tobacco" (p. 148). The same night he asks for tobacco, the Sidi interrupts his sad nightly chant to tap on the wall of No. 54's cell. Presumably, he is using a prisoners' code. But the letters he taps out make no sense: "C-Q-H did not make a word. The Arab could not know the letters of the alphabet, useless after all to try to communicate with him" (p. 150). No. 54's refusal to give the Sidi a hearing helps bring on disaster. The next day, the Sidi's failure to make himself understood kills him when a guard, rejecting his plea of sickness, clubs him. Everything tallies. Unable to earn a living in Paris, the Moroccan gets jailed. Then his nightly chant annoys both inmates and guards. Just as nobody sees piety or beauty in the chant, the prison guard, expressing his ignorance in the way he knows best, kills the beautiful chanter. An imaginative vision is not always communicable, either in music or painting. No wonder Verhausen hoards his canvases; no wonder he is the happiest of men. He has learned to temper his hopes.

A gentler reversal of romantic expectations comes in Story VI, "Mannequin," which is set in a *couturier's* Paris salon. On her first day on the job as a model, Anna finds bickering, hard work, and hard bargains made by tough, imaginative buyers. Here is her first look at the mazelike studio; again, Jean Rhys peeps behind a facade to reveal an unexpected reality; but this time, splendor hides drabness:

At the back of the wonderfully decorated salons she had found an unexpected sombreness; the place, empty, would have been dingy and melancholy, countless puzzling corridors and staircases, a rabbit warren and a labyrinth. She despaired of ever finding her way. (p. 161)

Anna's dreams of glamor and glory keep getting jostled. The dinnerware on the mannequins' dining table is not fine and delicate.

On a long, rough-grained wooden table sit "a thick and hideous white china plate, a twisted thin fork, a wooden-handled stained knife, a tumbler so thick it seemed unbreakable" (p. 163). The models' table-talk is vain, silly, and empty; Anna finds, to her chagrin, that the others scorn the only person at the studio who has been kind to her, the old dresser Mme. Pecard. But the story does not end sadly. As usual, Jean Rhys reverses an earlier reversal in order to show something new at the core of things. As usual, she manages the reversal through revelation rather than direct statement. The expanding image that ends "Mannequin," showing beauty absorbed and assimilated, softens Anna's disappointment over her new job. The bright beauty of the departing models at day's end passes into the city whence it came. Anna's vision of Paris as a well-tended garden rather than an aggregate of concrete slabs will encourage her to report to work tomorrow:

All up the street the mannequins were coming out of the shops, pausing on the pavements a moment, making them as gay and as beautiful as beds of flowers before they walked swiftly away and the Paris night swallowed them up. (p. 166)

At first look, the difference between "Mannequin" and story XXI, "La Grosse Fifi," resembles that between gossamer and sludge. The latter story's title character, Francine "Fifi" Carly, is a female blimp who looks as though she has rolled off a sketchpad of Lautrec or Degas. By contrast, her lover, who at twenty-four, is half her age, looks "dark, slim, beautiful as some Latin god" (p. 195). Appearances belie reality in both characters. Though Fifi's arrangement with the gigolo and her physical grossness both invite a comic treatment, she rises to a tragic grandeur unique in the collection. "Fifi was as kind as God" (p. 191), says Roseau, a young boarder at the Riviera hotel where Fifi and the gigolo are staying. After a romantic setback jars Roseau, Fifi comforts her, giving her, amid kind words, "the kindest, the most underttanding kiss she had ever had" (p. 191). Before saying goodnight, Fifi also advises her to do what she herself no longer has the looks or youth to dare—find another man. Then Fifi's lover bolts. But her bravery outdoes that of Roseau, her younger, prettier counterpart, despite her disadvantages. Fifi does not invite pity as Roseau did when *her* lover went away. Nor does Roseau comfort Fifi or defend her from nasty gossip at the hotel. Fifi's gloom lifts as suddenly as it descended, ironically just before Roseau rejects

her altogether. But the gigolo's return does not gladden Fifi for long. The day after his return, he stabs her to death in a Marseilles hotel during a lovers' quarrel. Her death shifts the narrative focus back to Roseau. A line from a poem Roseau had read during her doldrums, *"J'ai mis toute ma vie aux mains de mon amant"* (p. 201), tells her that she could never love as wildly or as beautifully as Fifi. That Roseau is also the name of Jean Rhys's birthplace in Dominica makes this failure a self-criticism. Jean Rhys deepens the motif by using intellectual history. As the story reminds us, Blaise Pascal, the seventeenth-century French philosopher, once compared the human self to a reed (the French word for which is *roseau*): though this reed snaps when shaken by the wind, it nonetheless thinks and feels. The comparison with the rest of the animal kingdom hurts Roseau, with her low-order sensibility. She forgets Fifi's death without thinking about its meaning; accordingly, her romance early in the story pales alongside Fifi's tragic passion. Fifi proved that only a person with a living heart can extend compassion. Insensitive to the needs of others, Roseau is merely vain and touchy. Her packing her clothes in the story's last sentence, in preparation for leaving the hotel where she knew Fifi, bespeaks a dead heart. Frightened and evasive, she solves problems by ignoring them.

The story that follows "La Grosse Fifi" and that closes the book also contains autobiographical elements. But rather than grazing autobiography with word play (Roseau-*roseau*), "Vienne" recounts personal experience. Its autobiographical thrust has been noted more than once. The "Jean Rhys" entry in *Current Biography* (1972) states that "Vienne" "has as its heroine a pursued woman whose husband is involved in a swindle and eventually arrested, a poignant tale not unlike an episode in her [the author's] own life." John Hall's January 1972 biographical sketch of Jean Rhys in the *Guardian* details the story's factual basis more closely: "Her husband, working with the Japanese Allied Commission [in Vienna], went smash in a bent money deal. 'Vienne' describes the whole business, culminating in a desperate flight across Hungary and Czechoslovakia by night and in a chauffeur-driven car."[5]

This exciting incident, though, comes near the end of a thirty-five-page story. For most of the way, "Vienne" reads like an outline or draft for a longer work. The brief appearance of two typists suggests that Jean Rhys may have modeled the story on the "Wandering Rocks" section of Joyce's *Ulysses*. Internal evidence sets forth the same line of descent. The action comes in scraps and the continuity is

choppy, one page containing twenty-three separate paragraphs. Also, each of the story's three parts is told differently. The first, done in an anecdotal manner, takes place in Vienna in 1921. A city of exiles, this former seat of the Hapsburg empire has a faded, battered charm in place of its former majesty. Pierre and Francine spend their time gossipping with and about the members of the Japanese military *attaché*. Writing for *Atlantic,* Ralph Tyler claims that "the disorder of their [Pierre and Francine's] life kept erratic step with the dissolution of postwar Europe."[6] He may be right. But if Jean Rhys aligns the breakdown of her two main characters with that of Europe, she does not do it dramatically. Instead, she cuts to Francine and to Francine's complaints about being a woman. Operatic and self-indulgent, this section explains the story's mood rather than describing the events behind it.

The final section, in which Pierre and Francine tear across Europe to avoid the law, lacks dramatic confrontation. In Budapest, a mistake or betrayal perpetrated by a Japanese officer Pierre had met in Vienna nearly causes the latter's arrest. (The bent money deal noted by John Hall takes place off stage, as does Pierre's discovery of it.) Fear drives him and Francine into the maw of central Europe. They stop at Prague, where Pierre, although shortfunded, buys her a string of pearls. Then, because Czechoslovakia is mobilizing, he sells his car to get traveling money to London. But the car's new owner will not take possession until the next day. On the last page, the couple make a last, wild protest against their fate—being absorbed into the middle class. They race their car at 100 miles per hour down a dark road, screaming and half-wishing to smash into a tree. (The mad, impulsive suicide as an escape from middle-class respectability had surfaced briefly in Story XVII, "The Blue Bird.") Yet their nerve fails, and they prepare to set out for staid, stuffy London in the final sentence.

Though poorly distanced, the story contains more data than any other in the book. Both this wealth of material and the moral passion infusing it save "Vienne" from failure. If an artistic comedown from most of the other stories in the book, it attempts much more—in characterization, setting, and idea. The fledgling artist cannot be faulted for trying to scale new heights. Yet the story's most serious fault—not developing its promising subject matter—throws the merits of the twenty-one earlier stories into sharp relief. *Left Bank* works best when it stays within its modest limits; its artistry is that of the impromptu freehand sketch. It celebrates little; nor does it offer

sustained, fully globed portraits. On the other hand, its discipline, clarity, and technical accomplishment give it some of the suddenness of good lyric poetry. Ford did well to give it his strong support.

## II  Tigers Are Better-looking

*Tigers Are Better-looking* (1968) consists of eight stories of the 1960s; to fill out the pages needed for a legitimate book, Jean Rhys's British publisher, Andre Deutsch, added a fragment of Ford's Preface to *Left Bank* and nine stories from the earlier collection. Perhaps the best-known story in the book, which came out in the United States in 1974, is the first, "Till September Petronella" (1960). It begins with its eponym, Petronella Grey, performing a characteristic act—packing her clothes. She is getting ready to go on a two-weeks sojourn to the country with a painter-friend, Andrew Marston, and another couple, a model named Frankie Morell and the mother-ridden music critic, Julian Oakes. Glad for the chance to leave dreary London, Petronella thanks Marston (who, with his "long, white face and . . . pale blue eyes" [p. 13], reminds Elgin Mellown of Ford)[7]. But she does not escape the tension that dogged her in the city. The local cottagers dislike the vacationing foursome. Then the vanity and backbiting infects the mini-upper-Bohemian society in exile. The long vacation brings out the worst in all. The vacationers idle away much of their time—walking, preparing and eating food, and, mostly, drinking. The restiveness bred by this dull routine brings on the bickering. Bored stiff trying to get through the long, hot, slow afternoons, the four turn on each other.

Fed up with the wrangling, Petronella, who has gotten the worst of the collective malaise, takes a walk. The fresh air raises her hopes. A farmer driving to market in nearby Cirencester gives her a lift to town. While the two drink champagne in a local pub, the anonymous farmer makes a bizarre offer—to keep Petronella: "I'd like to feel that when I go up to Town there's a friend I could see and have a good time with. You know. And I could give her a good time too. By God, I could. I know what women like" (pp. 28–29), he claims, naming "a bit of money" along with "pretty dresses and bottles of scent, and bracelets with blue stones in them" (p. 29). This crude proposition does not relieve the shrillness of the *haute-culture* Londoners Petronella has just left. Still, she lets the Norfolk farmer buy her some chocolates and a first-class coach ticket to London.

At ride's end, she meets her second stranger of the day. Outside

Paddington Station, a London fop, Melville, invites her to share his cab. But rather than parting, she and Melville walk in Hyde Park after the cab ride and then take a late dinner together. The story ends where it began—in her lonesome Bloomsbury flat. But not before Petronella tells how her brief stage career ended when she froze just before reciting her only speech in a play, "O Lottie, Lottie, don't be epigrammatic" (p. 37). (Autobiography keeps creeping into the stories; the undelivered one-liner deserves mention because its mangled execution also ended Jean Rhys's acting career.[8]) Petronella scares Melville away with material demands—appropriately, naming the same items she heard named by the off-putting Norfolk farmer a few hours before. "I'll see you in September, Petronella" (p. 39), Melville says, as did Marston earlier in the day.

In September? The month is July, Petronella wants company, and her one friend is out of town. Condemned to an empty present, she has to wait two months for the void to fill. As everybody knows, two months can be an eternity to the bored and the unhappy. The dismissal voiced in the story's title describes a life marked by goodbyes but no real chances for renewal. Another phrase she hears twice, "You" (or "Don't") "look as if you'd lost a shilling and found sixpence" (pp. 18, 27), sheds light on the title phrase: though the deferred (September) meeting will compensate for the present setback, it doesn't compensate *today*. Petronella is still bereft. The story's time-setting, 28 July 1914, i.e., a week before the outbreak of World War I, yokes her bereavement to the collapse of the West. Howard Moss does well to call the tale the book's best.[9] Petronella's unfocused life could easily drift into the madness that will soon overtake Europe. The young men she might expect to meet will probably spend the next five Septembers fighting at the front. But Jean Rhys offers no stony-jawed prognoses. Like Chekhov's best work, the story is free, open-ended, and uncluttered. While its details are vivid and its outlines clear, its characters do not dissolve into a plot or a polemic. Their freedom gives the underlying menace an extra charge of energy.

The menace erupts in the next story, "The Day They Burned the Books" (1960). Like "Petronella," "Day" takes place mostly in the afternoon, when time drags hardest on the idle. No careerist or gentleman-adventurer, Eddie Sawyer's English father came to the tropics for reasons known only to himself. Neither his job with a small steamship line nor his marriage to a mulatto native, whom he badgers in public, has fulfilled him. His sole pleasure, besides the

bottle, comes from his private library, which he stocks with books from England. When Eddie reaches puberty, the time he needs his father most, the father dies. The Rhys paradigm of the absentee father and the mad mother takes hold quickly. Long-suffering Mrs. Sawyer releases her madness at the first opportunity. Though Eddie takes over the library—"'My books,' he would say, 'my books'"— (p. 43) his mother has other plans for it. As a reminder of both her cruel husband and his English heritage, the library must go. Certain titles she slates for resale; the ones with words like *British* and *English,* she burns. A Christina Rossetti book also goes into the flames; having asserted herself in a masculinist society, Rossetti has reproached Mrs. Sawyer for her faintheartedness; now she pays for the reproach.

Burning her dead husband's books—a symbolic relegation of Sawyer to hell—beautifies Mrs. Sawyer. But Jean Rhys often lifts a character's spirits before raining down trouble. The widow's revenge is imperfect. Eddie and the nameless twelve-year-old narrator of the story both snatch a book from the fire and run away before Mrs. Sawyer can stop them. Symbolism extends the allegory. The narrator's remark about herself and Eddie after the theft, "Now perhaps we're married" (p. 46), fuses with the Sawyers' garden, the site of the book-burning, to convey the loss of innocence. Carrying the idea forward, the two salvaged books impart bitter knowledge. Eddie's book, Kipling's *Kim,* with its endorsement of British imperialism, is an apt legacy from his father. But the first twenty pages are missing, depriving the boy of his full inheritance. The narrator is let down still more. Just before opening her book, she calls it "the most important thing that ever happened to me" (p. 46). But the book, de Maupassant's 1890 novel of hopeless love, *Fort comme la mort,* is written in a language she cannot read. Though the book's theme has already touched her, she will never learn its wisdom. Sawyer's bequest obeys an iron logic. The legacy of an exile who never made sense of his life consists of two unreadable books.

"Let Them Call It Jazz" (1962) also features noncomprehension and bitterness. But we are no longer in the Antilles. The local reference, the cadencing, and the vocabulary of the first sentence identify the tale-teller straightaway as a West Indian black living in London: "One bright Sunday morning in July I have trouble with my Notting Hill landlord because he ask for a month's rent in advance" (p. 47). The Notting Hill riots of 1958 explain the unfair demands made on Selina Davis, the tale-teller. Though Selina has lived in the

rooming house for months, paying her rent regularly by the week, her landlord wants to evict her. The ouster comes at a bad time for Selina, who is out of work. She does leave, but not before a bitter scene, during which the landlord's wife, who may have stolen money Selina had tucked away, kicks her suitcase open, giving her best dress a special boot. Leaving this harpy brightens Selina's outlook, but only briefly. Her sudden turn of luck proves as deceptive as the false gleams sent out by the Norfolk farmer in "Petronella." A man Selina meets in a café, Mr. Sims, offers her the use of a vacant furnished flat. She accepts. But after she moves in, she has time on her hands. In her loneliness, she waits for the clock to toll the hour, gazes out the window, and, inevitably, drinks: "I get the habit of buying a bottle of wine most evenings" (p. 49), says she of her new routine.

Mr. Sims, the building's owner or manager, comes by after two weeks, carrying sandwiches and bottles. But he never says whether he wants Selina as a mistress or as an addition to a stable of prostitutes he may operate. Kissing her "like you kiss a baby" (p. 52), he asks her to stay another week at the house. Selina, curiously content with her new arrangement, accepts the offer, vowing privately to find work. But her resolve flags and, rather than looking for a job, she stays home and drinks. Then complaining neighbors get her hauled before a magistrate, who fines her £5 for being drunk and disorderly. Mr. Sims hears of her setback, and, though displeased, offers to pay her fine—an offer that worries Selina because he has not asked for anything in return. The trouble that follows has little to do with Sims, though. Selina stays sober for three weeks, but the frustration of not being able to reach Sims by phone starts her drinking again. Another complaint by the neighbor who engineered her arrest a month before angers her so much that she throws a rock through the neighbor's stained-glass window. Selina must face the judge again. But first she combs her hair and files her nails; though humiliated, the Rhys heroine always retains dignity and self-respect.

The judge comes down more heavily on Selina for her second offense than for her first. Her foul talk, obscene dancing, and window-smashing send her to Holloway jail. Her first stop at Holloway is the prison hospital, where she spends a week recovering from the stress that caused her outburst. Then, one day in the prison yard, she hears a woman singing. "That's the Holloway song" (p. 64), she is told in what proves to be the key event of her short prison term. The news of her release follows. During her third and last appearance before the bench, she learns that her fine has been paid. But by whom?

Demonstrating the lack of control she has over her life is her never
learning the name of her benefactor. Recalling Petronella Grey, she
feels, in her puzzled helplessness, like somebody who found sixpence
after losing a shilling. The feeling holds. After leaving jail, she finds a
job, a new room, and a friend. One night, a man she meets at a party
hears her whistling the Holloway song, rearranges it for a jazz piano,
and, some time later, sends her £5 for it. She takes the money with a
heavy heart: "I read the letter and I could cry. For after all, that song
was all I had. I don't belong nowhere really, and I haven't any money
to buy my way to belonging. I don't want to either" (p. 67). That her
private experience of the song remains inviolate does not comfort
her. The song has become cheap and confused, like everything else
she touches. "'So let them call it jazz,' I think, and let them play it
wrong" (p. 67), she muses. They have appropriated the song and
changed it; they might as well label it, too. Selina has nothing to call
her own. "I buy myself a dusty pink dress" (p. 67) with her royalty, she
says in the story's last sentence. The dress serves as a consolation
prize. One hopes that no shrewish landlady will kick it.

The story's great triumph consists of its bubbling, colorful
language. A remarkable impersonation, Selina's speech includes the
concreteness, the gently, swaying rhythms, and the attunement to
natural processes of native Caribbean English. Some sentences begin
with the adverbial, "Too." Others omit verbs, use present-tense verbs
in places where the past tense is called for, or select verbs that disagree
with their subjects in number. Though no handy passage will show all
these devices at work, the following paragraph conveys both the soft
birdlike lilt and candor trilling through the story:

So I agree that many things shameful. But what to do? What to do? I say it
have an elegant shape, it make the other houses in the street look cheap trash,
and she seem pleased. That's true too. The house sad and out of place,
especially at night. But it have style. The second floor shut up, and as for my
flat, I go in the two empty rooms once, but never again. (p. 49)

Selina's talk also separates her from all the other people in the story;
nobody else speaks as she does. A black woman from the tropics with
her own speaking style, she is a perfect example of the underdog, the
key figure in Jean Rhys's fictional world.

The Australian journalist, Mr. N. Severn of "Tigers Are Better-
looking" (1962), is another colonial-in-exile who has no chance in
London. Nor is he the story's only outsider crushed by the city. The

action opens with a farewell letter from Severn's friend, Hans. Hans writes, "I came to London with high hopes, but all I got out of it was a broken leg and enough sneers to last one for the next thirty years" (p. 68). After a day of work, Severn turns up in Soho with two young women—sensible Maidie Richards and a "sharp, bright self-confident" (p. 71) acquaintance called Heather. Heather suggests drinks at the Jim-Jam Club, where, it becomes clear, she has a personal stake. After paying an unexpected admission charge, Severn orders some gingerale. But Heather wants whisky, and the waiter who brings it wants his money straightaway. Our impression that Heather is fleecing her two companions deepens when she drinks very little herself and asks the headwaiter to join the threesome. The invitation reveals a great deal. Heather has invited the help to drink the same liquor they overcharge for. Naturally, the help refuses. The headwaiter despises his customers, for reasons given by Maidie in a remark about drink-peddlers: "People are funny about drinking. . . . They get you to buy as much as they can and then afterwards they laugh at you behind your back for buying it. But on the other hand, if you try to get out of buying it, they're damned rude" (p. 73).

Drink-buyers can be insulted openly, too. Her work done, Heather refuses more whisky to join some friends at the bar. Unsettled by having proved himself such an easy mark, Severn starts scribbling nervously on the tablecloth. A row with a waiter follows, which ends with Severn's being ousted from the club. Then the action peaks. His blood biting and snapping, the usually mild Severn swings "as hard as he could" (p. 76) at the waiter who had belted him on the way out of the club. Glorying in his manly self-esteem, he watches the waiter stagger and fall. His glory does not last long. Determined to retaliate, the waiter gets up, but, instead of charging Severn, hits—Maidie. Cowardice wins the day, as three men from the club pound Severn before seeing to it that he gets blamed for the fracas. The Jim-Jam incident fulfills a prophecy voiced in Hans's letter at the outset:

You people are exactly alike. . . . You'd pine to death if you hadn't someone to look down on and insult. I got the feeling that I was surrounded by a pack of timid tigers waiting to spring the moment anybody is in trouble or hasn't any money. *But tigers are better-looking, aren't they?* (p. 68)

To be whipped by the English is to lose face as well as territory or money. Though destructive, the English lack the barbarism and jungle wildness of tigers. Substituting guile for terror and ferocity, they belittle and betray anybody who cannot fight back.

But they are more than Severn can handle. In his fight against what Jean Rhys called in "Vienne" "the huge machinery of law, order, respectability" (p. 226), he loses hands down. The machine grinds relentlessly. He is cuffed about by the police, fined, sentenced, and locked in a cell, all within an hour of the skirmish outside the Jim-Jam. What happens to him after his release from jail shows that the meaning of the night's mishaps has passed him by. He snubs brave, sensible Maidie, who stood by him and who, being Irish and thus a fellow colonial, understands his problems. The last page shows him at a great distance from himself, as he goes back to the "swell article" (p. 69) he is writing on London life. Not only do his life and his work (he wants to call the article "Jubilee") remain miles apart; in rejecting Maidie he also loses his chance to heal the split. What is more, his cruelty to her, caused by his mistaking her generosity and openness for weakness, leagues him with his oppressors. The ease with which he takes his place in the pecking order shows his smooth adjustment to English ways. Severn is more socialized than he knows. But he has also lost touch with himself. Perhaps his friend Hans was lucky to escape England with only a broken leg. Severn's self-division will not mend as quickly as damaged bone.

The suffering that throbs through "Tigers" comes back in the hospital setting of the next story, "Outside the Machine" (1960). Like "Vienne" and the uncollected "Temps Perdi" (1967), "Machine" proves that the long, episodic tale does not unleash Jean Rhys's best energies. Unlike these two other works, though, it profits from having a unified setting—the women's ward of a clinic near Versailles "run on strictly English lines" (p. 83), which is to say that, with its high, inaccessible windows, mechanical routine, and self-important head nurse, it resembles a prison. Even on French soil, England remains Jean Rhys's metaphor for the drab and the loveless.

Her rouge, powder, and lipstick identify Inez Best right away as the story's heroine; the head nurse's objection to patients bringing cosmetics into the ward sharpens the identification: here, the repressive, establishment-backed authority is female. Inez prevails for the moment, using herself delicately and ignoring unfriendly criticism. But, as the story's title suggests, she and her fellow patients resemble defective or damaged parts of a machine. Inez befriends a young actress named Pat, fair Mrs. Wilson, and stout, elderly Mme. Tavernier. They and the others tell jokes and stories, write letters, and exchange personal histories while being reconditioned to meet to needs of their uncaring technological society. Then the action both focuses and blurs. Inez is to have surgery. A morphine shot, and then,

in Part II, she is wheeled to the operating room; the surgery (the nature of which is never revealed) occurs between Parts II and III, when she is unconscious. Though the operation succeeds, nobody rejoices; in III, the story's midpart, Inez, on waking up, notes that the comatose patient in the next bed is gone. No explanation is needed. The death of Inez's neighbor grips us all the more for not being mentioned. The scene is one of admirable restraint and tact:

> The screen round the bed on the opposite side had been taken away. The bed was empty. Inez looked at it and said nothing. Madame Tavernier, who saw her looking at it, also said nothing, but for a moment her eyes were frightened. (p. 94)

The death helps convey the rhythm of hospital life: some patients are known by their first names, some by their last; one dies, another is admitted, and still another goes home. Through it all, doctors and nurses stalk the wards, taking temperatures, giving drugs, and talking to the patients.

This banality lurches into terror when one of the patients, Mrs. Murphy, a married mother of two, tries to kill herself. The suicide attempt sends tension through the ward. Mrs. Wilson is outraged: "Oughtn't a woman like that be hung?" (p. 100). Her reaction is typical. As in "Tigers," the oppressed seize every chance to savage those more unlucky than they. Inez steps outside the pecking order, though, insisting that Mrs. Murphy belongs in a mental hospital rather than a general ward. Her compassion angers her friends. But neither Mrs. Wilson nor Pat daunts her. Calling them a "pair of bitches," she scolds them for maligning "a sad woman" (p. 101). Her remonstrances have little positive effect. Part V recounts her leavetaking. Still weak from surgery and upset over the suicide incident, she needs a few days more of bed rest to sort herself out. But she has already passed up the chance to extend her stay in the ward; and, now that her bed is needed for a new patient, Inez feels lost. She has alienated Pat and Mrs. Wilson; she must leave the ward before she is ready; she has nobody to look after her.

Hope comes from an unexpected source—soft, flabby Mme. Tavernier, who has been gone from the action since Part III and has not spoken since Part I. Mme. Tavernier's book is cracked open to the passage, *"De là-haut le paysage qu'on découvre est d'une indiscriptible beauté"* (p. 104). Inez soon learns that indescribable beauty exists outside of books. After complimenting her on her dress,

old Mme. Tavernier presses a scented handkerchief filled with franc notes into her hand. This stroke of surpassing kindness (from perhaps the only non-English patient on the ward) promotes in Inez new insight: "She had never taken money from a woman before. She did not like women . . . or trust them" (p. 105). The insight pales quickly, though. Symbolizing her return to the mentality of the machine are her first acts outside the hospital—calling and then boarding a taxi. "You can't die and come to life again" (p. 106), she mutters inwardly as she goes back to town, having rejected renewal through love as stupidly as Mr. Severn did in "Tigers" and Roseau did in "La Grosse Fifi."

"The Lotus" (1967), the most recent story in the book, also deals with woman's unkindness to her sisters. The unkindness cuts deeper here because it involves tenants of the same apartment building rather than people thrown together at random for a brief time. Christine and Ronnie Miles are discussing their basement neighbor, a late-middle-aged novelist and poet Lotus Heath. Like so many other Jean Rhys heroines, Lotus drinks too much. Her drinking becomes an issue early on. No sooner does Christine say, "Perhaps we'll have a bit of luck; she may get tight earlier than usual tonight and not turn up" (p. 107), than Lotus raps on the door. Frumpy, hoarse-voiced Lotus is returning a book she had borrowed, evidently for the purpose of having an excuse to spend time with the Mileses over a drink. "I get fed up, I can tell you, sitting by myself in that basement night after night. And day after day too if it comes to that" (p. 108), she says through her heavily made-up face. Perhaps the worst of her loneliness is that she needs the Mileses more than they need her and that the three of them know it. Gulping her whisky, she maneuvers polite, pliable Ronnie into pouring her a refill. Nor is she too drunk to let Christine's sarcasms go unnoticed. Wanting to save face, she offers to fetch a bottle of port she knows she does not have. Naturally, she does not hurry downstairs. Taking advantage of her weakness, Christine interrupts Lotus's drunken recitation of a poem by asking her to do a solo dance—ironically, it turns out, to the song, "Just One More Chance."

With Ronnie siding meekly with her, Lotus parries this cruelty with some barbs of her own. Then Jean Rhys removes her from the scene to let her neighbors discuss her. Ashamed of his kindness, Ronnie placates Christine by calling Lotus "the funniest old relic of the past I've struck for a long time"; Christine says with more malice, "She oughtn't to be touched with a barge pole" (p. 113). Lotus comes

back, announcing that she could not find the port. Then dizziness overtakes her. Ronnie helps her down to her foul-smelling basement flat. The action bends sharply here. Back home, she drops her defenses. "He takes everything he can lay his hands on. Never comes to see me except it's to grab something" (p. 115), she wails, neglecting to name the person who has let her down. (Her son? The poem she starts reciting at the Mileses' is "The Convict's Mother.") The platitudes of well-meaning Ronnie do not calm her. Soon after going back upstairs, he sees Lotus running naked through the streets, "a white figure . . . looking very small and strange in the darkness" (p. 116). Christine responds to Lotus's collapse with her usual sourness: "Good Lord. . . . Well, that's one way of attracting attention if all else fails" (p. 117). Cowed by her malice, Ronnie withholds compassion for the first time. He does not follow Lotus into the street, and he tells an investigating policeman that he hardly knows her. Following suit, the other tenants in the building hold back information, too. Nobody will help Lotus. At the end, Ronnie watches her being carried on a stretcher to an ambulance. Christine avoids the window. Looking "very pretty and warm" (p. 119), she has already drunk her fill of Lotus's pain and thrived on the draft. People benefit from each other's bad luck in the Rhys canon; people also flee unpleasantness when they can. The loveliness paid for by Lotus's sanity distracts Ronnie from the sad scene outside, and he starts making love to Christine as the story ends.

The moral outlook put forth in the closing pages of "The Lotus" is very dark, even for Jean Rhys: art has gone under, meanness has triumphed, and virtue has stood by ineffectively. Yet Jean Rhys's technique of angling the story from the standpoint of the Mileses tones down the severity. We see all that we need of poor Lotus to believe in both her anguish and its causes. A longer look at her would have lengthened the story and increased the danger of sentimentality. The printed version has no soft spots: suffice it that Lotus's artistic personality makes her vulnerable to pain; she need not have a tragic past or a special talent for moral virtue. "The Lotus" maintains both balance and perspective. A crisis story, it shows its main character from a sympathetic and an unsympathetic standpoint; it also notes, without analyzing them, the forces that drove her, first, to her cellar and, next, into the cold, dark street above. Any more detail would have distracted from the Mileses' response to her downfall.

Neighborly cruelty also runs through "A Solid House" (1963), which takes place in a London rooming house during the Blitz. The

five-part story is Jean Rhys's most Chekhovian: the owner of the house is away, creating a sense of loss among those left behind; the dialogue either stumbles or wheels in tired circles; their fixation on the past keeps the characters from coping with the fast changes going on around them. Lotus Heath lived in a cellar; "A Solid House" begins in one, with deaf, old Miss Spearman, the pushy building manager, waiting with a tenant named Teresa for the all-clear to sound. To pass the time, the women discuss the past, dotting their genteel talk with incongruous-sounding references to bombing casualties. The incongruous, the bent, and the broken dominate the story. Miss Spearman is as sharp-edged as a fragmented shell. Instead of worrying whether a bomb killed Nelly the char on her way to work, she complains of Nelly's lateness.

Part III of the story takes place in the afternoon, the time when disaster usually strikes in the fiction of Jean Rhys. Our fears are confirmed; though no bombs drop, the section recounts Teresa's suicide attempt. No heartbreak drove her to suicide, only the monstrous cruelty of neglect, which overtook her when the languors of mid-afternoon lowered her guard. The solid house of the story's title stands in a bomb-gutted city and lodges frightened, broken tenants. The exception is Miss Spearman, who dabbles in spiritualism and deals used ladies' clothes in her spare time. In Part IV, she opens the sitting room for Teresa to have her nap amid luxury. Teresa plods in after her and looks at the bookshelf, the wall hangings, and a case of stuffed birds. These trappings unnerve her, and she goes somewhere else to nap. This somewhere else is not the dining room setting of Part V, where she next meets Miss Spearman. The building manager asks her to join her for a seance and, having her invitation politely declined, reacts angrily: "Her friendliness seemed to float away in the act of putting the dishes on the tray and she slammed the door . . . violently" (p. 137). Her departure from the house some time later brings the peace Teresa needs for her nap. The noise tapers to silence.

The title, "A Solid House," proves ironical. The unnamed absentee owner, representing, like the many absentee fathers in the canon, the spirit of the house, has left the city; his tenants, most of whom never appear, stay trapped inside their private fantasies. Instead of bringing them closer, the Blitz has sent them scuttling to their goods and dreams. No symbol of solidarity, the architecturally sound house where they room has a hollow core.

A strong sense both of place and of mystery also focuses "The

Sound of the River" (1966). A nameless couple is staying at a friend's
moorland cottage. Although she chose the vacation site, the woman
is anxious. She frets, the man comforts and consoles. Then he turns
out the light in preparation for sleep. Lying awake in the dark
heightens her fears. Needing his strength, she pleads inwardly, "Stay
awake and comfort me. I'm frightened. . . . Don't turn away and sigh
and sleep" (p. 142). He has turned away from her for good. The next
morning, she finds him dead. As in James Agee's *A Death in the
Family*, the sick character languishes, and the strong, healthy one
dies swiftly. Why? Do her demands kill him? Her calling the coroner
from the house of a Mr. Ransom, the story's only named character,
implies that her comforter-lover has died to let her live. But the
action, told largely through symbols and images, ends in mystery.

The imagery and symbolism turn Jean Rhys's familiar failure-to-
connect theme into a category of natural law. Nature is askew. The
sunrise that awakens the woman ushers in the first fine weather of her
vacation. Yet this same sunrise reveals the corpse. The purling river
that runs near the death cottage also denotes life; its comparison to
"streaming hair" (p. 139) gives this life sexual force. The woman's
fear, caused by parental rejection, fixes on the river. Why, she does
not know. The story ends with her saying twice, "I heard the sound of
the river" (p. 144). Though able to isolate her malaise, she cannot
explain it. Her bewilderment touches us. As in "A Solid House," the
characters shrink from forces they cannot control. But "Sound" has a
trimmer line than its longer counterpart. Working within the tight
frame imposed by its materials, the story proves the value of shrewd
plotting. Its irony, balance, and control make it a brilliant rhetorical
exercise. The mystery sounding through it elevates it to something
more—a vision of horror and disaster.

### III  Sleep It Off, Lady *and the Uncollected Stories*

That Jean Rhys's uncollected fiction and the stories in the recently
published collection *Sleep It Off, Lady* resemble her collected work
of the 1960s shows clearly in the subjects, characters, and techniques
of "I Spy a Stranger." This story, which came out in *Art and Literature* in 1966, returns to the British pastime of picking on underdogs;
in "A Solid House," Jean Rhys called this practice "witch-hunting."
The object of the witch-hunt in "Stranger" hasn't a chance; as a
middle-aged intellectual spinster with a background in foreign travel,
she is a natural victim of her neighbors' war hysteria. The harshness

of her fellow boarders outdoes that described in both "Lotus" and "House." The most embattled, "Stranger" could also be the best of the three tales. Its people react to the war more believably than those in "House," and the nonappearance of its main character calls forth a bolder technique than does "Lotus." The whole story consists of two women gossiping. One, Marion Hudson, takes charge of the conversation; her sister, Mrs. Trant, exists to break up the recitation by asking the right questions.

Mrs. Hudson is complaining about the hubbub caused in her neighborhood recently by her cousin Laura. One anonymous letter warned her to "get rid of that crazy old foreigner, that witch of Prague," who has been staying with her. (In 1969, Jean Rhys told the *Sunday Observer* that one of her neighbors had called *her* a witch.)[10] Concurring with the British wartime sport of baiting foreigners, Mrs. Hudson asks Laura, who has been away from England long enough to be mistaken for foreign, to go to London. "It's no use thinking you can ignore public opinion," she says, reminding Laura that, having only come back home as a last resort, she should not complain about being the butt of local gossip.[11] This gossip, she admits to her sister, started with an ugly remark dropped by a Mr. Fluting, which Laura responded to in kind. The outcome of the incident could have been predicted: even though Fluting started the trouble, Laura, who is less able to defend herself, pays more dearly for it.

Mrs. Hudson takes this unfairness in stride, even though its victim is her cousin. The traditional British distrust of intellect expresses itself in her reference to Laura's "cracky ideas."[12] Cracky ideas to Mrs. Hudson mean Laura's dismay over the war—its origin, meaning, and impact on friends trapped on the Continent. Laura has written letters, scoured newspapers, and ordered books from London to get information about these subjects. In the meantime, she has taken to her room and put together a war scrapbook consisting of "headlines and articles and advertisements and reports of cases in court and jokes."[13] Though upset by the war, she has nonetheless tried to make sense of it. This courage marks her out for cruelty. After her neighbors drive her to her room, they resent her for keeping to herself. She can do no right:

She had some good clothes when she first came and she used to make the best of herself. "These refugees!" he'd say, "all dressed up and nowhere to go." Then she got that she didn't care a damn what she looked like and he grumbled about that. She aged a lot too. "Ricky," I said, "if you do your best

to get people down you can't blame them when they look down, can you?" Sometimes I wonder if she wasn't a bit right.[14]

The bitterness intensifies. The police confiscate her scrapbook, only to return it as harmless. But Ricky, Mrs. Hudson's querulous son or husband, wants it destroyed, anyway. Nor is he alone. Nobody understands the pressures Laura lives with. Nobody can afford to; it would mean suspending prejudice and challenging the majority. Mrs. Hudson admits that Laura is steady, helpful, and generous: "She paid well and she was good about helping me in the house, too. Yes, I was quite pleased to have her—at first."[15] The qualification spells the difference between recognition and action: to like unpopular people is dangerous. Regardless of who is to blame, Laura has enemies. Anyone who sides with her will also invite enemies.

Trouble comes after the source of trouble has been removed— Laura having agreed to go away. The worst air-raid to hit the town has upset the townsfolk. Nobody wonders whether the air-raid has upset her, too. She is too valuable as a victim. Even though she is leaving, Mrs. Hudson's Ricky storms, "That's enough now. She's as mad as a hatter and I won't stand for it a day longer. She *must* get out."[16] He is determined to hurt her. Under the pretext that her blackout curtain has been leaking light, he and Fluting try to have her arrested as a spy. (The cowardly Ricky also threatens to kick her door in until the door's sturdiness changes his mind.) Although their scheme fails, it does wound her heart. The only compassion she receives comes from a stranger, Dr. Pratt. A kindly local physician, he is nevertheless called "old-fashioned" and "obstinate as the devil"[17] for saying that Laura should not be on her own. Seeing her whipped gladdens Ricky, who takes her to the cab waiting to cart her away. "Come along, old girl," he says cruelly, "It's moving day."[18] When she protests, he responds with cheerful brutality—hitting and kicking her all the way out of the house.

The move to the sanitorium dooms her. "A large, ugly house with small windows,"[19] some of them barred, the sanitorium *is* ugly, Mrs. Hudson admits. But it costs far less than the one Dr. Pratt recommended. It also has a golf course, adds Mrs. Hudson with manufactured cheer, looking to clear herself for staying away from the rest home on visiting day. Avoiding Laura comes easily to her because it means avoiding guilt. It is also Mrs. Hudson's standard practice. So little has she cared about her cousin that she never bothered to know if Laura plays golf. In an indirect confession of

guilt, she ends the story with the groundless hope that golf is, in fact, Laura's game.

The wartime setting of the first part of "Temps Perdi" (1967) recalls both "Stranger" and "A Solid House." The fragmented, imagistic story also recalls the early "Vienne" in its episodic structure and Japanese characters. In fact, it repeats some phrases and ideas nearly *verbatim* from the earlier work.[20] The action does not begin in Vienna, though. At the start, the narrator is living alone in Rolvenden, a house belonging to an English school teacher who left the area in order to escape the Blitz. The war has insinuated itself into the daily lives of those who stayed behind. The two houses flanking Rolvenden in this "time of smash and grab"[21] have been taken over by the army, and tanks rumble through the local streets. A snowfall cheers the lonely narrator, sending her mind back to a Cuban high-wire act she saw years before on her small Caribbean island. But the festive memory only comforts her briefly. Yanking her back to the dreary present is the fear that some villagers have been taking her coal. The gay, colorful tropics have yielded to the biting East Anglia winter, where neighbors steal and where everything—faces, clothes, furnishings—is colored beige.

But no confrontation with a whey-faced thief occurs. In a Proustian motif hinted at in the story's title, a smell wafts her back to Vienna. Part II, "The Sword Dance and the Love Dance," begins immediately. The officers of the Japanese commission from "Vienne" have come back with names and personalities. One, "the tallest, handsomest, and best-dressed"[22] of the commission, likes to dance; another, who lost an eye in the Russo-Japanese War, hates all white people—except the Germans, whom he esteems as the future leaders of Europe. The narrator's husband has also gained definition; Pierre works as Hungarian interpreter to the Japanese. Neither he nor his wife makes much happen, though. Some political and military gossip promises to generate drama. But, instead, it flattens into an inventory of the narrator's wardrobe. A further train of associations leads to a reference to the Caribs, a mysterious West Indian tribe the narrator visits in Part III, "Carib Quarter."

"Carib Quarter" explains the Creole patois term, "Temps Perdi," as "wasted time, lost labor."[23] The explanation reveals little. Right after it, the action, what little there is, takes over. Accompanied by a handsome black man named Nicholas, the narrator goes to Salybia, the Carib enclave. As the story's title suggests, the visit falls short of her expectations—expectations created by books, illustrations, and

hearsay. If the Caribs have a secret language and live off buried treasure, as legend claims, they keep the information to themselves. The day brings no uplift. The narrator reaches Salybia by riding through scrubland on a morose, bony horse. The most notable Carib she meets is the town's main attraction, a beautiful girl who cannot walk. Every visitor to the Quarter photographs this symbol of wingless beauty and gives her some coins. But the crippled girl never intended to become a tourist attraction. She tells the narrator that, though she enjoys the attention, she came back to Salybia to spend time with her dying mother.

The remark dumps the narrator where she was at the outset: "It is at night that you know old fears, old hopes, that you know unhappiness, turning from side to side under the mosquito-net, like a prisoner in a cell full of small peepholes."[24] "Temps Perdi" is a looking-glass story. The West Indian who migrated to England returns to the tropics to find the same dreariness and dislocation that have always plagued her. Her travels have taught her that life everywhere is a prison. People are trapped behind mosquito nets, in remote outposts, or by crippling diseases. What looks like an escape is merely the substitution of one cage for another. The narrator has no more freedom at winterswept Rolvenden than amid the glitter and glow of Vienna. But her entrapment does not include us. As in "Vienne," wayward plotting and dim character portraits keep us outside the narrator's psychological cage.

The narrative focus sharpens in "Sleep It Off Lady" (1974), Jean Rhys's latest and perhaps best short story. The work embodies several familiar motifs: cruel neighbors whittling down a spinster who lives alone; old age as a crime; a sympathetic but ineffectual doctor. Jean Rhys distances this material with great skill; her Miss Verney, the aging woman broken by neglect and derision, tries people's patience as grievously as those two other tipplers, Lotus Heath and Selina Davis ("Jazz"). Miss Verney seems doomed from the start. Like "House" and "Stranger," the story begins with two women talking. Jean Rhys launches her theme by beginning, "One October afternoon Mrs. Baker was having tea with a Miss Verney."[25] The indefinite article before her name calls Miss Verney's identity into question. This is intended: the younger Letty Baker has both a first name and a husband; by contrast, Miss Verney is cut off from life's best chances by being single, by her sex, and, finally, by her age, which is "well over seventy."[26] But deprivation has not immobilized her. She has a project: to tear down an ugly old shed squatting on her

property. The project makes sense: "It was an eyesore," we learn of the shed. "Most of the paint had worn off the once-black galvanised iron. . . . Part of the roof was loose and flapped noisily in windy weather and a small gate off its hinges leaned up against the entrance."[27] But nobody will tear the shed down for her. The intimation that the hideous, sagging wreck will outlast *her* makes Miss Verney panic. The panic heightens when the shed acquires a totem—Super-rat, an imaginary or real rat she spots while emptying a small yellow dustbin. The fear symbolized by the color yellow (a constant in Jean Rhys) grips Miss Verney. Even after a local man mines the shed with rat poison, the rat mocks her with his presence; he thrives in the shed, intends to stay, and wants Miss Verney to know it.

Having committed us to Miss Verney imaginatively before telling us of her alcoholism, Jean Rhys can safely have the man who put out the poison attribute the rat to her heroine's tippling. This insult draws Miss Verney further into her obsession and further away from other people. As she withdraws from others, she understands less about the world around her and becomes more frightened. She shuts her windows; bolts the windows and doors of the shed; takes special pains storing and disposing of food, like cheese and pork products, that could attract a rat; cleans her house fanatically. Then she takes to eating less while drinking more. Naturally, her health declines along with her social image. A doctor who knows the dangers of loneliness as well as Dr. Pratt of "Stranger" advises her to get a telephone and to avoid heavy lifting. The visit to the doctor gives her hope. She feels younger, stronger, more relaxed; as soon as her phone is installed, she will invite Letty Baker to tea. Then she remembers to empty the little yellow dustbin. The chore does not faze her. The big bin that holds her rubbish is standing in its proper place near the shed, heavy stones on its lid to foil Super-rat, who seems to have been outsmarted.

Heartened, Miss Verney makes the mistake of removing the rocks holding down the dustbin lid. Although she succeeds, the subsequent effort of lifting her small pailful of paper, bread scraps, and eggshells knocks her down and clamps her to the cold earth. She still cannot move by nightfall, and none of the passers-by hear her cries for help. Frozen against the freezing darkness, she watches the road empty of people. Then she spots a twelve-year-old neighbor looking at her from her parents' gate. But Undine, or Deena, dismisses her pleas with the words, "Sleep it off lady."[28] The cold-hearted girl who loves cold weather and whose namesake in European folklore lacks a soul then turns soullessly away. The next morning Miss Verney is found

by a postman bearing a package of books for her. But she profits as little from the communication and interchange the book-bearing postman symbolizes as from her undelivered telephone. That evening she dies.

In ascribing her death to heart failure, her doctor never discovers its meaning. But this insult to Miss Verney is only one of several. She cannot avoid waste, decay, and vermin. The trash that spills from her little yellow dustbin festoons her body like a funeral wreath. And why shouldn't it? Her neighbors see no moral difference between her and the trash she lies in. The woman who had planned to come out of her lonely shell sprawls in a litter of eggshells, symbolizing her maimed rebirth. Miss Verney spends her last waking moments awaiting the assault of Super-rat. The slow romantic decline suggested in a line from Tennyson's "Ulysses" she recites, "After many a summer dies the swan,"[29] does not apply to her any more than the various symbols of communication that call attention to her hopelessness. Degradation is her lot. Dismissed as trash, she is done in by the job of emptying trash, and she dies amid trash. She could have spilled out of her dustbin with the other debris.

A remarkable achievement for an eighty-year-old, "Sleep It Off Lady" proves that, though basically a novelist, Jean Rhys can also do justice to the more exacting demands of the short story. Works like it, "Illusion," and "Petronella" come often enough in her career to show that some of her best work belongs to the genre. Although she sometimes misfires, her voice in the short stories is usually strong and clear, and her grasp of femininity, extraordinary.

## IV  Sleep It Off, Lady

*Sleep It Off, Lady* (1976) brings back many of the characters, settings, and attitudes of Jean Rhys's other fiction. Just as noteworthy is her ability, in her latest book, to write freshly and gracefully about grubby, formless lives. The exiles, outcasts, and dropouts peopling the book would escape notice but for the careful attention Jean Rhys gives them, her honesty and accuracy of observation creating poetical effects out of prosaic materials. Plot, style, and mood fuse easily in these bleak little encounters; one of the most touching, skilfully pointed stories in the book is only a page and a half long.

Several of the others have appeared in the (London) *Times*, *Mademoiselle*, and the *New Yorker*. Many have titles that are either

ironic ("Pioneers, Oh Pioneers," "On Not Shooting Sitting Birds") or flat ("Heat," "Night Out 1925"). Most include some item of autobiography—a young West Indian girl with a doctor for a father, a West Indian *émigrée* forced to drop out of London's Academy of Dramatic Art because her father dies, an elderly woman living alone in Devonshire. Then there is the book's careful organization. The stories look at Jean Rhys chronologically, from her island girlhood through her years in London and Paris; before providing a short parting glimpse at Dominica, the book inserts a group of stories about old people set in provincial England. But the stories trace a realistic curve from childhood to old age. A retired naval captain in "Goodbye Marcus, Goodbye Rose" and an old nun who dies at the end of "The Bishop's Feast" make age a force in the West Indian group of tales opening the book. Similarly, childhood counter-weights age in the last two stories. Besides twelve-year-old Deena, old Miss Verney's horrible neighbor in "Sleep It Off, Lady," Jean Rhys includes two little white children in "I Used to Live Here Once," the last story in the book. The story merits discussion. In it, Jean Rhys returns in spirit, through her anonymous heroine, to the Caribbean home she had revisited physically in the third story of the book, "The Bishop's Feast," a description of her first homecoming in twenty-five years. She is standing by a river, symbolic of the border she has just crossed, and looking at the local landmarks. A car parked in front of her family's summer home is but one incongruity in a parade of familiar and unfamiliar things. Then the drama starts. Two children she speaks to on a "rough lawn" (p. 175) disregard her; at her third greeting, one of them complains of a sudden chill in the air. Then they both go home. Their turning from the heroine to go indoors makes her see that the chill that touched them came from her. Having brought a chill to the tropics, she must be dead. Jean Rhys's tactic of delaying this recognition till the story's last sentence, "That was the first time she knew" (p. 176), makes for a powerful climax; the "rough lawn" where the aged heroine's recognition takes place refers to the loss of innocence and the shedding of illusions marking the passage from one stage of being to the next. Though given less than 500 words of foreshadowing, this passage touches our hearts.

The first brace of stories, to which "I Used to Live Here" refers, all take place around the turn of the century. The date of "Pioneers" is November 1899; "Heat," the fourth story in the book, is set 8 May 1902, the day Mont Pelée erupted, razing the city of St. Pierre in Martinique; some letters in the next story, "Fishy Waters," date the

action March 189—. The book's second story, "Goodbye Marcus, Goodbye Rose," varies the pattern subtly. Twelve-year-old Phoebe entices Captain Cardew, a handsome old battle veteran who has come to the West Indies to retire. Normally soft-spoken and reserved, the veteran officer slides his hand inside Phoebe's blouse, cupping her small breast, and soon starts telling her tales dealing with the violence and cruelty of sexual love. "The only way to get rid of a temptation was to yield to it" (p. 28), Cardew tells his wife. Phoebe is that temptation; she is gotten rid of. At twelve, she is already old enough to turn a man's head, even unintentionally. Her charms have made her a prey to danger. They have also cost Cardew his tropical idyll, his wife insisting that he take her promptly to England.

The Cardews' setback typifies the plight of English settlers in the Caribbean, be they planters, merchants, or retirees. As Edward Rochester shows in *Wide Sargasso Sea*, Europeans do not adapt easily to the tropics. The loneliness, the hanging heat, and the distrust of both the law and the police shared by the local blacks wreck the peace of white colonists. Often, trouble comes from other whites; British migrants to the West Indies have inherited the national disposition to hypocrisy evident in *Quartet* and *Mr. Mackenzie* while neglecting their nation's tradition of personal freedom. The title, "Pioneers, Oh Pioneers," refers ironically to the westering spirit—the wish to start anew in the new world. The story's chief character, Mr. Ramage, arives in Dominica "a handsome man in tropical kit, white suit, red cummerbund, solar topee" (p. 12). Two years in the islands change him completely. Shedding his imperialist trappings, he lets his beard and hair grow, stops wearing clothes, and marries a local black girl, an act that frets his British counterparts. (The Socialist carpenter from England, Jimmy Longa, also forfeits the benefits of white society by moving into a black district in "Fishy Waters.") Then his wife leaves him under conditions mysterious enough to make the local, black-operated newspaper suspect that he killed her. A "fiery article" (p. 19) sends a mob of black vigilantes to his home. The morning after their raid he is found dead. Though his shotgun is nearby, his death remains a mystery, along with his wife's disappearance and the outcome of the vigilante raid itself:

A crowd of young men and boys, and a few women, had gone up to Ramage's house to throw stones. . . . A man had shouted "White zombi" and thrown a stone which hit him. He went into the house and came out with a shotgun. Then stories differed wildly. He had fired and hit a woman in the front of the

crowd. . . . No, he'd hit a little boy at the back. . . . He hadn't fired at all, but had threatened them. It was agreed that in the rush to get away people had been knocked down and hurt, one woman seriously. (p. 20)

Jean Rhys's refusal to clear up the confusion extends an argument stated in "Temps Perdi" and *Wide Sargasso Sea*: Europeans cannot make sense of the tropics. If they veer from social norms, they cannot survive. His fellow whites snub Ramage because he does not attend church, dances, or tennis parties. Then the blacks savage him as soon as they see that his lack of white support will let them get away with it. As in her novels, the society that breaks the individual in Jean Rhys consists of broken individuals.

Displacement and homelessness also permeate "Overture and Beginners Please," the sixth tale in the book and the first one set in England. The nameless West Indian heroine is spending the Christmas holidays in a Cambridge boarding school emptied of its students; her only English relative, an aunt, whose mean, carping ways recall Anna Morgan's stepmother in *Voyage in the Dark*, has not invited her to spend the holidays. The story, which covers more time than any other in the book, then shows its heroine, a hit in a school play, joining the chorus line of a traveling musical comedy troupe. In the next story, "Before the Deluge," the heroine is an actress from the outset. Yet here, it is not she, but a colleague, an English soprano of twenty-four, who grieves (because her career falls flat). This stroke of misdirection imparts a lesson. Gloom can touch anybody in *Sleep It Off, Lady*, the unknown contents of an attic in "Who Knows What's Up in the Attic?" pointing up the possibility of the surprising amid the everyday. The commonplace houses danger in "Fishy Waters" and "The Insect World." The latter story features a London spinster of twenty-nine during the Blitz. No wonder she has hallucinations and nightmares: German bombs have flattened the street next to hers; the prospect of reaching her thirtieth birthday without a husband, at one time a vague worry, has become a real threat. Allowing herself to be talked into buying a dress whose color and size are both wrong and then not eating when hungry, she has lost her will. This shattering of her inner and outer defenses has made her see people as skin-burrowing insects.

"Fishy Waters," the longest work in the book, is one of several stories ending with a final and irreversible separation. (As has been seen, "Goodbye Marcus, Goodbye Rose" recounts the events forcing Captain and Mrs. Cardew from Dominica.) The separation can come

from a false start, a plan that miscarries, or a prospective friendship that never develops. "On Not Shooting Sitting Birds" makes the failed connection sexual. To please a London man on her first date with him, the heroine makes up a hunting story which she sets in the Dominican woods. The Londoner's riveting on a detail that means nothing to her causes a misunderstanding that spoils the evening. The date ends soon afterwards, both awkwardly and abruptly. Two Paris-based stories dealing with the failure to connect sexually after a sexual connection promises to develop are "Night Out 1925" and "The Chevalier of the Place Blanche," both of which end with would-be lovers exchanging final goodbyes.

Sex touches "Rapunzel, Rapunzel" more subtly. The irreversible farewell of this tender story involves the butchering of the long silky hair of an Australian patient in a convalescent home near London. Mrs. Peterson's beautiful hair conveys her womanly identity. Although Rapunzel's letting-down of her hair saved her in the fairy tale, the shearing of Mrs. Peterson's brings disaster. To the narrator's sympathetic, "Don't worry, you'll be surprised how quickly it'll grow again," she answers, with prophetic finality, "No, there isn't time." Then, to nobody in particular, she says, "Nobody will want me now" (p. 143). Life starts draining from her immediately. That night, after a violent spell of coughing and vomiting, she leaves the convalescent home. Was she taken away to die? Did her remark, "Nobody will want me now," mean that the promise of rousing male lust was all that kept her alive? Jean Rhys invites these questions with great compassion, the narrator noting of Mrs. Peterson, with whom she had quarreled earlier, "I can't say that we ever became friendly" (p. 141). The narrator does not reserve her heart for friends; that Mrs. Peterson has suffered entitles her to sympathy. A different sort of dead-end, freshened by an expansion of moral vision, comes in the West Indian story of a litigation, "Fishy Waters." The wife of the prosecution's star witness in a child abuse case believes her husband of many years guilty of having abused the child himself. Her belief is never confirmed or refuted. The story ends in darkness and estrangement as the English couple, the Penrices, agree to leave Roseau as soon as they can.

The story also blends different storytelling techniques. There are many ways to tell a story, and in "Fishy Waters" Jean Rhys moves smoothly between several of them. Some letters to the editor of a local newspaper about the upcoming trial yield to a letter Maggie Penrice writes to a friend in England about the defendant; next comes

the trial, including both the give-and-take between lawyers and witnesses and the judge's summing-up and verdict; finally, a short passage of domestic realism describing Maggie's uneasiness over the trial and Matthew's determination to leave the island ends the story. Although broken into several sequences, each of which features a different voice and mood, the story holds solid. This unity comes not only from the strong central incident—the alleged beating and torture of little Jojo—but also from the plot-twist at the end, in which Jimmy Longa, the hard-drinking working man, is replaced as Jojo's abductor by respectable Matthew Penrice. Jean Rhys maintains both unity and excitement, moreover, without introducing either Jojo or Longa, the story's two main characters for most of the way.

Other stories in *Sleep It Off, Lady* call for different strategies. For instance, "Night Out 1925" observes the unities of setting, time, and action. This tightly executed story recounts a visit to a private club in Paris featuring "a crowd of girls in varying stages of nakedness" (p. 103) who do sexual whirligigs with each other for a fee. Again, Jean Rhys refocuses her narrative elements in a marvelous stroke of misdirection, the scantily clad girls serving as plotting devices rather than as developed characters. As with Julia Martin's dreary visit to a London nightclub with Mr. Horsfield in *Mr. Mackenzie*, the barhopping couple in "1925" show that a man and a woman who cannot enjoy each other while out on the town do not belong together. The failure of the partying couple imparts a strong aura of futility. As has been said, they have no reason to spend any more time together.

Desolation of this kind runs through the book. The color yellow, symbolizing fear in Jean Rhys, appears often: describing a sun-stopped shopping street in Roseau in "Pioneers," the curtain of a boarding school dormitory in "Overture," some May grass in "Attic," and poor Miss Verney's dustpail in the title story; yellow-gray, the hue of an English sky in December in "Overture," is actually called the color of despair. This negativity, however, need not engulf or crush, thanks to Jean Rhys's balance, understanding, and sympathy. Though ending in confusion and bitterness, "On Not Shooting Sitting Birds" shows that setbacks can be shrugged off. Once again, Jean Rhys's conjury uncovers, at the end, the story's narrative focus in an unexpected place: reading the story prepares us to read it with the insight it deserves. Its main detail, apparently an incidental, is the pink underwear the West Indian heroine buys before her first date

with a man she has found attractive. The failure of the dinner date disappoints, without saddening, the heroine. As the story's last paragraphs show, the letdown, though regrettable, does not trouble her sleep. Her new pink underwear, which is mentioned three times in the three-page story, keeps its romantic promise. What is more, as the word, "perhaps," shows, the heroine will acquiesce even if this promise fails to materialize straightaway. It might be argued, similarly, that Jimmy Longa learns from his West Indian troubles in "Fishy Waters" and that the Cardews stand a good chance for happiness after leaving the Caribbean in "Goodbye":

I felt regretful when it came to taking off my lovely pink chemise, but I could still think: Some other night perhaps, another sort of man.
I slept at once. (p. 92)

# CHAPTER 3

# Quartet

F ULL of agonized, half-articulated emotions, *Quartet* (1928), first published in the United Kingdom as *Postures*, returns to the broken marriage with criminal overtones found in "Vienne" and "Temps Perdi"; a young Englishwoman and her Continental husband are living like vagrants in a large European capital. At age twenty-eight, Marya Hughes Zelli has spent the last five years in Paris; for four of them she has been married to Stephan, a Polish art dealer. Though their hotel existence lacks ballast, it makes for fun; they enjoy living from day to day and spending what they have. Marya is used to being left alone for days at a time while Stephan plies his wares. Rather than judging him or prying into his business, she has learned to relax. "She felt that her marriage, though risky, had been a success" (p. 22), Jean Rhys says of her, noting the easy secular morality she has acquired to fend off gloom. This casual life ends with Stephan's arrest and imprisonment for theft. Marya moves in with an English couple, Hugh J. Heidler and his artist-wife, Lois. Meanwhile, Heidler has been making sexual passes at her with both Lois's knowledge and approval. Zelli's release from jail some six hectic months later invokes Freud's famous definition of sexual love as a four-way relationship. Quoted by Lawrence Durrell as his epigraph to *Justine* (1957), and, by extension, to the entire *Alexandria Quartet*, the definition reads: "I am accustoming myself to the idea of regarding every sexual act as a process in which four persons are involved." The Freudian paradigm asserts itself costively in *Quartet*. Though Zelli's jail sentence allows Marya and Heidler to become lovers, the Zellis and the Heidlers only meet once as a foursome; so total is the latter couple's contempt for the shabby ex-convict that Marya never arranges another meeting. In fact she hardly has a chance; for soon after the foursome dine together, Zelli leaves Paris; and Heidler, tiring of Marya, sends her to the country. Nor does she get the chance either to give up Zelli for Heidler or to play off the men

against each other. Being left without a man immobilizes her; dazed by drugs and alcohol, she becomes a vacuum through which the interference of other people's selfishness rushes. The Heidlers both have their way with her after Zelli's arrest; Zelli joins them in tormenting her after his release. How does he smash her spirits? Like the absentee father of *Voyage in the Dark* and *Wide Sargasso Sea*, he and Heidler both exert their male force by being apart from the heroine; the Rhys heroine spends little time with the men who mean most to her. No punishment could be harsher. Stories like "Let Them Call It Jazz," "The Lotus," and "Sleep It Off, Lady" proved that the archetypal figure cannot survive on her own. These are not cheerful narratives. For the Rhys heroine, living without a man means loneliness, poverty, drink, and being stripped of defenses.

## I   *A Woman Falling*

Marya meets the Heidlers in Chapter 1 at a Montparnasse restaurant while Zelli is working. Heidler installs himself beside her and, during coffee and brandy, puts a heavy hand on her knee. In Chapter 3 she feels a more severe pressure; her husband is arrested. Suddenly, she has nowhere to turn. Her one friend, whom Jean Rhys introduced in order to whisk her away when Marya needs her most, has left town; she has no money; the police refuse to say why her husband is in jail. She must visit the Palais de Justice a second time to learn from a stranger that Zelli has been accused of theft. The frustration builds. Chapter 4 opens with a letter Zelli sends from jail, in which he denies stealing anything. The denial neither comforts nor convinces. Does he have a lawyer? When does his trial occur? Nothing makes sense to Marya. The homey familiarity of Paris takes on a terrifying aspect; it is a maze she cannot thread her way out of. She refers to "the endless labyrinth of Paris streets" (p. 47), and giving up her permit on visitors' day in prison reminds her of giving up her ticket at a local theater. No wonder she feels marked out for terror. Numb and empty, alone and moneyless, she has to sell her dresses to survive. But her survival is marginal. Within a week of Zelli's arrest, she gets sick and foresees having to write to England for money.

At this point, the end of Chapter 4, the Heidlers invite her to dinner. The action moves briskly. The first sentence of Chapter 5 shows her talking to Heidler at the chic restaurant where the dinner party is being held. Accustomed to squalor and negation, she has her guard lowered by this glittering amiability. The Heidlers, allegedly

worried about her health, invite her to use the spare bedroom of their Montparnasse studio-flat. The heavy news that opens Chapter 6 makes her fair game for their wiles: Stephan Zelli has been sentenced to a year in jail, to be followed by banishment from France. Seeing him crushed by the harsh sentence, she knows that he cannot help her. Her visit to jail, the day he breaks the heavy news to her, gives her the sensation of being eaten by a monster. Is her fantasy-monster a composite symbol of the Heidlers? Despite her fears and misgivings, she accepts their invitation. She moves in with them even though some money from her English aunt offers a reprieve. At the start of Chapter 8, she is already installed. The final push, ironically, comes from her husband, who speaks of the trouble she will have surviving on her own. To please Zelli, to whom she omits telling about Heidler's sexual interest in her, she agrees to the move.

For a while, the move suits her. She has but few chores in her new home—making Heidler's morning coffee, posing for Lois's paintings, and running small errands in the neighborhood. But this domesticity makes her long for her vagabond life with Stephan. "He made me come alive; he taught me everything. I was happy" (p. 60), she tells Lois. Lois is not impressed. She advises Marya to forget her marriage. "Your only chance is to put the whole thing behind you and start again" (p. 63), she says, offering to find Marya a job and looking at her all the while, "strangely without pity" (p. 64). But Marya believes in her marriage. No passive victim, she rejects Lois's advice straightout, insisting that her marriage lives in her heart.

The next chapter gives the motives behind Lois's unwelcome advice. Lois goes home early one night after a party, leaving her husband and Marya together. Then Heidler explains both Lois's conduct and his own: "She's gone away to leave us together—to give me a chance to talk to you, d'you see? She knows that I'm dying with love for you, burnt up with it, tortured with it. That's why she's gone off" (p. 71). Though this news surprises Marya, it has already reached several members of the Heidlers' expatriate set. A likeable American short-story writer named Cairn, believing Marya to have been appropriated by the Heidlers, is amazed that she shows up for a luncheon date with him: "I thought you weren't coming," he tells her, "I thought Heidler would stop you" (p. 75). Pressure from Heidler does come. Back at the studio-flat, he calls Marya a "cold and inhuman devil" (p. 76) for ignoring him. He also says that, since he and Lois tack separately, she would not object to an affair between him and Marya. Lois's conduct, as always, seems to confirm his

statement. In the next chapter, she goes out one evening and, giving Marya a small present, suggests that she fill in the time with Heidler. But neither the suggestion nor the gift, a lace collar, symbolizing the stranglehold Lois is applying, pleases Marya. She says she wants to leave immediately. Lois prefers that she stay, for reasons given in one of Jean Rhys's rare incursions into her mind. Marya, Lois believes, does not threaten her marriage. Letting Heidler indulge his fancy will get the fancy out of his system and then restore him to the roost:

> She twisted her hands in her lap, thinking: Oh, no, my girl, you won't go away. You'll stay here where I can keep an eye on you. It won't last long. . . . It can't last long. I've always let him alone and given him what he wanted and it's never failed me. It won't fail me now. He'll get tired of her as soon as she gives in. Pretty! She's revolting. You can see when you look at her that she's been chewed up. (p. 81)

The next chapter, the book's midpart, describes Lois's triumph. The triangle has been implemented on her terms: Marya is sitting with her and Heidler at their favorite table in their favorite restaurant. The chapter also provides an unsympathetic outsider's view of the triangle, balancing the sympathetic view of Cairn. The restaurateur, who esteems Lois as "a good-looking woman . . . who knew how to appreciate food" (p. 84), despises Marya for an upstart, an ingrate, and a homewrecker. Lois is making her sing for her supper. She plays the long-suffering wronged wife in public; in private, she snipes at Marya. Before Marya knows it, she is fencing hard with Lois. But she cannot win. Her heart defeats her. She has fallen in love with Heidler and will put up with any abuse from Lois to be near him. A second luncheon, in Chapter 13, with the well-wishing American writer, Cairn, charts her decline. When Cairn last lunched with her in Chapter 10, she had not yet moved in with the Heidlers. He invites her to lunch a second time because he has been hearing some nasty rumors about her. How much truth is there in the rumors? he wonders, looking at her sad, hardened face and noting, "She was not so pretty as he remembered her" (p. 91).

The lunch with Cairn helps the novel's well-regulated pace. Rather than advancing the action, it reflects on it. And reflection is what the novel needs here. Her emotions have been racing so fast that Marya needs a spell of self-inventory. Here is her view of the *menage à trois chez* Heidler:

> Heidler thinks he loves me and I love him. Terribly. I don't like or trust him. I

love him. . . . And Lois says that she doesn't mind a bit and gives us her blessing. . . . But she says that I mustn't give her away. So does Heidler. They call that playing the game. So I have to trail around with them. And she takes it out of me all the time in all sorts of ways. (pp. 91–92)

As demeaning as she finds this situation, she cannot free herself from it. She forgets Cairn along with his offer of money and friendship as soon as she leaves him. Half a page later, when Heidler orders her to stop seeing Cairn, she agrees on the spot, no questions asked. She has lost her will. Not only does she drop Cairn, she also lets Heidler talk her into skipping her weekly visit to Stephan in favor of a weekend in the country. The next chapter opens with her sitting with the Heidlers on a Paris-bound train some days later, the visit to their country cottage having already taken place.

In the cab that takes them from the train station, she sits wedged between the Heidlers. The discomfort does not let up after the ride is over. Lois leaves her and Heidler alone again, and Heidler again declares his love. The declaration surprises Marya because, the night before, she had overheard the Heidlers discussing her, burst in on them, and created a scene. Nervous, confused, and guilt-ridden, she finally leaves the Heidlers. But her new arrangement does not put her out of reach. Having no money, she lets Heidler install her in a hotel, appropriately named the Hôtel du Bosphore. The Bosphorus Strait, which runs through the city of Istanbul, divides Christian from Asian Turkey, the land of the legendary infidel. Infidelity rules Marya, a faithless wife with a married lover. A kept woman without a job or a friend, she only exists sexually. She has become nothing but what Heidler wants her to be; her being is enclosed in his. But what *does* he want her to be? In spite of his power, he, too, balks at Marya's hotel existence. His reason? The Englishman's special phobia, according to Jean Rhys: it violates the need to keep up appearances:

"I hate explaining these things," Heidler went on fretfully. "I hate talking about things, but you surely must see that you can't let Lois down. Everybody knows that you were staying with us and if there's a definite split it will give the whole show away. I can't let Lois down . . . we must play the game." (p. 114)

Marya cannot please anybody. Playing the game means posing as the husband-stealer in public and enduring Lois's sarcasm in private. Marya's world both shrinks and darkens. She drinks more; she stays off the Boulevard Montparnasse in order to avoid being cut by the

Heidlers' friends; she cannot sleep without drugs. Lacking sunlight, fresh air, and nourishing food, she grows ugly. She becomes a woman thing, as much of a prisoner as her husband. The chief conflict of her life has overwhelmed her: "I love him. I want him. I hate her. And he's a swine. He's out to hurt me. What shall I do? I love him. I want him. I hate her" (p. 124).

Nor can Heidler, the main cause of her plight, relieve her plight. Learning that Zelli is to get out of jail in a month, he refuses to see her again if she goes back to him. (Did Heidler give the police information that led to the arrest of his fellow art dealer and love rival?) She assures Heidler that she will never live with Zelli again. But she refuses to leave him flat. In the next chapter, she sets him up in a hotel, just as Heidler had set *her* up a few chapters earlier. Looking like "some frail and shrunken apostle" (p. 133), he needs her help; since his punishment includes banishment from France, he does not have much time to plan ahead. But plans must wait. Before going to Amsterdam with another ex-convict, he wants to thank the Heidlers for looking after Marya. The ironical meeting proves that Zelli can neither hold nor save his wife. Over his objections, she drinks brandy; then she leaves the restaurant with the Heidlers even though he asked to take her home himself. His first words, when he is next alone with her, show that he has lost her and, moreover, that he knows it: "You don't love me any more. . . . I feel it. I know it. You stiffen when I touch you. Well, I don't blame you. A year in jail doesn't make a man appetizing" (p. 141). The issue is dropped. In order to keep Zelli's new knowledge from taking over the plot before the plot is ready for it, Jean Rhys removes him from Paris. The chapter ends with his saying good-bye to Marya at the Amsterdam-bound train.

Restlessness soon overtakes her. Four days of being alone make her pine for Heidler, to whom she sends a *pneumatique* the same day she hears that Stephan is faring badly in Amsterdam. Her grief rivals his. Heidler accuses her of betraying him by having slept with Stephan before he left Paris. He defines traditional male sexual privileges very closely; the slight to his male vanity cannot go unpunished. Allegedly for the sake of her health, he sends her to Cannes with an allowance of three hundred francs a month. She agrees to go. But before leaving, she sleeps with a nameless pickup. "Why not?" (p. 152) she says to his proposition, acquiescing in her identity as a sexual creature and going to his room "silently—like a sleep-walker" (p. 152). The incident means so little that she never mentions it again.

The stupor induced by Stephan's absence stays with her in Cannes. Her heart drooping and sluggish, she finds the beautiful Riviera squalid: "The beach was strewn with old sardine tins and fishing nets spread to dry in the sun" (p. 155). She fails to recover her sense of beauty or her will. Her landlady tells her to go to Nice, and, even though she dislikes the place, she goes there the same afternoon. A tormented letter to Heidler ("I am horribly unhappy. I'm simply going mad down here" [p. 156]), asking for trainfare to Paris, heightens her anguish. Heidler never answers the letter. Instead, Lois sends an American friend staying at Antibes, a Miss Anna Nicholson, to look in on Marya. "Neat, full of common sense, grit, pep, and all the rest" (p. 158), Miss Nicholson shocks Marya by assuring her of Lois's great liking for her and of Lois's promise to make Heidler answer her letter soon. Marya is crushed: Lois knows of her sorrows and is using a friend, who may know of it, too, to mock her.

The setback caused by Miss Nicholson's visit she never shakes off. Behaving again like a sleepwalker, she is either drunk or drugged most of the time; she reverses the natural cycle, sleeping days and waking at two o'clock in the morning; her head roars. Then hope stirs in the form of news from Stephan. She uses the money Heidler had sent her for her hotel bill to visit Stephan, who has stopped in Paris en route to Argentina. As a mark of her degradation, he gets *her* a hotel room. He also introduces her to his fellow ex-convict and friend, Jacques Bernadet, and Bernadet's "astoundingly pretty" (p. 168) friend, Simone Chardin. The spirit governing their dinner together differs greatly from that of the meal she and Stephan took with the Heidlers in Chapter 18. As soiled, frayed, and battered as he is, Marya knows that she's lost without Stephan. Yet he rejects her pleas to go with him, telling her, misery's intimate, "You don't know what it is, *la misère*" (p. 172).

A new misery assaults her at the end, where a last try at communicating with Stephan fails. His reaction to the news that Heidler has been her lover shows that she cannot count on his help. Hearing her confession turns this social outcast into the conventional heavy husband of nineteenth-century bedroom farce. "He chucked you, hein?" (p. 181), he asks derisively, even after she says that she defied Heidler by coming to Paris instead of staying in Nice, as ordered. Still pleading for his kindness and assuring him that she defied Heidler for his, Stephan's, sake, she is called trash. Jealousy continues to madden him. He asks her to help him ambush Heidler. Foiled, he threatens to go after Heidler with a revolver, which he brandishes pathetically. Following a series of defeats, the news of her

infidelity has broken him. His eyes "miserable," he looks "small, shrunken, much older" (p. 184). Seeing this whipped, disheveled ex-jailbird putting on airs makes her lose grip. She tries to fight her way out of the room, screaming her love for Heidler.

Although Elgin Mellown believes that the finale of *Quartet* "degenerates into melodrama,"[1] the violence of the last scene shows artistic control. When Marya threatens to betray Stephan to the police, he swings her "with all his force" (p. 185), slamming her head accidentally against the edge of a table. The ending is both tentative and conclusive, surprising and inevitable. Whether Marya dies cannot be known. Stephan leaves her lying "crumpled up and . . . still" (p. 185), and, quickly forgetting his jealousy, starts chatting with Simone Chardin, whom a farfetched coincidence has produced in the street below. Simone is better equipped for survival than Marya. Though she has broken with Jacques Bernadet, she fills the rift quickly, convincing Stephan in less than a page to take her with him to Argentina. He thus grants a stranger a prize he had withheld from his wife. The last sentence of the novel shows them rattling to the train station in a cab.

## II  *A Tangle of Motives*

Jean Rhys puts more distance between herself and Marya than Mellown credits when he says of Marya, "Because she is an autobiographical projection . . . she fails as a fictional creature."[2] A much more balanced reading comes from Shirley Hazzard, who explains Marya as "an imaginative, susceptible nature destroyed by the assertive, unyielding world." The argument continues: "Marya is helplessly disadvantaged by . . . the ironic, tender view that enables her to understand her fate while making her incapable of preventing it."[3] The argument has merit; although Marya knows her duty, she cannot perform it. She said of herself, even before moving in with the Heidlers, "I'm a soft, thin-skinned sort of person and I've been frightened to death these days" (p. 51).

As has been seen, her fears sharpen as her fortunes drop. Her drinking habits chart her sad tailspin. The first paragraph of the book shows her drinking coffee while sitting alone for ninety minutes in a café. In Chapter 5, she is drinking vermouth, a mild enough drink. In Chapter 10, two chapters after moving into the studio-flat, she drinks two brandies and half a bottle of champagne at a dinner party. The spirits keep flowing. By Chapter 17, drinking

has made her sound "as hoarse as a crow" (p. 130), and she spends much of her dreary Riviera sojourn drunk on Pernod. The end of the book shows her drinking her Pernods straight, despite a friendly bartender's warning. Her worst fears, though, do not come from the bottle. When her husband smashes her head on the table-edge, a page from the end, she has reached her nadir. Though she is sober at the time, it is difficult to imagine her sinking any lower.

But she surprises us with her pluck—standing up to everybody who tries to bully or patronize her. "Don't poor-little-thing me" (p. 92), she snaps at a condescending Cairn; she defies Lois more than once; she barges in on her and Heidler, opening the door "as noisily as she could" (p. 102), when she hears them discussing her. Then she slaps Heidler "as hard as she could" (p. 103) in Lois's presence; at other times, she calls him a "cold and inhuman devil" (p. 76) and "the cruellest devil in the world" (p. 100). Even though she loves him, she gives him no quarter. The only advantage he can claim over her is his money; his social connections do not impress her, and he lacks the tenderness to be a good lover. Her final overthrow, a matter of crude physical strength, comes, not at his hands, but from those of Stephan.

The basis of her attraction to Heidler? The best explanation comes from Rosalind Miles. Marya, she says, "is a bewildered expatriate whose marriage to a foreigner has robbed her of her own sense of nationality without providing a new one."[4] The insight can be extended. Stephan's arrest intensifies her smothered nationality, leaving her adrift in a foreign city without a job, friend, or fixed residence. During this time of upheaval and stress, the Englishness of the Heidlers represents home. That her husband and her lover are both art dealers also shows the pull of England. An ex-chorus girl who chose exile over suburbia, she would never have opted for a middle-class marriage. Stephan's arrest throws her options back in her face. The chance to become Heidler's mistress looms as a recognition, a self-reproach, and an expiation. A successful art dealer from England, Heidler is a socially acceptable version of mousy, Continental Stephan. Marya has not shaken off England. To convey her lingering national ties, Jean Rhys gives her closest living relative, an aunt, Marya's name before her marriage; Maria Hughes is Marya Hughes Zelli's alter ego, the self that settled for a life in England.

Does Heidler, "a rock of a man with his big shoulders and his

quiet voice" (p. 43), mean more to the fatherless Marya than security and ballast during a crisis? Does he risk anything for her? Howard Moss calls him "a monster of selfishness,"[5] too cocksure to be wounded in life. Moss may be right. Never to Marya's satisfaction does Heidler rise above either his self-absorption or his adherence to "playing the game." Yet satisfying Marya is not easy work. This allegedly vain, selfish man has had a nervous breakdown about a year before she meets him. His nerves and heart are both raw. He insists that he is burning up with love for her and that he would leave Lois if she asked him to. Does he make the offer because he knows that Marya will not accept it? Is he obtuse or supremely clever? Though we never gain access to his mind, we can assume that he responds to her as candidly as the prevailing double standard of sexual morality lets him. The standard decrees that women exist sexually; they are sexual creatures, and they are to be both used and judged sexually. Whereas Heidler prizes her mystery, he also wants to penetrate it and thus violate it. The falling woman might as well fall his way. Her having a husband in jail resolves his dilemma: nobody owes an adulteress a fair deal. Thus he uses her and then casts her off, lest he find himself on the same footing with her or her convict husband. He will accept moral and financial responsibility for her, lodging her at his expense, but he will not spend time with her. By withholding himself, he deprives her of what she needs most—a sympathetic heart. But he cannot stop judging her long enough to understand her. He cannot afford to. Extending imagination and sympathy might loosen his hold on the gentlemanly privileges that social tradition has given him.

Though no English gentleman, Stephan Zelli has inherited Heidler's sexual morality. His mother, believing that "honorable intentions were unnecessary when dealing with a chorus girl" (p. 18), advised him to drop Marya. His marriage has not freed him from his background. He takes sexual license for granted while discussing Simone Chardin and Jacques Bernadet, who stay together the same night they meet. Then he fumes after learning of Marya's affair with Heidler. Curiously, he denies the affair any free-standing reality, regarding it solely as an insult to him. It threatens him. He is sure that it would not have happened if he had not been in jail.

He is right. As far-fetched as his thinking seems, it does have a basis in fact. His year in jail hammers him down. At the outset, this shady dealer who speaks six languages has managed to keep the police at bay. "A short, slim, supple young man of thirty-three or four, with

very quick, bright brown eyes and an eager but secretive expression"
(p. 17), he fences stolen goods; his wife both loves and enjoys him; he
maintains his boyish, reassuring manner. Gentle, quick, and sweet-
tempered, he shrugs off bad luck and shares his good luck generously
with her. His prison term puts an end to good luck. Nobody gives an
ex-convict a break: he cannot defend himself against the Heidlers'
rudeness; he is exiled from France, where his friends are; he falls back
on crime to earn a living. In Chapter 22 he admits, "You understand,
don't you, that I must get away? I've lost my luck. I care too much. I
did my best but it was no good. I've lost my luck" (p. 171). As has been
seen, his run of bad luck expresses itself physically. His voice goes
rusty; his buoyancy flattens; frays and seams undermine his dapper
good looks. Jail has sapped his manhood. Marya calls him "my poor
boy" (p. 36) during her first prison visit; after his sentencing, he
whines in "a little boy's voice" (p. 49). Nor do the tears dry after his
release. The modern city has crushed him as relentlessly as it has
Marya. Knowing the handicaps facing an ex-convict, he never
bothers looking for honest work: "I don't think any respectable
gentleman would risk lending me his flat, and I have to take what I
can get in the way of friends" (p. 171), he says with glum accuracy.
Constantly on the move, he cannot hold his marriage together. He
cries himself to sleep every night "like a little boy" (p. 171). Can this
desperate, hammered-down soul be blamed for lashing out when he
learns of his wife's unfaithfulness?

His opposite number is Lois Heidler; that her husband is his wife's
lover gives them a common standpoint and perhaps even a common
purpose. Yet while the Chaplinesque Zelli is playing out a slapstick
gutter tragedy, Lois, a stranger to the grime of the crowded streets,
enacts a comedy of manners in salons, chic restaurants, and country
houses. Perhaps correctly, Alvarez calls her "crushingly understanding and emancipated."[6] Highly informed and serious, she enjoys
taking charge. Marya says to herself, soon after meeting her, "Lois is
as hard as nails" (p. 62). Heidler strengthens this impression several
chapters later, when he tells Marya, who is having qualms about the
affair, "I shouldn't worry too much about Lois if I were you" (p. 107).
He judges his wife's resourcefulness well. Lois controls the affair. She
leaves Marya and Heidler alone for hours at a stretch; she invites
Marya to live at the studio-flat; several times, she chides Marya for
being "too virtuous" when Marya complains about Heidler's sexual
advances. At one point, Lois says she values good dancing in a man.
Yet on the next page, at a party, Marya learns that Heidler cannot

dance. Did Lois time her remark to give Marya the impresssion that her marriage was unhappy?

Raising Marya's hopes fits her strategy. What she wants most is to preserve her marriage. A page after inviting Marya to share the studio-flat, she says to herself, "The poor little devil has got no harm in her and I shouldn't mind doing her a good turn. She won't be much trouble" (p. 49). What Marya will not trouble is Lois's marriage. Lois knows that her husband is both a womanizer and a sentimentalist. Confident that he will tire of Marya quickly, she gives him a free hand. Her scenario accounts for everything but Marya's heart, which she does not care about, anyway. She seems to have everything under control.

Yet there is also evidence that her plans have backfired. In Chapter 6 tears come to her eyes as she speaks tenderly of her husband: "I love him so terribly . . . and he isn't always awfully nice to me" (p. 53). In the next paragraph, Marya sees her as a "soft creature" and a "fellow-woman, hurt and bewildered by life" (p. 53). In Chapter 11, as she sends Marya and Heidler out for the evening, her eyes again glaze with tears. The tears move Marya, who later implores Heidler, "Be good to Lois, be good to Lois, you must be good to Lois" (p. 107). Even as her love rival, Marya sympathizes with Lois. Her compassion typifies the novel. The emotional outgoings and retrenchments of the three parties involved turn the love triangle into a duel with invisible swords. The original British title of the novel, Postures, which Jean Rhys liked less than its present one, suggests the formality of a fencing match. The three duellists strike poses; the Heidlers put style (Heidler's "playing the game" and Lois's credo of "grin and bear it") before content in order to protect themselves. Whereas Marya's role grants her little freedom, the Heidlers try to impress outsiders with their role-playing. Yet again, the charade defies the script. The roles overtake the players, and the invisible swords draw blood. The phrase, "the essential craziness of existence" (p. 55), describing Marya's state of mind while she visits her husband in prison, accounts for much of the bloodshed. Plans miscarry; effects do not follow from their causes; nor can the characters predict either the quality or results of what they do. Nobody performs evil willingly. Each figure in the love triangle tries to protect the other two. But because their common situation brings out their worst—their dishonest, possessiveness, and insecurity—they butcher one another.

And each feels butchered by the other two. In Lois's presence, Heidler refers to Marya as "this sort of woman" (p. 103) and then ac-

cuses her of wanting this money. Yet on the next page, he staggers to bed drunk, looking at Lois "with hatred" (p. 104) and pushing her out of his way. Then Lois, his victim, consoles Marya "in a sisterly manner" (p. 104), politely offering her a drink and rehearsing Heidler's moral failings. The way the three characters align and realign recalls the shuttlecocks metaphor in the climactic love triangle of Ford Madox Ford's *The Good Soldier*. Just as the metaphor is used by a young woman driven mad by conflicting loyalties to the man she loves and his wife, so might it apply to the trio in *Quartet* who sow madness by exposing, shielding, and sniping at one another. Written while Jean Rhys was both Ford's literary protégée and mistress, *Quartet* came out a year after the 1927 printing of *The Good Soldier* (1915), which contains a long, loving dedicatory letter, dated 9 January 1927, to Stella Bowen Ford. *Quartet* refers not only to *The Good Soldier* but also to its author and his wife. (It is a tribute to Jean Rhys's literary judgment that she admired a novel in 1927 that critics in both Britain and the United States took another thirty years to find merit in.)

The metaphor of the maze dominates both books along with the color, blue. Matching the many blue color patches in Ford's book are Heidler's blue eyes, the blue rabbits on the wallpaper of Marya's room at the Heidlers, a blue and mauve background in a nightclub before which two naked girls dance, and L'Heure Bleue of Guerlain perfume, which is worn by a woman who lives on Paris's Rue Bleue. Ford's title character, Edward Ashburnham, and Jean Rhys's H. J. Heidler, both of whom feel trapped in mazes they help build, resemble each other, too. Sentimentalists both, they have the same complexion, build, and eye-color. As the following passages show, the first of which describes Ashburnham, they have also cultivated the vacant look prized by the English upper classes:

His face hitherto had, in the wonderful English fashion, expressed nothing whatever. Nothing. There was in it neither joy nor despair; neither hope nor fear; neither boredom nor satisfaction. . . . I never came across such a perfect expression before and I never shall again. . . . His hair was fair, extraordinarily, ordered in a wave, running from the left temple to the right; his face was a light brick red, perfectly uniform in tint up to the roots of the hair itself; his yellow moustache was as stiff as a toothbrush.[7]

He was a tall, fair man of perhaps forty-five. His shoulders were tremendous, his nose arrogant, his hands short. . . . The wooden expression of his face was

carefully striven for. His eyes were light blue and intelligent, but with a curious underlying expression of obtuseness—even of brutality. (pp. 10–11)

The similarities between the two men prompt a search for similarities between their wives, whose first names both begin with the letter L. The most vivid parallel refers to motives. Leonora and Lois both prescribe love affairs for their husbands in order to encourage the men's future fidelity. In each case, the protective shell they build around their men shatters, causing unlooked-for damage. Although not as artistically accomplished, *Quartet* puts forth as dark a vision as Ford's classic.

The novel has roots in reality as well as in fiction, much of its darkness stemming from the close resemblance between Heidler and Ford, the tormentor-lover of *Quartet* and his real-life counterpart. Just as Ford was called either Ford or F. M. in conversation, so does his fictional stand-in answer to Heidler or H. J. But the name parallel extends still further. Jean Rhys may have been mocking the literary judgment of her former mentor-lover by giving her destructive male lead the same initials as those of her mentor's mentor, Henry James. That Ford's name until 1919 was Ford Madox Hueffer also provides a real-life context for Marya's insult, "Horrible German" (p. 104); Hueffer and Heidler are both bisyllables beginning with *H* and ending in *er*. Still another echo comes in the Heidlers' practice of wintering in Provence. The Roman Catholic convert Ford studied the troubadour tradition of southern France, especially as it applied to religion. (In one scene in *Quartet*, Heidler prays alongside Marya in a Roman church.) Although unintended, Ford's 1935 book, *Provence*, coming out seven years after *Quartet*, gives Jean Rhys's reference to the Heidlers' winter home the look of prophecy.

The mention of Provence and Marya's denunciation of blond, fair, broadshouldered Heidler as a horrible German make us ask how many of the events in *Quartet* came from life. The question cannot be answered definitively. The time Jean Rhys lived with Ford and Stella provides the central dramatic conflict of *Quartet*. On the other hand, very little information about the arrangement has survived. In *Quartet*, Heidler sends Marya away after six months; Ford's letters say that Jean Rhys stayed with him and Stella in Paris for "many weeks."[8] Ford's commitment to Jean Rhys may have been as scant as the difference between "many weeks" and six months. Arthur Mizener says that, in Ford's quest for "an ultimately satisfying woman," Jean Rhys, his junior by twenty-one years, was one of the

"less serious relations."⁹ Impressed by her writing, Ford asked her to live with him and Stella (who, it bears repeating, painted pictures, as does Lois) when the collapse of the *Transatlantic*, his magazine, made him crave excitement. Her inability to slake his craving led to her being ousted.

Though instructive, the biographical record of Jean Rhys's romance with Ford matters less than its imaginative transformation. The process by which Jean Rhys converted fiery subject matter into fiction shows real skill. Judith Thurman miscues when she calls *Quartet* "aesthetically off guard." It doesn't have "the faults and youthful excesses of its heroine."¹⁰ Pared down and selective, it hews to a consistent method—that of recounting the effects of time rather than imitating the passage of time, like the Victorian chronicle novel. Marya's point of view, besides providing a steady focus and, because of what happens to Marya, an accelerating tempo, also determines narrative selection. Thus the novel says no more about the Heidler's marriage than it must to make it believable; Stephan serves his prison sentence off-stage; if Anna Nicholson discusses her visit to Marya with Lois, she does it out of our hearing. Jean Rhys keeps her narrative elements sketchy in favor of recording their impact on Marya. Other examples of her rigorous selectivity come to mind: Stephan's arrest also happens off-stage; we never read the letters Heidler sends Marya after she moves into the Hôtel du Bosphore; nor do we watch their affair develop or end—the speech in which Heidler drops Marya in Chapter 19 coming to us as a summary:

> He cleared his throat. "My dear Mado. . . ." He began to talk dispassionately and deliberately. He spoke with dignity and with a certain relief, as though he were saying something which he had often longed to say. Towards the end of his explanation he became definite, even brutal, though not to excess. All the time that he was speaking she was looking into his eyes. (p. 147)

Accordingly, Jean Rhys summarizes rather than dramatizes many of Marya's other dark moments. But she also avoids the lowering and flattening that often go with summary. As the following passage shows, her summaries sometimes gain vitality by being phrased as dialogue:

> She [Marya] persisted. "Everybody cuts me dead all along the Boulevard Montparnasse, anyway. . . . I'm the villain of the piece, and they do know. They say that Lois picked me up when I was starving and that the moment I got into her house I tried to get hold of you." (p. 120)

Passages like this also reveal that, rather than being self-indulgent, the action is too lank and stripped; more than once, dramatic tension builds, only to be released summarily or out of our view. Jean Rhys's strategy of recording the effects of Marya's sad affair, rather than its causes, has both merits and faults. Whereas it promotes unity, it also thins and narrows the action. The bloodstream of *Quartet* needs an infusion of Victorian robustness. Although some of the character sketches are sharp and clear, they remain sketches. Nobody besides Marya is fleshed out. Surrounded by characters who exist to badger her, she steers the novel down a narrow track. When the track threatens to thin into inconsequentiality, Jean Rhys will reset her course—but often disastrously. Her reporting the thoughts of other characters, for instance, derails the action. The worst violation of narrative unity comes at the end of Chapter 15; here, Anna Nicholson shows her face for two little paragraphs in order to make some judgments that Jean Rhys should have smoothed in dramatically:

She was Lois's friend and confidante and, as she talked, she watched Marya. . . . She was thinking:
"The idea of a woman making such an utter fool of herself. It's hardly to be believed. Her hand is trembling. No poise. . . . Lois needn't be afraid of her. But then, Lois is a bit of a fool herself. Englishwomen often are. (pp. 115–16)

Acts of authorial clumsiness like Anna's walk-on occur rarely in the later work. The mature fiction also maintains greater stylistic control. The heavy alliteration in a passage describing Marya's terror, during a visit to prison, dulls, rather than sharpens, the woe: "She crossed a cobblestoned courtyard and a dark, dank corridor like the open mouth of a monster swallowed her up" (p. 55). An earlier visit, in which noise bombards Marya, also fails because of unrestraint. So clogged with metaphor and simile is Jean Rhys's description that we can hardly trudge through it:

She sat down on a wooden bench and stared steadily through bars that were like bars of an animal cage. Her heart began to beat heavily. The buzzing noise deafened and benumbed her. She felt as though an iron band were encircling her head tightly, as though she were sinking slowly down into deep water. (p. 35)

Verbal snarls like this are rare. For most of the way, *Quartet* moves nimbly through heavily mined psychological terrain. The novel depicts a young woman's emotional stress accurately and honestly.

Though it risks more psychologically than technically, its craftsmanship displays both schooling and skill. Jean Rhys's eye rarely slides from her subject. Chapter 2 summarizes the courtship, the marriage, and the daily routine of the Zellis. But the summary is not a digression. We need this information to credit the faith Marya has in Stephan. What more sensible and economical a way to convey the data than through a series of time glides?

*Quartet* has both a temporal and spatial structure. Its pinpointing of character and incident through summary, description, and editorial comment controls the flow of emotion. Not an original strategy of narration but one that suits the novel admirably: the bipolar tension between the book's conventional technique and bizarre, driven characters has created a field where Jean Rhys can convey moral passion without haranguing or boring the reader.

### CHAPTER 4

# After Leaving Mr. Mackenzie

FRANCIS Wyndham catches the spirit of *After Leaving Mr. Mackenzie* (1930) in his reference to the book's "clear, bitter quality."[1] Still believing in the truth of her vision, Jean Rhys neither heats up nor structures her material as she did in *Quartet. Mackenzie* deals more quietly with the same horror that ran through the earlier novel. But the treatment is less literary. *Mackenzie*'s ambience is not narrative; lacking a well-hewn central action, the book does not give its heroine's desolation the quality of art. Characters do not develop; the dialogue sounds improvised, as if the characters are saying the first thing that comes to mind; their deepest thoughts they keep to themselves. Often, they act like people in a play who will not say their lines. The heroine says, without much ado, "It's funny how you say one thing when you're thinking of quite another, isn't it?" (p. 93). The insight is right on target. But it does not help regulate her life. Though Julia Martin both watches and judges her conversation, she does not channel her talk into the vital currents of her life. To use E. M. Forster's term from *Howards End*, she cannot connect: her acts have a low degree of successful completion, making her life a series of disjointed episodes. This disjuncture affects the book's structure. The refusal to face conflict, while freeing character from the rigors imposed by plot, both clogs dramatic incident and blocks forward drive. When Julia hears that her weekly allowance from an ex-lover, her sole source of cash, is drying up, her thoughts do not turn to the ordeal of coping. "She thought of new clothes with a passion" (p. 20), Jean Rhys says of Julia's desperate search for ways to splurge rather than save. Because Julia splurges quickly, her desperation fades quickly. Her life follows this pattern. Another crisis will emerge, which Julia will either ignore or buy her way out of with some man's money. But cadging cash from men is hard going for a woman of thirty-six; crises leave deeper scars. Judith Thurman has related the novel's randomness to the heroine's sad self-knowledge: "*After*

*Leaving Mr. Mackenzie* is a vision, in slow motion, of a woman coming apart. Julia is used to being turned out. But this time it comes at the wrong moment, the changing season, the onset of the loss of beauty, her one resource."²

## I   *A Labyrinth of Streets*

Had Marya Zelli walked into a novel set six or eight years later than *Quartet*, she might look, feel, and act a good deal like Julia. Julia's marriage to a Continental who "went absolutely smash" (p. 82) has ended, and with it comes a carefree round of wild spending; the death of an infant son, from the same period, is an episode she has nearly wiped from her memory. For the past ten years she has been living off men, "a very easy habit to acquire" (p. 26), she admits. The action begins six months after her latest patron, Mackenzie, drops her. Jean Rhys places this event at the novel's central nerve because of its impact on Julia. The jilting by Mackenzie has weakened her—sapping her strength, lowering her self-confidence, and filling the future with dread. Here is Julia's own view of her predicament:

I was all right till I met that swine Mackenzie. But he sort of—I don't know—he sort of smashed me up. Before that I'd always been pretty sure that things would turn out all right for me, but afterwards I didn't believe in myself any more. I only wanted to go away and hide. (p. 49)

The predicament worsens. In Chapter 2, Julia learns that, besides doing without Mackenzie's company, she will also have to forego his weekly check of 300 francs; Mackenzie has told his lawyer to accompany a final payment of 1,500 francs with the notice that no more money will be sent. Although the month is April (of 1930 or 1931, if Julia was born in 1894, like her author and the heroines of the other novels through *Good Morning, Midnight*), she does not partake of the renewal and rebirth surging forth around her.

The novel's opening sentence, which has the same first word as the novel's title, hints at her run-down, chewed-up life. Could the mention of Augustine yoke the Augustinian creed of original sin to Julia's hopelessness? "After she had parted from Mr. Mackenzie, Julia Martin went to live in a cheap hotel on the Quai des Grands Augustins" (p. 9). As has been noted, Julia is not a complete person: she lacks family love and friendship; she does not have a happy sex life; she does not work at a job she enjoys for a living. A sign of her

dim, out-of-kilter life is the window of her room. Windows in rooms occupied by Jean Rhys heroines (in "Outside the Machine," "I Spy a Stranger," and *Wide Sargasso Sea*, for instance) can be too high, too small, or set to one side. Julia's window fits the pattern: "Her room . . . had a somber and one-eyed aspect because the solitary window was very much to one side (pp. 9–10). Julia spends most of her time in this room, "not altogether unhappy" (p. 11) with her books and bottle. Though escapist, the reprieve comforts her. So long as she can count on her weekly check, she does not have to risk rejection from another man. Mackenzie's weekly check has given her a threadbare security because it frees her from testing her ability to charm and attract men.

Unlike the Jamesian heroine who often defeats herself by asking for too much, the archetypal Rhys figure demands little and gets nothing, anyway. Julia no longer thinks of men; she has put on weight; she eats, dresses, and applies her makeup mechanically. Yet this half-life ends when Mackenzie stops her allowance. Several hours after receiving the bad news, she walks to the "narrow, rather deserted street of tall, quiet houses" (p. 21) where he lives. A wait of half an hour produces him, and Julia, after watching him leave his apartment building, follows him to a restaurant—the place where they last met, six months ago. Their reunion in the restaurant, Jean Rhys's most original scene to date, bristles with incongruities. First, Mackenzie, the standard-bearer of organized society, with all its legal ways of hurting Julia, looks too dry and stiffnecked to harm or save anybody. V. S. Naipaul calls him "a man of fifty [he is forty-eight], middle class, correct . . . hardly an object of passion, a nobody."[3] Jean Rhys describes Mackenzie, whose family earned enough in shipping to let him retire early, in just these terms: "Mr. Mackenzie was a man of medium height and coloring. He was of the type which proprietors of restaurants and waiters respect. He had enough stomach to look benevolent" (p. 23). Evasive about sex, he tries to dodge his moral responsibilities to Julia. Though he admits theoretically that he misused her, he will only help her from a distance or through his attorney. He dismisses her woeful recitations as either exaggerations or the just deserts of a fallen woman. Having condemned her for giving him what he asked, he is Jean Rhys's classic English hypocrite:

She had obsessed him. He had lied; he had made her promises he never intended to keep. . . . All part of the insanity, for which he was not responsible.

Not that many lies had been necessary. After seeing him two or three times she had spent the night with him at a tawdry hotel. Perhaps that was the reason why, when he came to think of it, he had never really liked her. (p. 25)

On the other hand, he is not fact-ridden. His heart pumps real blood. Though distrustful of impulse, he has not regimented his life. Unafraid to invite his soul, he published a book of poems in his youth; he likes sex well enough to support a mistress who moved him enough to make him say, "I would like to put my throat under your feet" (p. 28); he prefers to live freely in foreign parts rather than staying pinned to a desk in London.

Sitting in the restaurant where he last saw Julia, six months ago, turns his thoughts to her. Motivation in the scene runs strong and true. Besides dovetailing his thoughts into the coming encounter, Jean Rhys also touches in some important background data on her heroine—her divorce, her dead baby son, and her career as a model. But her encounter with Mackenzie would go flat unless we first knew of his disapproval of her. Thus Jean Rhys cites her inability to save money, her practice of drifting from man to man, her disorganization. Mackenzie's disapproval is meant to carry the force of common sense: "Something which rose from the bottom of Mr. Mackenzie's soul objected to giving her a lump sum of money, which of course she would immediately spend" (p. 27). In view of Julia's poor instinct for self-preservation, the moral issues at stake do not split into neat categories of good and evil. Can the self-doubting Mackenzie be blamed for not wanting to saddle himself to a loser? Should he judge her by standards other than those imposed by common sense? Like so many of her sisters in the canon, Julia can fret anybody's nerves with her impracticality and lack of purpose. The inevitability of her ruin would drive away the most ardent lover. How can moral judgment be withheld from someone who has condemned herself to futility? What Jean Rhys objects to is Mackenzie's refusal to sympathize. Julia, she reminds us in her opening chapter, stands for an international class of discardable mistresses. To damn her is to damn the thousands of women who, like her and Blanche Dubois of *Streetcar Named Desire*, can no longer find men to give her money. Julia's frayed, battered look gives her away immediately; she is one of life's losers: "Her career of ups and downs had rubbed most of the hall-marks off her, so that it was not easy to guess at her age, her nationality, or the social background to which she properly belonged" (p. 14).

The entrance of that loser into the restaurant where he is dining

shocks Mackenzie. Her rundown life style had already offended his tact, breeding, and instinct for caution. The nasty public scene she seems getting ready to create threatens to shatter his peace altogether. He starts to panic over his veal. Is his alarm justified? Whatever purpose Julia wanted to accomplish by following him into the restaurant miscarries. Her first words, "Tell me, do you really like life? Do you think it's fair?" (p. 30) betoken a loss of grip that lasts throughout the scene. Her purpose is unclear. While wanting to hurt, or, at least, embarrass, Mackenzie, she also wants to reopen options. Thus she neither attacks nor cringes, though she is inclined to do both. The psychological effort of following Mackenzie into the restaurant has sapped so much of her energy and resolve that she can only blather about the bullying letters his lawyer has been sending her. So inane is the blather that, rather than cluttering her novel by quoting it verbatim, Jean Rhys summarizes it: "She began to talk volubly, in a low, rather monotonous voice. It was like a flood which has been long dammed up suddenly pouring forth" (p. 30). In the meantime, Julia's shakiness has given Mackenzie the heart to join the issue. His speaking out addles Julia's nerves even more than before. When he asks, "Well, what exactly did you want when you came in here?" (p.33) she cannot answer. With a breeze, she returns his 1,500-franc check, and, as a feeble anticlimax, slaps his cheek lightly with her glove. The pressure of living on the edge has wrecked her judgment along with her poise: returning Mackenzie's money, her entire bankroll except for a few francs, is one of the most stupid, self-defeating acts she could have done.

The travesty plays on. The indifferent world does not respect our purposes or needs. Thus Jean Rhys intrudes two Englishmen into the scene during Julia's prattling recitation. Mackenzie now has more than one reason to squirm; the sight of the visitors, one of whom he knows, turns him livid with worry. Reluctant to interrupt the funny-sad meeting of ex-lovers with this intrusion, Jean Rhys carries the incident forward. One of the English diners, the one Mackenzie does not know, a "dark young man" (p. 36) called George Horsfield, had indeed watched the awkward confrontation. But his reaction to it frees Mackenzie from worry. Forgetting English propriety, he follows Julia to a nearby café, sits next to her, and starts talking. Their conversation does not sharpen his impression of her. Though she looks an ill-used thirty-five, her ability to compose herself quickly after the scene with Mackenzie bespeaks freshness and bounce. Horsfield likes her well enough to see her home in a taxi and, to prolong their time together, take her to a cinema.

The evening takes some turns that rattle his English calm. Julia starts crying in the dark movie-house; and Horsfield, annoyed and embarrassed, regrets having first approached her. Yet, his impulse ruling his reason, he invites her to his hotel for a talk. Jean Rhys continues to portray the effects of emotional choice rather than, like Henry James, analyzing the complex of causes behind them. There is no comprehending her characters' turns of mood or self-definitions. Perhaps to show off, to feel strong, or, simply, to be kind, Horsfield gives Julia fifteen hundred francs. But braking his impulsiveness, he shrinks from having sex with her: lovers in Jean Rhys do touch, but briefly and infrequently. Julia, too, settles for talk. And what she says makes sense. The upshot of a long, semi-drunken speech she makes on her past is her recognizing her lack of free will. She has become the sum of her mistakes. "Everything I had done had always been the only possible thing to do" (p. 52), she says, recalling an incident where she felt less real than a woman in a painting. The recitation touches Horsfield's heart. Besides giving her money, he also lets her have his address in London, where he plans to go soon and where she mentions having a rich friend.

Should she go to London, too? Julia hates making practical decisions. Knowing that she will squander Horsfield's fifteen hundred francs anyhow, she leaves the means of her thriftlessness to chance. "If a taxi hoots before I count three, I'll go to London. If not, I won't" (p. 57), she reasons. A nearby horn blast makes her London-bound. But before she leaves, she needs new clothing. New? So empty is her purse that she can only afford cheap, ill-fitting clothes from a second-hand shop. A wiser person would not have bought these. Julia's purchases added to her train fare leave her only thirty shillings with which to manage in London. But Part One ends hopefully. Eager to return home for the first time in ten years, she writes to her sister, and, heartened by the speed with which she spurns a would-be pickup, leaves for London the next day.

The opening of Part II blunts some of this affirmation; aimless and alone, the Rhys heroine never keeps hope alive for long. With barely enough cash to live on for three days, she checks into a cheap Bloomsbury hotel. Immediately, her English past begins to haunt her. Her cold, cramped room with its tumbledown dressing table and dingy curtains calls to mind her last hotel room in Bloomsbury ten years ago. So vivid is the identification that it gives her the helpless feeling of having moved in a circle. The helplessness deepens when, on the next page, she sees a florist selling violets on the same street-corner where he used to peddle them. To shed her discomfort, she

goes to a movie house playing the film, *Hot Stuff from Paris*. She sheds nothing; the city she came to London to forget flashes before her in a reel of bygone romantic images. This gay, glittering past threatens her; she feels unreal. The end of the chapter resurrects still another element from the past—her sister, Norah. Norah Griffiths' pale lips, set jaw, and stout peasant build all bespeak self-denial. Stiff and withdrawn, Norah has denied herself excitement to stay at home with her ailing mother. Naipaul calls her "an embittered, unmarried sister, imprisoned in suburban Acton by poverty and a family responsibility: an invalid mother . . . in a coma and dying."[4] Though the resentment the sisters feel is mutual, that of unprodigal Norah cuts deeper. Norah hates whereas Julia registers only dry-eyed spite. During a later meeting between the sisters, Jean Rhys notes of Norah, "Every time she looked at Julia she felt a fierce desire to hurt her or to see her hurt or humiliated" (p. 102).

Norah's large, soft eyes convey her flair for romance; her cold, fixed expression conveys her bitterness over never having indulged the flair. To dramatize this tension, Jean Rhys gives her the same first name as that of the heroine of Ibsen's *A Doll's House* (1879), Western literature's exemplar of the home-bound woman who bolted from her family to test herself in the great world. At age thirty, Norah, no breakaway, has stayed home and tested only her domestic skills: "Norah herself was labelled for all to see. She was labelled 'Middle class, no money,' Hardly enough to keep herself in clean linen. And yet scrupulously, fiercely clean, but with all the daintiness and prettiness perforce cut out" (pp. 73–74). Thus she probably enjoys denying her better dressed, more sophisticated sister's request to stay at the family flat. Norah gives both the real and overt explanation backing her denial. A trained live-in nurse who came to care for the comatose mother has taken all the available space. Besides, Julia has no right to ignore the family for years and then expect to be lodged. Disregarding both Norah's rebuff and her "fierce expression" (p. 75), Julia sidesteps conflict. As well she should, if only for the novel's sake: the major clash between the sisters must await further developments in the plot.

Julia agrees to visit her mother the next day and, after telling Norah goodbye, turns her thoughts to the job of coping with cold, drab London: "She made anxious calculations and decided that with about another couple of pounds she could be all right," she reasons, adding, "The thing was to keep calm and try everything possible" (p. 77). Money can only be had from a man. Thus she welcomes the chance to make a dinner date on the phone with George Horsfield.

But, in keeping with the book's sure, unforced pace, the next man she sees, and seeks money from, is her sixty-five-year-old Uncle Griffiths, the family head. Predictably, this large, solid patriarch (her natural father died when she was six) spurns her. He tells her straightaway to leave London; he insults her former husband; forewarned by Norah of her visit, he refuses her money in terms both degrading and painful to her: "He said that he had not got any money and that if he had he would not give it to Julia, certainly not, but to her sister Norah, and that he would like to help Norah, because she was a fine girl, and she deserved it" (p. 83). Having thus humiliated Julia to scale down her financial demands, he offers her a pound to put toward her train fare to Paris. His strategy fails; Julia has more iron in her than he had credited. She takes his pound without intending to use it as traveling money and, on her way out of his hotel, rejects his extended hand.

The interview with the older man gives way to one with a man her own age. The next chapter restores Horsfield, looking "very tidy and precise" (p. 87). As with the resemblances between Marya Zelli's husband and lover in *Quartet*, Horsfield shares traits with Julia's earlier protector, Mackenzie. Neither man works for a living. They also have the same heart, the kind that comes from having been trained to hide their feelings. Emotionally escapist, both distrust impulse, yield to it grudgingly, then blame Julia for having tempted them with their own desires. But whereas his affair with Julia has soured Mackenzie on sex, Horsfield is ripe for rutting. "Lamentably deficient" in his "love life and humanity" (p. 36), he must keep his heart from shriveling further. "The habit of wanting to be alone had grown upon him rather alarmingly" (p. 36), he worries. Thus Julia, though lowdown and threadbare, promises renewal. That she has touched something vital in him shows in his sensitivity to her. Having heard of her bad times, he does not want her to bracket him with her selfish, unimaginative lovers of the past. He knows that she needs sympathy and understanding, not as a member of a class of unfortunates, but as a person. What is more, he knows that her need calls for immediate action:

Suddenly he saw Julia not as a representative of the insulted and injured, but as a solid human being. She must be taken somewhere—not later than the next morning. She must have a bed to sleep in, food, clothes, companionship—or she would be lonely; understanding of her own peculiar point of view—or she would be aggrieved. (p. 168)

But he does not let moral impulse rule for long. Not that he denies Julia outright; when he sees that a delay will work the same effect as a

denial, he dallies. His chance to clear himself morally without lifting a finger lessens the urgency of her need. His failure is clear; he lacks the fiber to act on his good instincts. He does not want to feel responsible for another person. Aware of both her need and his own chance to help, he always feels relieved to part from her. "He understood her, but in a cold and theoretical way" (p. 174), Jean Rhys says of him as he tells Julia goodbye for the last time.

Only rarely will his understanding glow with warmth. For most of their dinner outing of Part II, Chapter 4, he does little to help her from feeling poor, lonely, and unwanted. "He's been taught never to give himself away" (p. 88), Julia observes correctly of him. He has observations of his own: that she looks older, more worn, and less pretty than in Paris. This comedown lessens his enthusiasm for her. Nor does the falling-off bypass her. "I thought from the way you were staring at me that I must be pretty ugly" (p. 92), she says, out of wounded vanity. Her brutal honesty disturbs Horsfield, who lacks the self-confidence to beat back adversity. Being shamed makes him shrink from her. He sits away from her in the taxi, and, when the taxi pulls up short, flinging her "soft and yielding" (p. 93) body against him, he blushes and flinches. Pressing a pound note in her hand, he drops her with great relief at her hotel.

The action of the next chapter moves to Julia's mother's flat in suburban Acton. Julia is ushered into the flat by Miss Wyatt, the brisk, determined live-in nurse. (Her mannish gestures, necktie, and reference to faded Norah's youth suggest that Miss Wyatt is lesbian. But anything more than this whisper of homosexuality would distract from the plot. Suffice it that Julia returns home to find the life pulse dried, shrunken, and twisted.) Entering her mother's room gives Julia a series of shocks: she is stunned that her once-vibrant mother has become a "huge shapeless mass" (p. 97); that her mother's face is still beautiful; that the juddering encounter with her paralyzed mother means so little to her. "Silence—the best thing in the world" (p. 98), she thinks, as she sits in the quiet, thickly draped room.

But the novel has other work to do besides watching Julia indulge her languor in the womblike sick room. To show the different ways women can come to grief, to give another picture of Julia, and to prepare for the final rift between the sisters, it cuts to the point of view of Norah. As has been seen, Norah has spent the last six years buried under a mound of domestic chores. Seeing Julia looking more stylish than herself makes her ask if her years of drudgery have wiped out her youth, her beauty, and her verve. What is worse, her self-questioning

cannot help her; she still lacks the money and the freedom to start afresh. Hope keeps eluding her. "Nothing mattered except sleep (p. 105), she observes, trying to suppress her grief. She is not a woman for nothing. Some hurts can be eased by simply ignoring them, she has learned, applying the logic of Joyce's Molly Bloom in *Ulysses*.

The grip of the past persists through the next chapter, prosaically entitled, "Mr. James." Nobody in London welcomes Julia and she knows it. "Dry, distant" (p. 112) Neil James, with whom she had an affair some sixteen years ago, is no exception. So strapped is she for friends that she has no more recent an ex-lover to write to in London. Though knowing that she wants money, Neil James agrees to see her. Their meeting, like all of Julia's others with (English)men, goes badly. "That wasn't what I wanted" (p. 116), she says of her tears, her inability to charm James, and her failure to speak her deepest thoughts. Still, he does agree to send her some money. He will have to send it to a new address. The next chapter, "Change of Address," shows her moving from the Bloomsbury hotel to a boarding house in Notting Hill. The move reinstates her gnawing earlier impression of going around in circles. Protesting, "I'm not walking in a circle" (p. 117), she gets lost for a second time in a week in London's maze of streets; she goes to her third cinema; looking back, she sees that she has taken money from three men, all of whom want her out of London. All of her options seem to have dried up.

## II  *Swallowed Up by Drabness*

The following chapter, in which she sees her mother die, darkens her hopes. What happens to her afterwards shows a part of Julia to have died together with Mrs. Griffiths—a warm-blooded Brazilian who never got used to cold, gray England. What dies in Julia is this tropical inheritance of color, warmth, and zest. The process of attrition begins immediately. Showing no will, she lets Miss Wyatt keep her out of her mother's death room until Miss Wyatt is ready to admit her. On her way back to her rooming house, she improvises an ironic dirge to the events of the day, "Go Rolling Down to Rio." She will never know festive, flavorsome Rio first-hand; nobody will put *her* on an ocean liner. But her predicament goes beyond being trapped in Europe. "Fathers are brutal and remote; mothers are feeble, remote, and a bit mad,"[5] writes Judith Thurman of the Rhys heroine's parentage. The definition fits Julia. The little she gets both from her mother and from her stingy Uncle Griffiths rules out a

legacy from the older generation; her dead infant son, the only child mentioned in the book, has sealed her off from the future. Rather than fitting into a British literary tradition, she belongs to the lost generation of the Americans Gertrude Stein and Ernest Hemingway. Her chance of linking herself creatively to those around her matches that of sailing to Rio.

Coinciding with her arrival at her boarding house the day her mother dies is a characteristic craving for sleep. The hours of rest she grabs at the end of Chapter 8 must not be decried or begrudged; they may be the last peace she enjoys for some time. Beginning with the next chapter, where her mother is cremated, Julia's fortunes dip sharply. She runs out of money; her judgment plays her false; that old standby, indifference, no longer solves her problems. While her mother's remains are burning, she compares herself to a comet—skying upward in a blaze but then, having risen to the top of her fiery parabola, sinking fast. The second half of her comparison, anyway, is accurate; she has become a guttering flame, emitting little warmth or light in her down-rocketing course: "She was a defiant flame shooting upwards not to plead but to threaten. Then the flame sank down again, useless, having reached nothing" (p. 131). In keeping with this description, the dull, drab world reasserts itself right after the funeral; even in her privation, Julia cannot feel special for long. She is smashed down quickly. Hostility spoils her final moments with Norah. As if their mother's death removed all traces of family love, the fated interview between the sisters occurs in their mother's bedroom. Only misunderstanding and rancor come to life in the dark, heavily curtained womblike room.

The interview starts well enough. Norah, having decided to leave London immediately with Miss Wyatt, gives Julia their mother's ruby and gold ring. Her generosity, though, cannot erase years of mutual resentment. Julia repays her kindness poorly. Usually compliant, she begins quarreling. Suspecting that she may not see Norah for another ten years, she seizes the chance to vent her anger full blast. The anger is both social and personal. Norah she aligns with the respectable middle class that has excluded and besmirched her for the past fifteen years:

People are such beasts, such mean beasts. . . . And do you think I'm going to cringe to a lot of mean, stupid animals? If all good, respectable people had one face, I'd spit in it. I wish they all had one face so that I could spit in it. (p. 135)

All you people who've knuckled under—you're jealous. D'you think I don't know? You're jealous of me, jealous, jealous. Eaten up with it. (p. 136)

Is the charge fair? Self-denying Norah does envy Julia's having bolted from the family. Does she also envy Julia's obvious failure to rise out of her shabby-genteel class? A younger sister who stayed at home, Norah views Julia's tattiness as her comeuppance. But Julia's harsh words have silenced her. She runs from the room in tears; Uncle Griffiths, on hand for the ritual postfuneral dinner, attacks Julia—ironically, for not knowing how to act among respectable folk—and is called "an abominable old man" (p. 136) for his meddling. The speed with which her long-overdue insult routs him comforts Julia. The comfort is welcome. The ordeal of fighting with her two closest relatives, within hours of her mother's funeral, has tired Julia, and she starts dozing in the darkened room. But her rest is broken by capable Miss Wyatt, who accuses her of having harmed her family. Then she sends Julia away, without Julia's ever challenging her authority. Julia's final, and perhaps worst, setback in the sad family scrap comes right here—in being put out of her mother's house by a stranger.

Walking in the fresh air of the tube station boosts her briefly. As in Chapter 4, she shores herself up by rejecting an overture from a strange man. What she rejects is a dinner invitation from a respectable-looking South African businessman. Dignity has been maintained. Though she looks like an easy pickup, she refuses to act like one—especially for the benefit of a squat establishmentarian. Besides, she has already planned to have dinner with George Horsfield. The evening follows an unpredictable course, Jean Rhys tempering her sense of incongruity with craftsmanship. At her rooming house, Julia finds a note in which Horsfield regrets that urgent business has forced him to break their date. But Horsfield, probably yielding to impulse, shows up after all, stopping Julia on the street on the very next page. In the course of the evening, the couple meets various lost city types, both on the drizzling streets and in the dance hall they go to after dinner. The couple communicate badly at the dance hall; their evening together seems to have gone flat. While their conversation flags, Horsfield has coffee and Julia sips a brandy. Then she dances with an elderly man. As usual, she gives very little of herself, neglecting to mention to either man her mother's death or her quarrel with Norah. But these events *have* upset her. At the end of the cab ride home, she implores Horsfield to stay with her. Nothing that happened in the course of the evening has led up to this urgent plea.

A puzzled Horsfield accepts her offer blankly. Nor does his enthusiasm rise as the night wears on. Because neither he nor Julia is a voluptuary, they do not interact any more vitally from the loins than they did in conversation. But Jean Rhys never blitzes a character or relationship without first sending forth some rays of false hope. Julia's talk of cracking up, in her darkened room, touches Horsfield's heart. Stroking her hair and listening attentively, he answers her in kind; he, too, knows mental disorder firsthand: "I know something about cracking up too. I went through the war, you know" (p. 152). But the sexuality these confidences lead to dissatisfies. Not only do the lovers avoid calling each other by name; to help block the growth of intimacy, Jean Rhys even refers to Horsfield as "Mr. Horsfield" (p. 153) at the hottest moment of the encounter. Nor does she describe the sexuality, as if anything so rundown did not deserve the effort—hers or ours. Instead, she has Horsfield stroke and kiss Julia mechanically and then, rather than feel elated by his lover's charms, listen to a train rumbling in the distance. Would he rather be riding the train than lying in the dark with Julia? How much time must pass, he wonders, before he can go home without offending her? The end of the chapter stresses his noncomprehension and discomfort rather than fulfillment: "'The worst of it is,' he thought, 'that one can never know what the woman is really feeling'" (p. 153).

Horsfield's attempt to slink away and Julia's sharp displeasure with him further discredit the sexuality. Sex has alienated the couple rather than uniting them. Jean Rhys distances this effect well. To undercut the somberness, she intrudes an unexpected comedy. Slipping out of Julia's boarding house at five A.M., Horsfield spots a policeman watching him from across the street. His sheepish look and tumbled evening clothes convey an inescapable meaning. The proper English gentleman has paid for his gentlemanly folly with an awkward public exposure. And he did not enjoy himself. The disapproving policeman is the logical offspring of his carouse with Julia.

The sexual bout did not move her much, either, as can be seen in her reaction to the dutiful note he wrote before leaving the room: "She read Mr. Horsfield's note, and it was as if she were reading something written by a stranger to someone she had never seen" (p. 157). The new chapter, entitled "Childhood," besides hinting at the meaninglessness and sterility of the night before, adds to the regressiveness that has ridden Julia since Mackenzie put her out. The chapter is deliberately undramatic—sifting affections, measuring

feelings, and, as the following extract shows, telescoping past and present: "When you are a child you are yourself and you know and see everything prophetically. And then suddenly something happens and you stop being yourself; you become what others force you to be. You lose your wisdom and your soul" (p. 158). Recent chapters have hummed with action and incident. The reminiscences of Chapter 12 create a resting place before Julia's last reversals. The novel needs this relief. It also profits from the smoothness with which Jean Rhys tones Julia's self-inventory into the plot.

However awkward their night together, it has encouraged Julia and Horsfield to try another go. He takes her to dinner, as he promised in his goodbye note; he commends her for restoring his youth; the evening goes well enough for them to plan to spend the night together. What happens next is only clear from its effects. Julia wrecks any intimacy that may have been costively building between her and Horsfield. Either by accident or design, she becomes hysterical when he touches her on the dark staircase (the chapter is called "The Staircase") leading to her room. Has she wilfully thrown away her chance for security? The self-defeating scene with Horsfield on the stairs looks back to the one with Mackenzie in the Paris restaurant. Germane to an understanding of both scenes is Judith Thurman's explanation of the Rhys heroine's tendency to defeat her best hopes as "a symptom of advanced loneliness."[6] Having climbed the dark stairs several times in the past, the night before with Horsfield, she has no cause for panic. On the other hand, her mother's death and the fight with Norah may be troubling her more than she lets on; later, she reports having had the impression that a corpse touched her in the dark.

In either case, her screams wake the other tenants and the landlady, and the next day brings an eviction notice. On the brink of gaining security, i.e., what she most wants and needs, she wastes her best hope: the conventional English gentleman George Horsfield can be counted on to flee from emotional outbursts, especially when they take place around other people. Without him, London offers Julia nothing. She prepares to head back to Paris rather than look for new lodgings in London. During an uneasy interview with Horsfield, whose relief in her impending departure shows in his helping her to pack, she opens a letter from her old beau, Neil James. Options are drying up quickly. Accompanying a present of £20 is the declaration that no more money will be sent; Julia's setbacks with men are multiplying. The pattern is extended. In a scene resembling Marya

Zelli's guilty confession to Stephan at the end of *Quartet*, Julia talks to Horsfield about James. The resemblance includes the men as well as the women and their truthsaying. Like Stephan and Heidler before him, James deals in paintings. This shared interest is thematic: all three men keep the heroines at a distance. But, signalling the superiority of *Mackenzie* over *Quartet*, Jean Rhys tells us that Julia posed for portraits at the time she knew James. The low-key relationship between the artist's model and the art connoisseur need not have been so low-key; they had something in common besides sex. Their failure to cultivate this fertile common ground speaks badly for both. More pathetic than tragic, Julia has connived at her downfall. As her words to Horsfield show, she probably has not brought any candor to a sexual relationship for the past sixteen years: "He collects pictures, this man," she says of James. "I don't know anything about him, really. You see, he never used to talk to me much. I was for sleeping with—not talking to" (pp. 172–73). No wonder that the prospect of needing a man two straight nights makes this apathetic woman hysterical. For all these years, she has equated sex with self-suppression, not communication, expression, or joy.

Her return to Paris in Part III is a letdown: nobody meets her at the station; she has no prospects; all she craves is sleep. Nothing good came from her ten days in London. Needing a job, she writes a résumé for the classified section of a magazine. But she does not send it: the Rhys heroine does not work. The novel ends in a series of missed chances, false starts, and disconnected scraps. Horsfield sends her £10 by registered post. But rather than saving the money, she spends it all on clothing. This rashness stems from her double vision of herself. Knowing her inability to make money last, she throws it away on things she likes; pretty things mean more to her than sensible things. But anybody with such a poor sense of self-preservation cannot fend off sorrow, prettiness notwithstanding. Her new dress and hat neither gladden her nor help her defy her fate. She wears her depression openly. A policeman who sees her peering into the oily Seine fears her as a potential suicide.

The rest of her wayward afternoon carries no hint of violence. She drifts into a café, a "low-down place" (p. 184), for a brandy. On her way home, it starts to rain, so she ducks into a music store, where she buys some phonograph records to listen to until the showers subside. In another café, she starts a letter to Horsfield, but, uninspired, draws lines and faces instead. Even in small incidentals, her life lacks control: in the previous scene, she bought some records she did not

want; here, the letter she starts dwindles into childish scrawl. She no longer cares. This novel about an indifferent woman ends indifferently. Rather than smashing her with a cruel blast of fate, Jean Rhys shows fate helping Julia in the last chapter. She and Mackenzie meet by chance—again, in a café. When she walks silently past his table, he follows her and invites her for a drink. She answers his impulsive act with one of her own; living near the edge can rouse boldness as well as fear. She asks him for two hundred francs, which, caught off guard, he gives her. Then he leaves, presumably to get ready for a trip. She finishes her Pernod by herself. The novel's brilliant last paragraph shows her walking to her hotel—the same one she occupied at the outset. Returning to her starting point confirms her London fears; her life *is* wheeling in circles. Yet these tired, diminishing circles, brightened by occasional spots of good luck, could form her last line of defense; moving in tired, worn grooves beats standing still and marking time. Any distraction is welcome. The shadows lengthening around her do not bear thinking about: "The street was cool and full of gray shadows. Lights were beginning to come out in the cafés. It was the hour between dog and wolf, as they say" (p. 191).

As has been seen, the threat of circularity emerges first in England; coming home haunts her rather than giving comfort or strength. It also makes her feel unreal—insubstantial and removed from time. She refers to herself as "an importunate ghost" (p. 66) in a letter to Neil James. Walking through the fog the next day, she wonders whether "the ghost of herself" (pp. 67–68) is coming toward her. On the next page, a stranger in a restaurant exclaims that he just saw a man who died in a Japanese earthquake. The stranger is never named; he never reappears. Jean Rhys does not need to flesh him out or to develop his story. A device more than a character, he adds to the mood of frustration building both around and within Julia. This mood had already asserted itself. Thus, Chapter 1 introduced two women worse off than Julia—Liliane, the "big, fair . . . sullen and rather malicious" (p. 12) chambermaid and Julia's malevolent-looking upstairs neighbor, "an old forsaken woman" (p. 15) with frowzy salt-and-pepper hair. These women, exemplars of female experience, fall within the range of Julia's moral possibilities. Although they are not to be equated with Julia, they do represent variants of the same social type—today's dispossessed urban woman. Several other reminders of woman's low estate accompany Julia's downfall. These vivid images generalize Julia's story. On their way to a London dance hall, Julia and Horsfield spot a woman wandering in

the rain; her mackintosh, as in Joyce and Graham Greene, is the uniform of the loser; no stranded notebook entry to the novel, the foundering woman is living a real drama whose pathos we can imagine:

Outside a fine rain was falling. The darkness was greasy in spite of the rain. A woman in a long mackintosh passed them, muttering to herself and looking mournful and lost, like a dog without a master. (p. 145)

Some seemingly irrelevant footage from a film ties in directly with this waywardness; tradition has taught us to laugh at women who try to do what we see men do without blinking:

After the comedy she saw young men running races and some of them collapsing exhausted. And then—strange anti-climax—young women ran races and also collapsed exhausted, at which the audience rocked with laughter. (pp. 117–18)

### III    Carving a Vortex

Most of the criticism of *Mackenzie* has been favorable. A dissenting voice comes from Mellown, who brackets the book with *Quartet* as an early misfire:

Her first two novels are flawed by her failure to control the point of view. . . . Rhys's point of view is so patently that of the main female character and so biased in her favor that the abrupt shifts into the thoughts of another character . . . destroy the continuity of the narrative and weaken its psychological verisimilitude.[7]

These objections apply less to *Mackenzie* than to *Quartet*. Jean Rhys approves neither of Julia's bullying of Norah, when Norah's guard is down, nor her practice of inviting men to use her as a sexual object. Besides, the later novel shifts point of view smoothly, mindful of both motivation and setting. For instance, the shift from Julia's mind to Norah's occurs on Norah's home ground—the seedy flat she has occupied for many years. The shift both extends and deepens the action. Besides adding freshness and variety, it also shows Julia from the standpoint of somebody whose opinion deserves a serious hearing—a sister who has not seen her for ten years. The final row between the women thus stands as the climax of an ongoing rivalry rather than as an arbitrary piece of plotting. Mellown's objections to

the book's alleged discontinuity can be dismissed. *Mackenzie*'s shadows and silences are as carefully prepared for as the clamor. The subdued tones of the novel shape and adumbrate, abstract and embody. Rebecca West has explained the power generated by the novel's bleak, flat images and played-down style: "It is a terrible book about the final foundering to destruction of a friendless and worthless but pitiful woman. It is terrible, but it is superb."[8]

Echoing Dame Rebecca, Naipaul, calling *Mackenzie* "the most brutal" of Jean Rhys's novels, discusses its quiet horror: "It doesn't dissect a passion. It examines solitude and the void,"[9] Naipaul says of the book's ability to keep passion from breaking through the skin of the story. Though pulsing with fears, stresses, and uncertainties, the book slews its technique away from its underlying melodrama. Julia lacks the verve and wit to make her life a racy romp; her heart is not supple, open, or loving. Her practice of coping with problems by ignoring them, while reflecting her psyche, also infiltrates the novel's tone. Jean Rhys's deadpan effects rarely shrill or grate. The flat, toneless chapter titles help create an unforced revelation of actual experience; few readers of the novel would indict Jean Rhys for not telling the truth.

Her technique conveys the same sure-handedness. Narrative selection both keeps options alive and opens psychological vistas. Our never being told Mackenzie's first name draws us into the indifference of Julia's relationship with him. Yet this lack of intimacy never troubles Julia as much as it does us. She helped foster the depersonalized relationship, consented to it, and wanted it to last. Structure also lends meaning to the events Julia passes through. Though supple and random enough to look spontaneous, *Mackenzie* has a definite organization. We have already seen Jean Rhys unifying the action with images of female desolation, like the mackintosh-wearing woman in the London drizzle. Another unifying device she summons is that of matched scenes. Julia meets Mackenzie both before and after her London trip. Both meetings occur in restaurants. This equation of food and death (the death of the affair having devitalized Julia) points to the tense family dinner following Mrs. Griffiths's funeral. More cruelly, it likens Julia to a slab of decaying meat in the butcher shop of sexuality.

Again, paired scenes make death the logical product of her spiral existence. Chapter 4, "The First Unknown," shows her rejecting money from a strange man. Her decisiveness cheers her: "I'm not finished at all" (p. 59), she exults, refreshed and strengthened for her

London trip. Chapter 20, "The Second Unknown," which takes place after the trip, shows how much the London trip has wasted her. A young man looking for a pickup trails her and then, walking up beside her and seeing her face, turns away. This time *she* has been rejected. Her rejection is foreshadowed structurally. Midway between the chapters featuring the two unknowns falls Chapter 12, entitled "Death." Midway into the three-part chapter, Julia's mother dies. Death, the supreme imponderable, stands dead-center between the two unknowns; similarly, Julia occupies the middle ground between her dead son and dead mother. Death is the black hole at the center of her spiral half-life. Death beckons from the widening vortex.

# CHAPTER 5

# Voyage in the Dark

IF Julia Martin is a later version of *Quartet*'s Marya Zelli, Anna Morgan, the young heroine of *Voyage in the Dark* (1934) is an earlier incarnation. Jean Rhys's personal favorite among her works[1] goes back in time to 1912–14, roughly the date of her own arrival and early days in England. Jean Rhys's traveling to England with an aunt suggests Anna Morgan's having her sea passage paid by an English stepmother who looked after Anna for some months after her arrival. Other resemblances between author and heroine can be invoked. Anna, an eighteen-year-old Creole, or fifth-generation White West Indian on her mother's side, is working in the chorus line of a traveling musical comedy. Though not identified as little Dominica, Jean Rhys's birthplace, the unnamed island where Anna was born and reared is, like Dominica, one of the smallest in the Antilles. Similarities between Anna and Jean Rhys's other heroines are also vivid. In an August 1967 issue of *Punch*, Martin Shuttleworth called the archetypal figure "a female utterly impractical, incompetent, generous, passive."[2] The adjectives all fit Anna. Though she does not wreck her best chances like Julia Martin, she does little to help herself, throwing away money, misjudging people, and tending to do what comes easiest, like drifting by slow, easy stages into prostitution. Marcelle Bernstein's remark about Jean Rhys's women, "They are passive . . . soft, sad uncertain creatures with pretty faces and a liking for liquor,"[3] besides touching on Anna's large intake of gin and vermouth, also refers to her tendency to let herself be used. She rarely starts or ends a relationship; people move close to her and, after taking what they want, disappear. These acquaintances, lovers, and relatives all refuse to accept her as she is. Yet their schemes to help her, while beneficial to themselves, usually leave her worse off than before.

Help is what Anna needs. Like Julia before her, she is depressed by London's dishwater uniformity. But her island background and

speech, like the possibility that she has a spoonful of Negro blood, make her more of an outsider than Julia. Where can she turn? While exluding her from respectable English society, her theatrical career withholds compensations of excitement or fame. The singing lessons a lover pays for do not help her get better stage roles; in fact, she gives up the stage around this time—when she is training to get ahead. The decision comes easily. No adventure, her life in the theater never rises out of the dull, weary sameness characterizing England in general:

After a while I got used to England and I liked it all right; I got used to everything except the cold and that the towns we went to always looked so exactly alike. You were perpetually moving to another place which was perpetually the same. There was always a little gray street leading to the stage door of the theater and another little gray street where your lodgings were, and rows of little houses with chimneys like the funnels of dummy steamers and smoke the same color as the sky; and a gray stone promenade running hard, naked and straight by the side of the gray-brown or gray-green sea. (p. 8)

I . . . slid off into thinking of all the bedrooms I had slept in and how exactly alike they were, bedrooms on tour. (p. 150)

This sameness bewilders and then demoralizes, belying the glamor, energy, and high spirits usually associated with a career in musical comedy. Suitably, the London theater where Anna's touring company performs is in Holloway, a famous prison-site; Anna says, "The dark streets round the theater made me think of murders" (p. 18). Her intimation prefigures the main lines of the plot. Her moral darkness will mesh with the dinginess of the streets she prowls; her abortion, ten pages from the end, refers back to the murders conjured up by Holloway. But her descent both to the dark streets and the abortionist's couch is conveyed so casually that it packs no punch. This casualness is intended. Only when we realize that the meaning of her acts strikes Anna no more than it does us do we feel their force. The Rhys touch is so light and graceful that some of its best effects can be overlooked. Anna is a victim whose innocence produces other victims. The following summary of *Voyage*, from *Current Biography*, sets forth the materials which Jean Rhys shapes and tones to create her deadpan drama of derailed innocence:

Eighteen-year-old Anna Morgan, a newcomer to London, hovers on the edge of the theatrical world as a chorus girl and fantasizes about the warmth and

ease of the West Indies, where she was born. Loneliness and despair lead her to her casual affair with a "gentleman" who, quite as casually, drops her. But the experience was so easy that Anna finds herself drifting without much resistance into prostitution. The inevitable pregnancy occurs, followed by an induced miscarriage, and she awakens to hear the doctor say that she will be "ready to start all over again in no time."[4]

## I   *Barriers of Futility*

*Voyage* spans more time than any of the novels through *Good Morning, Midnight*. The date at the outset is October 1912, and the setting is Southsea, where Anna's troupe has been performing. But, ignoring the professional side of traveling musical comedy, like rehearsals, costume fittings, and back-stage chatter, the book focuses on Anna's private life. Two years in ragged, featureless England have sapped Anna's pep: she rarely smiles; she moves slowly; she is often sick. England's thin, pale sunlight and drizzling gray streets depress her after the bright sun-heat, the rich, moist smells, and the street clamor of her home town. Work offers no release; a chorus girl's life, reputed to be gay and carefree, is only drab, loveless repetition. Repressiveness dogs her from the start. Her Southsea landlady complains about the irregular hours kept by Anna and her roommate and fellow trouper, Maudie Beardon. She has grounds for complaint. The girls do not take breakfast with the other roomers; they troop through the corridors in their negligees; Maudie's wearing a torn kimono in the common sitting room, in clear view of the window, *could* hurt the house's reputation. This sloppiness has a more corrosive effect. A sullen, promiscuous street brat of twenty-eight, Maudie influences Anna for the bad: she makes the word, "swank," sound like the definition of a moral value; she cares little about music and acting; she takes money from men. A missing tooth in clear view when she smiles conveys the futility of her low-life vanity.

One day, she and Anna go shopping for stockings. On the street, they start talking to two men, pair off with them, and then, after getting the stockings, invite the men to their boardinghouse for tea. Anna gets along well with her new friend (the same "gentleman" mentioned in the summary above), a pleasant softspoken man about twice her age. Politely, he takes her address and assures her that he will invite her for dinner when she gets to London. Anna's meeting with Walter Jeffries points up her self-destructive innocence. Five

minutes after meeting him in the street, she lets him pay for her stockings; within half an hour, she is serving him tea in her room. Girls who acted this way in 1912 did not appeal to a man's noblest instincts; a friendship that starts in the gutter usually stays there. Were Anna more worldly, she would know to expect the worst from Jeffries. The worst shows itself quickly, though disguised by good manners and expensive trappings. Jeffries writes, as promised, and within a week is dining with Anna in a hotel suite. The warm, companionable glow imparted by their wine chills when he starts kissing her in earnest and steering her toward the bedroom. He cannot see his plans through. Right away, he can tell that she does not welcome his sexual overtures. After she pulls away from him, he apologizes and then takes her home without making another pass. (The expensive dinner taken with a bedroom in the background that the diners never use recurs in the one-page story, "On Not Shooting Sitting Birds," *New Yorker*, 26 April 1976, p. 35; reprinted in *Sleep It Off, Lady*.

But the red-shaded lamps, the red carnations on the table, the painted red fire in the cold grate of the bedroom, and perhaps even a pain in her side, all prefigure the sexual downfall of the shivering virgin from the tropics. The prefiguring is fulfilled quickly; the next morning Jeffries sends a letter, a large bunch of violets, and some money. This appeal Anna cannot resist. Her eagerness for Jeffries's £25 recalls Julia Martin's statement in *Mackenzie* that taking money from men is an easy habit to acquire: "I took the money . . . and put it into my handbag. I was accustomed to it already. It was as if I had always had it" (p. 27). What she does with the cash also recalls Julia's behavior in similar circumstances; like Julia, Anna is mad to buy new clothes: "All the time I was dressing I was thinking what clothes I would buy. I didn't think of anything else at all" (p. 27). The next scene, in Cohen's, a Shaftesbury Avenue dress shop, is one of the book's best, even though it lasts less than two pages. Having located their shop smack in London's theater district, i.e., the West End, the two Misses Cohen thrive on chorus girls. Knowing that Anna has money to burn makes their blood sparkle and they use all their tricks to lower her sales resistance. Subtle predators, they flatter her on her appearance, praise a friend from the chorus line (whose name they have carefully noted), and, experts in the psychology of merchandising, quiet Anna's fears about money: "We're having some new dresses in next week. Paris models. Come in and look at them and if you can't pay at once I daresay we can make an arrangement" (p. 29). That

Anna leaves the shop wearing, unaltered, the first dress she tries on betokens the triumph of salesmanship over innocence.

Does Anna feel cheated? The search for an answer overrides cause-and-effect materialism. No sooner does she leave the dress shop than her side begins hurting for the first time since she opened Jeffries's letter hours before. Her run of bad luck continues. The same landlady that brought her Jeffries's present now evicts her for a tart as soon as she returns from her shopping spree. Anna cannot bask in her windfall. The pain in her side races through her system and flattens her. Jeffries, to whom she had written after her eviction, comes to her sick room with food, drink, and an eiderdown. Then he arranges both a medical examination and a reprieve on Anna's eviction. The same room that had begun to shrink menacingly around her now grows back to normal size. Anna can now get the rest and nourishment she needs to recover. After a meal, she goes to sleep right away. But she overlooks the fact that Jeffries did not share her meal. This delicately nuanced portent exerts its force immediately, keeping alive the alternation between cheer and depression that helps unify the early chapters. The alternation holds as the action jumps ahead a week. Having recovered from the flu, Anna complies with her eviction notice. But rather than describing her new digs or the details of settling in, Jean Rhys cuts to Jeffries's house, where, without much ado, Anna is deflowered. As usual in Jean Rhys, the lovers are not shown enjoying sex or its tender afterglow. The writer continues to criticize the action through narrative selection. Instead of describing intimacy, she shows Anna and Jeffries going out into the street for a cab at four o'clock in the morning, Jeffries's putting some money in Anna's purse, and Anna's ignoring the knowing wink of the cabdriver who drops her at her new address.

How cogent is this denial of membership in London's crew of nighthawks? Jeffries never lets her spend the night with him. Nor does she ask, both of them complying with a tacit code governing the conduct of gentlemen and their mistresses. The routine Anna slips into signals further adherence to the code. Beyond finding out that he sells insurance, she knows little about Jeffries. And even though he pays her rent and sends her gifts, he never comes to her room. She questions neither his conduct nor her own. While waiting for him to call or write, she gets up late, lazes around her room, and buys new clothes if she has the money. But the time she spends with him does not seem worth the long waits in-between. Another night in his bed ends with her hailing a cab on a dark, lonely street; solitude has

become coextensive with his embraces. One unshaped, truncated scene showing her with him follows another. Observing a loose time scheme, the novel glides and hops ahead. The next scene describes Anna's nineteenth birthday in January 1913. Maudie Beardon comes over for a birthday drink. Her working-class obsession with social rank shows in the hungry, covetous look she gives Anna's well-appointed rooms, dress collection, and fur coat. Anna has acted wisely to trade the touring company, with its tedious rehearsals, busy travel schedule, and changeless regimen of cold rooms in strange dark towns for this largesse. But Maudie's voice is edged with spite; she seems determined to score a point on her friend. Anna thwarts her by ignoring her recitation of the tart's code: "The thing with men is to get everything you can out of them and not care a damn" (p. 44). When told, next, to make Jeffries set her up in an expensive flat in Park Mansions, Anna changes the subject. Although her heart has mellowed while she has been out of our view, she has come to love Walter Jeffries. She refuses to exploit him.

The issues raised by her loving loyalty come into question right away. Does Walter love her, too? The next scene takes place at his house, where he is talking about buying Anna music lessons and helping her find work as a singer. His plans seem not to impress her. She communicates as badly with Jeffries here as she did with Maudie in the last scene. When asked if she would like to get ahead in her career, she answers, her mind full of the promise of having sex with him, "I want to be with you. That's all I want" (p. 50). Now Jean Rhys does not accept this romanticism outright; mistresses must make their patrons feel strong and important, especially when the patrons are being generous. But neither does she approve Jeffries's impatience. Jeffries admonishes Anna, "Don't be like a stone that I try to roll uphill and that always rolls down again" (p. 50). His annoyance persists. On the next page he refers to her predecessor, as if he wants her to know that she may have a successor, too. The subtle warning escapes her. Brimming with emotion, she talks of her West Indian family and home. But her island heritage means nothing in London; rather, it is despised. Jeffries listens politely, even dredging up the effort to ask questions in the right places. Clearly, her recitation has touched nothing vital in him. He replies thickly to her most heartfelt disclosures. "You sound a bit tight" (p. 56), he says, when he tires of the conversation, ignoring her words and leading her to the bedroom, upstairs.

Naturally, the narrative breaks here; for Jean Rhys to show Anna

happy would go against both the book's intent and mood. In the next chapter the month is March, and Anna is entertaining her step-mother, who came back to England after her husband's death. Hester always lorded it over Gerald Morgan and his West Indian family. The device with which she raised herself over her adopted culture was her immaculate English speech. Brilliantly, Jean Rhys fixes her character in a few sentences:

She had . . . an English lady's voice with a sharp, cutting edge to it. Now that I've spoken you can hear that I'm a lady. I have spoken and I suppose you now realize that I'm an English gentlewoman. I have my doubts about you. Speak up and I will place you at once. (p. 57)

Now living in Yorkshire, Hester has come to London both to judge and to carp. Her self-serving talk with Anna in Chapter 6 helps justify the following judgment of Anna by Francis Hope in the London *Observer Review*: "She shivers in feverish delirium half the time, suffers from step-parents, cannot enjoy her legacy. The date is 1914, but the misery is timeless."[5] Her plight is certainly widespread. Money has cut across love and duty, making her reel. As Uncle Griffiths did with Julia in *Mackenzie*, Hester tells her to leave London: "I feel it's altogether too much responsibility for me" (p. 59). Anna's Uncle Ramsay, or Bo, back in the West Indies, voices the same attitude. But he refuses to pay half of Anna's passage home, as Hester has asked. His reason? Hester inherited her husband's Caribbean estate and then sold it in order to decamp to England.

Anna stands in the middle of a financial brawl. Uncle Bo, wanting her to stay in England, where he is not responsible for her, offers Hester terms too insulting for her to accept: "If you feel that you don't wish her to live with you in England, of course her aunt and I will have her with us. But in that case I insist—we both insist—that she should have her proper share of the money you got from the sale of her father's estate" (p. 61). Money has infected all. If Uncle Bo is right, then Hester cheated Anna out of her inheritance. Hester parries this charge by itemizing the money she has spent on Anna. Her breathless self-justification includes both a dentist's and a doctor's bill, Anna's fare to England, and a complete winter wardrobe for school. This generosity comes with a moral surtax. Anna must hear Hester explain it genetically and environmentally. Living in the Caribbean detracts from your whiteness, Hester argues, citing the bastards, "all the colors of the rainbow" (p. 63), fathered by Uncle Bo. She rides the

color issue hard, censuring Uncle Bo for laughing like a black man and even implying that Anna's mother had black blood. Nothing can stem the flow of her venom. When Anna balks at the remark about her mother, she is accused of saying "wicked and unforgivable things" (p. 65). "I'm not going to argue with you," Hester rattles on, anxious to clear herself of any misconduct against Anna. "My conscience is quite clear. I always did my best for you and I never got any thanks for it" (p. 65). Anna cannot win. Hester wants to be rid of her; yet she also resents her independence. Without a shred of supporting evidence, she accuses Anna of living improperly and of turning out badly.

Hester's resentment of Anna has deep roots. Its seedbed is Francine, the fat Black Christian cook who helped rear Anna after her mother died. Because Francine was everything to Anna that Hester should have been—seeing Anna through her first menstrual pains and thus guiding her into womanhood, for instance—Hester wanted to send her away. (A similar conflict will recur in *Wide Sargasso Sea*.) Yet Gerald Morgan overruled her—on the basis of Francine's cooking, since he knew nothing of her closeness to Anna, a subject Hester could not afford to raise with him.

This background material comes into the novel as a time glide. The next chapter restores the action to the present and to England. Except for always having to leave Jeffries in the middle of the night, she enjoys being his mistress. Her spirits rise when he proposes a weekend outing to Savernake Forest with another couple—his cousin Vincent and French-Irish Germaine Sullivan. As she showed in *Mackenzie*, "I Spy a Stranger," and "Tigers Are Better-looking," Jean Rhys will sometimes use either a non-English woman or an English woman who has lived abroad as a lens through which to look at England. A choric figure, Germaine voices objections to Englishmen Anna lacks the seasoning to make—that they are rude and insensitive, that they dislike women, and that they are too selfish to make women happy. Coming midway into the book, these complaints focus Anna's decline; they both pertain to her at the moment and forecast what awaits her. The wait is not long. The day after crying with happiness, Anna learns that Walter and Vincent are going to New York for several months. She receives the news more quietly than Germaine, whose outburst ends the weekend party early. Back at Walter's house in London, Anna lauds Germaine's judgment of the English. Then, after doing what she was brought to do, she goes home, saddened by Walter's coming departure.

Her sadness does not lift. The next subchapter starts with an admonition from her landlady: "This is no way for a young girl to live" (p. 90). Anna's lack of purpose justifies the reproof: "For a week after Walter left," says Anna, "I hadn't gone out; I didn't want to. What I liked was lying in bed till very late, because I felt tired all the time, and having something to eat in bed and then in the afternoon staying a long time in the bath" (p. 90). Then a letter comes from Walter's cousin, Vincent, which saddens her still more. Too timid to do the job himself, Walter has used Vincent to fob her off. The letter is full of patronizing evasions. (Francis Hope, while dismissing Walter as "a decent man by the standards of his time," calls Vincent "something of a monster.")[6] Everyone wants to drop Anna; everyone feels guilty about it; all want to shed the guilt. Calling her "a nice girl" (p. 93) several times and referring to her as "dear Infant" (p. 93), Vincent keeps downgrading both sex and the sexual tie. Yet this same man who insists that "life is chock-full of other things" (p. 93) like books and games, lavishes heaps of time and cash upon sex himself. Incongruously, the thought of false teeth runs through Anna's mind as she reads the letter. Then she telegraphs fangless Walter, asking him to see her that evening. He agrees. Avoiding her eye at first, he later admits over coffee that he asked his cousin Vincent to write and told him what to say. But Anna fails to carry the day with him completely. Though he agrees to give her some money, the details to be arranged through Vincent, of course, he will not be alone with her. Part I ends shortly after he leaves her. Needing a new set of realities with which to steer her life, she gives notice at her rooming house and begins looking for new quarters: "I walked straight ahead. I thought, 'Anywhere will do, so long as it's somewhere that nobody knows'" (p. 100).

Her wanting to forget both Walter Jeffries and places connected with him makes sense. But forgetting is not easy. Her regrets over being discarded cut too deeply. He treated her well—giving her money, housing her comfortably, and caring for her as much as the code that regulates gentlemen's conduct with their tarts allows. His failure stems largely from his conventionality, i.e., his slavish adherence to the code. Too lazy and ineffectual to be cruel, he worships girlish purity with all his sentimental heart, calling female chastity "the only thing that matters" (p. 36). Perhaps this Victorian attitude (along with the fear of catching venereal disease?) explains the big age difference between lovers in Jean Rhys: men have the same sexual needs at forty-five that they had at twenty-five—virgins

to despoil and appropriate. Where does the practice of using women in this way lead? Besides handicapping marital sex, it hamstrings young single women like Anna. Walter only wants her as a toy, and this hurts her chances with men who may have nobler intentions. But can these men be found above the lower middle class? Using women as ciphers makes little boys of men. Ironically, Walter lives on Green Street. Nothing can grow on the slablike pavements where his house stands; no life can sprout from a moral dwarf.

## II    *Some Disconnected Episodes*

Anna's story continues to move us, both morally and viscerally. Recovering from another influenza attack in a Camden Town rooming house, Anna is drinking vermouth while writing a long, incoherent letter to Walter which she will never mail. Her practice of drawing her curtains during the long, lonely hours she spends in her room shows how far she has withdrawn into herself. But the withdrawal is not total. Pulling her out of her dark shell is a short, fat masseuse of forty named Ethel Matthews. In another context, Ethel, Anna's upstairs neighbor, might be called a spiv, an operator, or a wheeler-dealer; she keeps her eye on the main chance. The main chance now is symbolized by Anna's fur coat. As soon as Ethel rivets her gaze on the coat, she starts looking for ways to fleece Anna. (She admires the coat three times within four pages.) "Why don't you come along and live with me for a bit?" (p. 112) she wastes no time asking, offering her spare bedroom in a flat across town for £25. While deciding whether to accept the offer, Anna meets her former chorus line chum, first introduced in Chapter 1, Laurie Gaynor: to make the action more realistic, Jean Rhys knits the different strands in Anna's life rather than setting them forth sequentially.

Jean Rhys's craftsmanship continues to work at a high level, as talk and movement follow solitude and stasis. Her voice coarsened by drink, Laurie invites Anna to join her and two American businessmen for dinner. Anna is not sure that she wants an evening of gaiety. When she explains that her spirits are low, she is asked, for the second time in a day, if she is pregnant. Relieved to hear her negative reply, Laurie takes her friend to her flat to get ready for dinner. Her bedroom suprises us. Like her hennaed hair and heavily blued eyes, the blatant functionalism of the room—avoiding all personal touches—labels Laurie a prostitute: "Her bedroom was small and very tidy. There were no photographs and no pictures. There was a huge

bed and a long plait of hair on the dressing-table" (p. 116). Based on a chapter count, *Voyage* reaches the halfway mark here. The action calls for a shift of direction. The jilting by Walter has stunned Anna. Meeting Laurie by chance on Oxford Street, London's main shopping street, soothes her nerves. More comfort seems at hand in the form of a gala evening. But again she is bilked. Laurie spoils the dinner by calling the waiter a bloody fool and by trying to impress the table with her command of foreign languages. After dinner, Carl Redman, the American Anna prefers, goes off to gamble. The stranded trio then go to a hotel suite, where Anna gets giddy from drink, nearly passes out twice, and hears Laurie and her new friend mocking her. Then, she and Laurie quarrel drunkenly, after which she finally dozes off in an adjoining room.

Several hours later, the girls are friends again. They take a taxi back to Laurie's flat, where they breakfast together. Before Anna leaves, Laurie, the good-hearted, quick-tempered Cockney tart, kisses her roundly. This impulsiveness works thematically, yoking narrative structure to motivation. Though preparing to remove Laurie from the action, Jean Rhys wants to restore her friendly feelings for Anna before bringing her back; for Anna will later ask Laurie for help appropriate to their friendship. Taking Laurie's place in the novel is the false friend, Ethel Matthews. The last chapter of Part II shows Ethel and Anna making their bargain: Anna will pay £8 a month for room and board; in addition, she will learn manicure from Ethel and keep half of what she earns manicuring Ethel's clients. Anna pays a month's rent from a large bankroll. Seeing that Anna has cash to spare, Ethel regrets not having hiked the rent bill. But, biding her time, she settles for calling herself the best masseuse in London and for trying to impress Anna with her respectability.

By Part III, which occurs a fortnight or so later, her partnership with Anna is running smoothly. The first paragraph shows her referring again to her respectabiilty. But what, we ask, has this cherished respectability to do with her taking on Anna as a boarder? Does she want to share Anna's earnings as a prostitute? Has Anna gone on the game? Though Ethel never sends her into the streets, she does encourage her to cook fees with her sexual charms. "You must be a bit nice to them," she says of her customers, assuring Anna, "that when it comes to it they're all so damned afraid of a scene that they're off like a streak of lightning" (p. 140). The ease with which Ethel's judgment plays her false calls into doubt the value of her advice. For instance, she later mistakes the Cockney tart Laurie Gaynor for a

lady. (Her bedazzlement is not mutual, for Laurie refers to her as "a funny old cow." [p. 141]). Anna goes off with Laurie and two men for a drive in the country. The next day is not nearly as relaxing. Ethel's massage couch tips over, spilling a basin of hot water and scalding a customer. When Anna comes upstairs to help repair the mess, Ethel loses her temper. Anna has disappointed her; she should clear out for good. Though never mentioning sex directly, Ethel attacks her for not being friendly enough to the customers. But the clincher for her dismissal of Anna is Anna's having gone out with Laurie the day before and leaving her flat: "You clear off with your friends and you don't even ask me to come with you," she wails. "Well, clear out and stay out" (p. 145).

Despite this outburst, Ethel does not want Anna to go. While she spits out her anger, she is standing against the door, blocking Anna's path out of the room. When asked to move aside, she sinks to the floor in tears. The pressures fretting a single woman of forty who must fend for herself have undone her. Again, she says that Anna hurt her feelings by neglecting to take her motoring: "You went out with your pals and enjoyed yourself and you didn't even ask me. Wasn't I good enough to come?" (p. 146). She ends the melodramatic session by begging Anna to stay and then warning her that, if she does not return from her walk in an hour, then, she, Ethel, will kill herself.

Presumably, Anna returns within the hour. By the next morning Ethel has recovered but, curiously, Anna is drooping (from walking in London's dank air?). She spends the morning in bed with a headache, yearning for the tropical greenery she forsook for cold, murky England. These daydreams are broken by Ethel, "wreathed in smiles" (p. 152). Only the prospect of quick, easy money makes Ethel smile, a response that does not flatter Anna, considering what it presumes about her sexual morality. The two Americans Anna had dinner with the day of her reunion with Laurie have come to fetch her. Again, she pairs off with dark, broken-nosed Carl Redman. They go out for dinner and then return to Ethel's Bird Street flat, where they have sex. The whole escapade is recounted briefly. Jean Rhys omits the events that led up to the lovemaking, Anna's feelings, and Redman's departure in the middle of the night. (Like Walter Jeffries before him, he will not stay the night with Anna.) Instead, she concentrates on Ethel's attempt to coax more rent money out of Anna the next morning: if Anna gets money from men, Ethel will take her mite: "You know, kid," she tells Anna, "I've been thinking you'll want to go out more with your friends and not feel you've got to be in

all day. I don't mind, but we may have to talk it over a bit about the rent" (p. 156).

Redman keeps seeing Anna. During one of their dinners, he says that he is married and adds "after a while" (p. 158) that he has a daughter. Why the pause? He refuses to talk about his little girl, as if her purity would be smirched if discussed with a tart. Anna has no right to pry into his family affairs. The inevitable has occurred: his moral conscience has been roused, and it finds Anna wanting. But what has she done? Though he condemns her for a slut, he has always used her like one. To solve the moral conflict, he gives her up. Her innocent remark about laughing a great deal recently he interprets sexually, and, perhaps out of wounded vanity, drops her soon afterwards. In the meantime, her chum from the touring show, Maudie Beardon, has turned up in London. Maudie needs help. She has met an electrical engineer she would like to marry, but her shabby wardrobe is hurting her chances—lowering both the engineer's estimate of her worth and her own self-confidence. Can Anna loan her money? Of course, Anna can. Her mistake with Maudie echoes the one she made by giving Carl Redman the impression of having a busy sex life. (Is the impression false? Because it is no *verismo*, or slice-of-life, report, like so many other novels about street walkers since Zola's *Nana*, *Voyage* avoids a close detailing of its heroine's private life.) Whether Maudie wins her engineer is never revealed. We cannot even say whether she uses Anna's eight pounds ten to buy new clothes. She does not reappear; and, although Anna never mentions the subject, apparently she never returns the money she borrowed, either. That Anna's poor judgment of Maudie follows her last evening with Redman tallies the high cost of her mistakes. But the final reckoning is yet to be made. Poor street sense will cost her more than eight pounds ten.

Several months pass. It is now March 1914. Besides sending her into the streets, the experience of being dropped by Redman has also made her bad-tempered and reckless. The next scene shows her bringing a mustachioed man with a liking for classical music to her room at Ethel's. Perhaps Jean Rhys gave him his muscial tastes to imply a sensitivity in both him and Anna greater than that of either Redman or Walter Jeffries. But the nameless pickup's ability to fulfill Anna is never tested. Anna gets sick while dancing with the stranger and smashes his bandaged hand to free herself. Before she drives him away, though, she throws her shoe at a framed picture, causing a racket and strewing the room with glass. Thus Ethel's letter to Laurie

(letters in the canon always bring bad, or, at least, unwelcome news), complaining about Anna's destructiveness and asking for more money, has some justification; for besides smashing the picture, Anna also spilled wine on the eiderdown and left cigarette burns on the furniture. Another link with her nameless pickup comes in an offhand reference to her pregnancy, which probably nauseated her. It is as if her destructiveness were the child of her failure with the pickup; Jean Rhys's oblique method would not rule out assigning such thematic prominence to a minor figure.

Or to an unborn one: Laurie, who used to call Anna the Virgin (p. 16), can now find her an abortionist, but the cost will be £50, a sum Anna is unable to raise. Because she has already sold her fur coat—another sign of her decline—she tries to pry the abortionist's fee from her ex-lover, Walter Jeffries. The action moves quickly. The sentence after she starts a letter to Walter jumps ahead to the afternoon she is to meet him. But, evasive to the last, he sends his cousin, Vincent, to stand in for him. Vincent agrees to give her the money. But he makes conditions: he wants all of Walter's letters plus Anna's word that she will not write to Walter anymore. Part III ends with the abortion. But in view of the scene's spareness and deadpan tone, Jean Rhys might be describing a minor business transaction. The potentially moving scene prompts little emotion. The fat Swiss-French abortionist who calls herself Mrs. Robinson pockets her money, induces the miscarriage, and sends Anna home within a few hours. Then dizziness strikes. After reeling through the streets, Anna makes it home. But no warm homecoming greets her. Her friend Laurie, who may have gotten a commission for sending her to Mrs. Robinson, deserts her. Nor does Laurie's unwillingess to help upset Anna. As Laurie's last words in the chapter show, neither girl belongs in the tradition of the tart who has a heart of gold: "I should go slow on the gin if I were you. You've been taking too much lately" (p. 179). The phrasing that ends both the chapter and Part III resembles that which began Part II. No less a prisoner of cities than Julia Martin, Anna leads her shadow life amid the interstices of standardized lengths of steel and concrete: "Everything was always so exactly alike—that was what I could never get used to. And the cold; and the houses all exactly alike, and the streets going north, south, east, west, all exactly alike" (p. 179).

The short (five pages) fourth part of the novel introduces terror into the gridwork. Anna has been losing blood for six hours as she lies, semidelirious, in a dark room. The only light is the squib of

yellow—always the color of fear in Jean Rhys—that leaks in under the door. Worried about Anna's loss of blood, the charwoman has called Laurie to her friend's bedside. But Laurie wants no part of Anna's trouble: "It's nothing to do with me" (p. 183), she shrills, adding, in a fillip of self-justification, "She'll be all right. It's bound to stop in a minute" (p. 183). Anna is not all right. A minute later brings, not consciousness, but visions of a wild masquerade or street dance she attended as a girl. Her fall at the end of the hallucination coincides with Laurie's advising her to tell the doctor that she hurt herself falling. "Oh, so you had a fall, did you?" (p. 187) the doctor asks in the next sentence, adding, "You girls are too naïve to live" (p. 187). The sarcasm speaks home. Anna had kept her innocence while losing her virtue. Single women who live alone do not always become prostitutes or drunkards. Anna might have supported herself honorably. Somebody with more fiber would not have slid so easily into her groove of sameness. The best reading of this slide comes from Alvarez: "At the beginning . . . the nineteen-year-old virgin chorus girl is reading *Nana*; at the end she like Nana, is on the game."[7]

### III  *From Stage to Street*

Jean Rhys's publisher judged wisely to overrule her original intention to kill Anna;[8] Anna grips the imagination more as a member of the walking dead than she would have as a corpse. Besides, she never lived full tilt. Since childhood, when she wanted to be black, because West Indian blacks enjoyed life more than the whites, she has felt excluded—from fun, from the tropical abundance streaming up around her, and from the people she loved, like Francine and, later, Walter Jeffries. "I hated being white," she recalls feeling during her first menstrual cramps, "And I knew that day that I'd started to grow old and nothing could stop it" (p. 72). The coincidence of this recognition with the onset of womanhood yokes whiteness to alienation. In England, she does not fit, either. She has inherited a tradition the others neither value nor try to know; one of her landladies refers to her "drawly voice" (p. 30); her stepmother Hester says she talks "like a nigger" (p. 65); her first lover, Walter Jeffries, barely disguises his boredom when she tells him of her island life.

In England, the chill also foils her. She shivers; her hands always feel cold; she drinks partly to keep warm. Yet she is not obsessed, wasted, or driven to the edge. Midway into the book, she says, "I'm

nineteen and I've got to go on living and living" (p. 109). Her problem
is how to fill in the stretch of time. Poor judgment keeps her from
filling it creatively. When asked by Walter how she spent her day, she
answers, "I don't know" (p. 86). We have already seen her foolishly
loaning Maudie money and driving Carl Redman away by mis-
speaking herself. While pouring herself a whisky, she also tells Walter
that everybody in her family drinks too much. She neither acts nor
looks bright. Ethel refers to "that potty look of yours" (p. 145), and
Redman says she looks as if she takes ether. This drugged look
reflects her inner disposition. She does not know her life well enough
to control it. One night after coming home from Walter's bed, she
says to herself, "My God, this is a funny way to live. My God, how did
this happen?" (p. 40). As the question shows, her life lacks purpose
and definition. She stops reading. She will take singing lessons if
somebody pays for them; but the lessons are not her idea, and she
doesn't use them to make headway on the stage. Except for one time
with Walter, she says next to nothing about her deepest feelings and
concerns. We hardly know her because she has given us so little to
know her with. Her lackluster response to the disclosure that Laurie
is a prostitute typifies her: "Why shouldn't she be a tart? It's
just as good as anything else, as far as I can see" (p. 127).

This apathy shows in her effect upon others. Resembling Redman's
reference to her drugged look are Laurie's remark that she always
looks half asleep and Ethel's belief that she lacks a sense of humor: On
the day her couch tips over into a tub of hot water, Ethel says to a
laughing Anna, "This is a bit of a change—you laughing" (p. 144); in
her letter to Laurie, Ethel also calls Anna "sulky. . . . I have never
seen a girl like that—never a joke or a pleasant word" (p. 166). Ethel's
complaint is not surprising. Anna has little to smile about. What is
more, her deadpan look annoys people, possibly because it brings out
their worst. Most of this worst comes from women. Jean Rhys serves
notice in *Voyage* that women get scurvier treatment from other
women than from men. Practically every woman in the book fleeces
Anna—the Misses Cohen, owners of the West End dress shop; her
business partner and quasi-landlady, Ethel Matthews; Maudie Beardon, who borrows money she never pays back; Hester Morgan, who
cheats her out of her father's money; Laurie Gaynor, who could have
earned a fee for sending her to Mrs. Robinson for an abortion.
Readers who have made Jean Rhys a guiding spirit of the Women's
Liberation movement in the 1970s need to look again at *Voyage*,
where women of different ages and backgrounds selfishly exploit the

innocent heroine. The only wicked man in the book is Vincent Jeffries, much of whose wickedness comes from the nasty job he is asked to do. Anna has much more to fear from Hester and Ethel than from Walter and Carl Redman, who want mostly to give her a good time.

Neither the good times nor the hard times get much attention. Tone, narrative selection, and scenic arrangement all take Anna's descent for granted. Put simply, we fear the worst for Anna early on, and our fears are confirmed with few rays of false hope intervening. Avoiding any strain between its subject matter and form, *Voyage* is not rich, bright, or spacious. Its smooth, even flow comes, ironically, from its discontinuity. Causes produce unlikely effects throughout. But Anna takes it all in stride. On her first date with Walter, she notes, "He started kissing me and all the time he was kissing me I was thinking about the man at the supper party at the Greyhound, Croydon" (p. 22). We never saw Anna at the Greyhound, Croydon; we do not know why she went to the supper party or how long she stayed. Also, the man at the party lacks all definition; his name and job, age and family, are never revealed. Jean Rhys refers to him to show Anna's preference for him over Walter and thus to describe the disjointedness of her life. Foreshadowing this disjuncture was a conversation four pages before in which Anna replied to Maudie's question, "I'm getting lines under my eyes, aren't I?" (p. 18) by saying, "I've got a cousin out home, quite a kid. And she's never seen snow" (p. 18). She represents the boundaries of her tiny world; the only things that matter are the things that touch her. This attitude filters into the first-person narrative. No developing central action holds the plot together, freeing Anna to travel her own tack. Further openness comes from Jean Rhys's refusal to take sides: the experiencing self and the narrating self fuse closely in *Voyage*, squeezing out the moralizing author. Too innocent, uncaring, and morally green to judge social behavior, Anna simply reports events without explaining or connecting them. We must fill in the gaps, draw our own inferences, and make the connections. Anna does not foresee the effects of her actions well enough to reason from them. Often, she will charm or offend somebody unintentionally. But she lacks the self-awareness to discern both her mistakes and her windfalls and thus can't learn from them. Whatever sense the book makes bypasses her. Life is all the same to Anna, who does not know that accepting £25— a huge sum in 1912—from a man obligates her to sleep with him.

Yet the novel is not thin, random, or vague. Rigorously selective,

Jean Rhys only includes data that either lead to or express the meaning of her heroine's decline. Thus a great deal of material goes unreported because of its irrelevancy to the novel's main business. Jean Rhys leaves out Anna's life backstage, her singing lessons, and her treatment for flu in Part I by Dr. Ames; in fact, we never meet the doctor or the singing coach. What Jean Rhys does include deserves a close look. She gets the novel off to a good start by introducing Anna and the characters who will have the greatest impact on her, Walter, Maudie, and Laurie, in the opening chapter. She uses variety to build the narrative—interspersing dramatic scenes with daydreams, reminiscences, and letters. Letters serve well; people will write things they lack the courage to say. In addition, because letters obviate the give-and-take of conversation, they can convey information and attitudes quickly. Thus the letters of Uncle Bo, Vincent Jeffries, and Ethel Matthews both bring in important new material and speed the narrative. This acceleration helps maintain tempo. Much of the book consists of Anna's recollections of her island girlhood, her first impressions of England, and her thoughts on subjects like men, clothes, and family. These loosely connected ideas and images alternate well with the letters and the conversations to smooth the book's pace. Something is always happening to hold the reader. This freshness helps make *Voyage in the Dark* Jean Rhys's most beautiful, dangerous, and, in view of its grimness, distressingly clear novel to date.

# CHAPTER 6

# Good Morning, Midnight

ALL who have written about *Good Morning, Midnight* (1939) agree on two points—the book's high merit and its unstinting gloom. Ralph Tyler calls it the darkest of Jean Rhys's novels set in modern Europe, "as wounding as jagged glass. It marks some final inner shattering."[1] Using a different metaphor but reasoning similarly, Sara Blackburn finds reading the book "like literally drinking the essence of despair."[2] This bitter brew has been winning friends as it ages. Noting that the novel sold badly when first published, John Hall, in a January 1972 issue of the *Guardian*, calls it "the best of the pre-war novels,"[3] and V. S. Naipaul, writing the following year, prizes it as "the most subtle and complete of the novels, and the most humane."[4]

The novel's epigraph, from Emily Dickinson, captures some of its grimness. Although the heroine, at age forty-three or so, carries forward from Julia Martin rather than from Anna Morgan, *Midnight* marks another voyage into darkness. The daytime world of brightness and cheer offers Sasha Jansen no friendly port, and she must sail forth into the night without steering instruments or lights. (Fittingly, her Paris hotel is on an impasse.) Like so many of Emily Dickinson's poems, *Midnight* is a very personal work, or self-exploration, many of its sentences beginning with the word, "I." A first-person narrative, like *Voyage*, the memoirlike book has a confidential tone; Sasha stands close to the events she describes, drawing us into her mental processes. Jean Rhys's throwing in a minor character named Dickson (Dickson-Dickinson) serves as a warning that the novel will not try for narrative continuity any more than most of Emily Dickinson's work aims at smooth phrasing, logical development of idea, or defining a neat value system. Though controlled, *Midnight* is neither schematic or predictable.

Its control comes from Sasha, its narrator-heroine. Rightly called by Francis Wyndham "the culmination of Jean Rhys's composite

heroine,"[5] she lacks the resources and outlets of her earlier counterparts, like friends, family, or lovers, past or present, to cadge money from. Jean Rhys begins her brutally accurate portrait of faded, deenergized Sasha at that time of enervation and looming darkness, autumn. Sasha's fight against the drift to winter has caused some critical disagreement. Wyndham calls her story "the tragedy of a distinguished mind and a generous nature that have gone unappreciated in a conventional, unimaginative world."[6] Most of the novel's other commentators blame her seediness, estrangement, and degradation on herself. Mellown explains her as "a woman so overwhelmed by the passing of her youth that she allows herself to be humiliated, degraded, and finally destroyed by her own self-hatred."[7] Stressing both Sasha's self-protective indifference and Jean Rhys's indifference to the writing of social criticism, Judith Thurman reads the novel as "the tragedy of a sufferer who has ceased to respect her own grief. . . . Her days are really assemblages of random sensations and events."[8] Thurman grazes an important point. Sasha does not struggle because she cannot afford setbacks; better to be displaced than a loser. This attitude explains her indifference to success. She does not try to excel, win distinction, or even get ahead. Her motto, "*Faites comme les autres*" (p. 106), or, Do as the others do, conveys her fear of risk. Reversing the migratory pattern of Julia Martin of *Mackenzie*, she goes from London to Paris, where she tries to live as quietly and as regularly as she can. The routine of the displaced, however wild and broken it looks, follows a slavish logic; attending to domestic trifles eases the pressures of loneliness. Sasha's self-summary captures both the randomness and ritual of her closely watched life:

My life, which seems so simple and monotonous, is really a complicated affair of cafés where they like me and cafés where they don't, streets that are friendly, streets that aren't, rooms where I might be happy, rooms where I never shall be . . . and so on. (p. 46)

Sometimes loneliness saddens her; too many drinks or some cold words can also throw the ritual awry. "I'm sick of being laughed at" (p. 151), she says near the end of the novel, after being insulted, both with words and looks, by strangers, acquaintances, and relatives. Yet the laughter and the insults keep echoing in her ears. Frenetic and weary, manic and exhausted, she listens to the sounds of derision while watching her face go to ruin. Waiting and watching take up much of her time. Although worldly, she lacks charm; she has no gift

for conversation; her faded looks keep her from leaning on men. Neither an amused spectator nor desperate participant, she doesn't know where she stands. And she does not want to know. Organizing the sensations and events of her life into pale patterns delays the recognition that her life cannot improve, a recognition her survival demands that she avoid.

## I  *Arranging a Little Life*

To summarize *Good Morning, Midnight* is unfair, since the book's strengths owe little to sustained plotting; it attempts to convey Sasha Jansen's psychic reality through discontinuity and disjuncture rather than through a closely knit sequence of events. Communicating feelings rather than the kinetic drive of adventure, it relies more on accurate observation than on technical virtuosity. The self-mockery of the book's opening paragraph, stopping just short of sarcasm, sets the tone for what follows: "'Quite like old times,' the room says, 'Yes? No?'" (p. 9). Jean Rhys's giving the hotel room a speaking part forges a close link between the room and Sasha; her fate is nearly fixed. "I have arranged my little life" (p. 9), says she, keeping an eye on both order and its opposite, chaos. The trifles she worries about— where to eat, where to have her after-dinner drink, which route to walk home—are all she has. And she must take care lest she lose *them*. Living on a small fixed income and having no friends or job, she has forgone excitement for the consolations of a routine. She longs for the neutrality of middle age: "That's the thing," says Sasha to herself; "to have a plan and stick to it. First one thing and then another, and it'll be all over before you know where you are" (pp. 52–53).

She has come back to Paris from her London bedsitter, where drink had nearly destroyed her. But, as Alvarez shows, the change of venue hasn't helped her: "Her Paris is haunted: her baby died there; her marriage broke up; affairs have torn her to shreds. There are bars she can't enter, hotels she daren't pass."[9] Still drinking, she uses up time by sleeping long hours and by sitting through movies twice at the cinema. Like Julia Martin, she craves the oblivion of forgetfulness or sleep: "I get up into the room. I bolt the door. I lie down on the bed with my face in the pillow. . . . What do I care about anything when I can lie on the bed and pull the past over me like a blanket?" (p. 57). Oblivion protects her from the hysterics that take her without warning and also from the fear of seeing the face of a hag-worn

middle-aged drinker in the glass. Her dream about her father being shot through the head in a London tube station gives way to a ghostly apparition in the hall of her rooming house—the wraithlike commercial traveler who has the room next to hers. Though she dislikes her emaciated neighbor, she returns his "Bonjour" (p. 14).

But she quickly forgets the unpleasantness he generates. Her dividend check has just come, and, providing that she can control her impulses, she has a nice treat in store: "Careful, careful . . . ! Not too much drinking, avoidance of certain cafés, of certain streets, of certain spots, and everything will go off beautifully" (p. 15). Coming back from the inevitable cinema, though, she passes the street where, several years ago, she worked as a receptionist in a dress shop. The street brings back the memory of her last day at the shop. The shop's owner, a gruff Londoner, was making his quarterly visit. The first person he saw entering the shop was, naturally, Sasha, the receptionist. Anxious to do well on her first job in nearly five years, she tries to impress her chief. But the chief, upset because the shop has been losing money, does not impress easily. Hearing that Sasha last worked as a model, he asks, disbelief edging his voice, "How long ago was this?" (p. 20). Then, after making her wait in front of his desk for five minutes, he sends her on an errand in mixed French and English. He could have given his order more conveniently in English. And more effectively: for because he slurs his French, saying *kize* for *caisse* (the French word for cashier), he flusters Sasha. She cannot carry out his order, even though she wanders through the maze of show rooms and fitting rooms making up the salon. Her confusion prompts the chief of the firm to call her, to her face, "the biggest fool I've ever met in my life" (p. 27). The local branch manager, who hears the insult, says nothing on Sasha's behalf. He would not dare. To fault his chief's pronunciation would be dangerous; so he stands by silently as Sasha, victim of two injustices, bursts into tears and bolts from the room.

The lesson conveyed by the incident is grim: she cannot defend herself against her superiors, and she cannot expect help from anybody with a conflicting vested interest. Recognizing herself as somebody most people can insult without risk, she resigns. (She had said of the London manager, moments before, "He knew me right away, as soon as he came in at the door. And I knew him" [p. 28].) Jobs she held in the past continue to come to mind. She fastens onto another post she held in Paris—that of an American Express tour guide. Her record here is unclear. Possibly because she did not prey upon the family she took around town, she never got a second assignment; her job at American Express lasted less than a day.

The action swings back to the present, i.e., fall 1937. Her despised next-door neighbor, the *commis voyageur*, or traveling salesman, knocks timidly at her door, presumably for sex. She repulses him, pushing him backwards and slamming the door in his face without resistance. But the repulsion does not comfort her. As effortlessly as she spurned the *commis*, she cannot drive his timid overture from her mind. The next morning she looks into the possibility of moving to another hotel; new lodgings might produce better neighbors. But her search for a new place to live only heaps on more confusion and frustration. Though willing to be overcharged, she cannot get the room she wants. Her futile search ends with a passage that recalls the ending of *Mackenzie*: "A room is a place where you can hide from the wolves outside and that's all any room is. Why should I worry about changing my room?" (p. 38). Sasha cannot stop living her drab, hammered-down life in drab, lonely rooms. Coming home, though, soothes her; sometimes, she can still shake off bad luck. Rooms for her have become hiding places. Any room will protect her from hurt as well as any other.

Her return home, punctuated by another chance meeting with the *commis* in the hall outside her room, summons up one of the worst hurts of recent years. While drinking at a Montparnasse pub, she heard a young Englishwoman call her a drunken old woman. It is material that the young woman was English and that the pub, with hunting pictures decking its walls, looked like an English tavern. The cultural heritage Sasha spurned by choosing to live abroad is now haunting her. The London chief of the dress shop and the London Turkish bath smell given off by her boardinghouse point up the futility of her exile: there is no escape from the self. Free association continues to join the scenes in the novel. The nastiness of the young Englishwoman—an earlier embodiment of Sasha condemning her present self—summons up the London winter of five years ago when Sasha inherited the money the meager interest from which still supports her. Rather than freeing her, the inheritance choked off life, teaching her to settle for the shabby. The absence of a challenge wastes the lackadaisical Sasha. She calls her legacy "the end of me, the real end. . . . The lid of the coffin shut down with a bang. Now I no longer wish to be loved, beautiful, happy, or successful. I want one thing and one thing only—to be left alone" (pp. 42–43). For at least five years, she has not had a romantic dream or hope. The accumulation of £35 interest on her legacy, in fact, once inspired her to drink herself to death. It was then, her face looking like "a tortured and tormented mask" (p. 43), that a friend convinced her to go back

to Paris. The intervening years vindicate Alvarez's judgment that returning to Paris has not helped her.[10]

The novel's structure reflects careful planning. Because the action needs brightening at this point, Jean Rhys introduces a small drama. Two Russians who start talking to Sasha on the Boulevard San Michel invite her for a drink. Her evening with them goes well enough for her to accept a date with the younger of the two, Nicholas Delmar. Yet, blocking the romantic drive, Jean Rhys ends the chapter ironically, even trivially. Lying in bed the night before her date, Sasha longs, not for Delmar, but for the prospect of dyeing her hair. And why not? Her spirits need a boost. Fair game for anybody's insults, she had recently heard herself mocked by another young English-woman: *"Et qu'est-ce qu'elle fout ici, maintenant?"* (Now why is she messing around here? [p. 50]). The scurvy treatment she keeps getting from her compatriots helps sustain the novel's psychological drive. A more ironical incarnation of Sasha emerges immediately in the memory of a sick, malnourished kitten who slinked into Sasha's flat after being persecuted by her original owners. Annoyed with the kitten's rejection of both food and affection, Sasha shooed her away, only to learn that, within hours of the time the kitten left the flat, she was run over. The memory of the hectic, scruffy kitten strengthens Sasha's resolve to dye her hair before her four o'clock date. Though somebody as marginal as she cannot expect to be coiffed by the shop's manager, she nonetheless hopes for one of the better assistants.

The symbolic tie-in between hair and sexuality helps explain Sasha's memory of the time she had her baby son. After her delivery, the midwife bound her torso tightly in bandages to remove her stretch marks and restore her pre-pregnancy muscle tone. The treatment worked; she had neither birth scar nor corrugation when the swathing was unwound. But she has no baby, either. Her pregnancy and delivery have changed neither her body nor her life-style. Except for the inner scars it left, the drama in the hospital might never have happened. When released, she simply goes back to her hotel room— an unlikely place to bring a newborn child, in any case. But the inner scars go deep. The swathing that restored her beauty becomes winding sheets rather than swaddling for two people: "And there I lie in these damned bandages for a week," Sasha says. "And there he lies, swathed up too, like a little mummy" (p. 60). The next scene refers to her sad lying-in; joining the two sections is the coincidence that the midwife and the hairdresser of the present action both call Sasha "*ma petite dame*" (pp. 58, 61). Sasha's dyeing her hair ash blond, both

a cover mechanism and a self-unfolding, tightens the link between the scenes still more. Although coloring her hair constitutes a sexual disguise, the ashen color of that disguise implies death—of her charms, her zest, and her son. As with the Blooms' baby son in Joyce's *Ulysses*, a work that may have influenced *Midnight*, the death of an infant mangles the sex drive. Her loss of sexual appetite and reversionist fascination for some immobile fish in a public fountain both depict Sasha trapped in a death-drift.

Jean Rhys shows uncommon skill in sustaining her symbolic rhythm. The concurrence of some prams being wheeled through a park and her date, Nicholas Delmar, "tightly buttoned into a black overcoat" (p. 63), keeps the birth-as-death motif before us. Delmar, a naturalized Frenchman, says ponderously, "If someone had come to me and asked me if I wished to be born I think I should have answered No" (p. 64). But, having more options than Sasha, owing to both his youth and his sex, Delmar has brightened his melancholy; besides changing his citizenship, he spends more time socializing than before. Today, he wants Sasha to meet one of his friends, Serge Rubin, an artist who lives nearby. But, to describe the brokenness of Sasha's life, Jean Rhys sends her heroine shopping first, thus creating a gap of time she promptly fills by bringing Sasha together with another younger man. The meeting takes place near the terrace of the Dôme, where Sasha had gone for a drink. Possibly a French-Canadian who came to Paris from Morocco, the young man has singled her out because of her expensive-looking fur coat. Referred to earlier by her as "this damned old fur coat . . . the last idiocy, the last incongruity" (p. 15), it has given the good-looking, French-speaking young man the impression that Sasha has money. Will she pay him to make love to her? Again, the experience of seeing herself from another's point of view stings her; does she look like a wealthy dame on the prowl for a lover?

Despite the wound to her vanity, she agrees to have a drink with him. Part I interposes a dramatic encounter just before the end, but not involving Delmar, with whom Sasha had a date. She goes bar-hopping with the gigolo, Rene, who claims to have deserted from the French Foreign Legion. (His naming Franco Spain as his escape route from Morocco dates the action later than 1936). Of course, Rene denies wanting either money or sex from Sasha. He would settle for a forged passport, and he buys Sasha drinks in the hope that she can lead him to one. Tired and cranky, she lets him take her home in a taxi, but will not let him into her room. But, she wonders, Was

turning him away a mistake? Part I ends the next morning, with Sasha getting ready to shut out light, hope, and interchange altogether: "I'll lie in bed all day, pull the curtains and shut the damned world out" (p. 81).

## II  *No Tears for the Half-Living*

At the start of Part II, Sasha is dressing for her date with Delmar, The meeting with the gigolo at the end of Part I seems both digressive and climactic, an imponderable that will puzzle us until Part IV, when Rene reenters the action. Winter, the season Emily Dickinson equated with desolation, is approaching. There is, thus, little in the air to thaw Sasha's icy heart. Her first act in the new section combines thoughtlessness and discourtesy. Though she knows he is not rich, she insists that Delmar take her by taxi to the flat of Serge Rubin, the Russian artist awaiting their visit. Delmar seems determined to save money whenever possible. Her short walk with him after the cab drive calls to Sasha's mind a time when *she* was stone-broke. She had not eaten anything for three weeks except croissants washed down with coffee; she was also sleeping fifteen hours a day. One day an acquaintance took her out for drinks and dinner. But the drinks meant more to her than the food. Soon they overtook her: "Food? I don't want any food now. I want more of this feeling—fire and wings" (p. 88), she remembers feeling. She also got so drunk that she could hardly walk. Although the acquaintance drove off alone in a cab, he did not offend her. So numb was she that her vanity was beyond wounding. Her "heaven of indifference" (p. 91) resembled the self-detachment that helped Julia Martin dodge sorrow in *Mackenzie*: "People talk about the happy life, but that's the happy life when you don't care any longer if you live or die" (p. 91).

Back to late October 1937 and the flat of the Russian artist, Serge Rubin. While the recorded music and the drink are both flowing, Sasha starts crying for no apparent reason. But she has tea instead of the brandy she would prefer and feels better for it. After she composes herself, she asks Rubin if she can buy a picture he painted of a Jewish musician, i.e., an outsider on two counts and thus a kindred spirit. Though offered the painting free of charge, she insists on paying. She will meet Rubin at ten thirty that evening to make the transfer. Delmar shows up in his place, making Sasha wonder if he is getting a commission on the sale or even if he plans to pocket *all* the money. She pays him the agreed-upon sum, anyway, before going to a café to

celebrate her new purchase. (She need not have worried about Delmar's embezzling the money; men usually treat her well.) The scene breaks, and she is next seen at a cinema—a dark place where the unhappy can escape into celluloid fantasies. Part II ends grimly. Sasha sees another movie, has too many drinks afterwards, and staggers home. She has done nothing to improve herself. The sullen last paragraph of Part II shows her wheeling in the same tired grooves that trapped Julia Martin: "This damned room. . . . It's all the rooms I've ever slept in, all the streets I've ever walked in. Now the whole thing moves in an ordered, undulating procession past my eyes. Rooms, streets, streets, rooms" (p. 109).

The opening of Part III does not relieve the sullenness. Going back to 1920 or so, this unit deals with Sasha's marriage, which, we already know, has come apart. Though Enno seemed rich when Sasha met him in London, he ran out of money quickly. He and Sasha marry in Paris and spend their wedding night in Amsterdam. As this activity implies, marriage does not mean settling down for the pair; Jean Rhys's married couples travel more than her single people do. Nor does movement promote solvency. Two pages later, Sasha and her journalist-song writer husband, now living in Brussels, have only thirty francs. Sasha outdoes Enno in raising cash at this dire time, although she acts in keeping with the betrayal suggested by their remaining thirty francs. While he is out looking for work, she remembers a Mr. Lawson, whom she knew first in London and then met on the way to Brussels. Lawson comes into the novel just long enough (nobody besides Sasha sustains an appearance) to give her two hundred francs. She uses the money to send Enno and herself to Paris via Calais; Enno has friends in Paris who will find him work. But the strain of living hand-by-mouth has already undermined Sasha. Enno's happy prospects do not erase the impression that, though still in her twenties, she has grown lank and haggard.

Paris soothes her. After spending all but her last few francs drinking coffee in a café for three and a half hours, she sees Enno coming hopefully toward her. He has money, some of which he spends on a big ravioli-and-wine dinner. Sasha is overjoyed: "I've never been so happy in my life. I'm alive. . . . A door has opened and let me out into the sun. What more do I want?" (p. 124). Not even the bugs in the fourth-floor hotel room she shares with Enno rattle her. Then, within less than a month, Enno says that he is bored with her and walks out. He leaves without any heartrending goodbye or row. This novel about a disconnected life abounds in smudged, discon-

nected scenes, time and setting both shifting too quickly to evoke an emotional response. Enno walks out within a line of saying goodbye, robbing the novel of a dramatic scene. All that Sasha reveals is her certainty that she is expecting a baby. But she only reveals her knowledge to us. It is not clear whether Enno ever knew of her pregnancy or delivery; he says nothing about these subjects within our hearing. Now Sasha does not hide this information from him; she loves Enno and enjoys sharing with him. Yet she does not show her deepest self to anybody, including us. She never tells us her feelings about being abandoned. Nor does Enno explain *his* motives for coming back to her three days later, smiling and carrying a bottle of wine under his arm. The people in *Midnight* do not act like characters in a novel. They have a life beyond that recounted by their author; besides holding back important information both from each other and the reader, they drift aimlessly; their words do not meld with their thoughts.

All the same, the marriage rights itself after veering off course. Enno has sold two articles, and Sasha, now pregnant, gives English lessons to two private pupils. As her belly grows, her hair spreads luxuriantly on her shoulders. Yet the snow falling on Paris and the calm she feels as she goes to have her baby both prefigure the death she must soon face. Life will become so awful that she will start schooling herself not to think about it. But the image of a dead baby with a ticket tied to his wrist has etched itself on her mind. As well it might: presumably, the death of the baby wrecks her marriage. The red apparitions beginning the next section—"the lights are red, dusky red, haggard red, cruel red"(p. 140)—symbolize the blood hacked from Sasha's soul during the breakup of her marriage. Jean Rhys often substitutes this symbolic shorthand for domestic realism. Symbolism helps her convey information that, for purposes of thematic unity, she does not want to dramatize or ponder philosophically. The collapse of the marriage, although probably the main event of Sasha's life, is neither described nor analyzed:

This happened and that happened. . . .
And then the days came when I was alone. (p. 142)

Did I love Enno at the end? Did he ever love me? I don't know. Only, it was after that that I began to go to pieces. Not all at once, of course. First this happened, and then that happened. (p. 143)

The loss of husband and child shatters her. She moves to another hotel, where, in a rare literary allusion, to the *Eumenides* of

Aeschylus, she finds herself plagued by flies. While awaiting a reply to
her request for money from England, she eats at a convent "where
nuns supply very cheap meals for destitute girls" (p. 143). The money
does come after a long wait, but it is accompanied by a warning and a
moral reproach: "We can't go on doing this. . . . You insisted on it
[leaving England to live abroad] against everybody's advice" (pp.
143–44). The scolding she ignores. The money she spends. But it
does not rescue her from the mechanical routine that has trammeled
her since her divorce, c. 1924, when, significantly, she turned thirty.
"Eat. Drink. Walk. March. Back to the hotel" (p. 144), she notes
wearily as she turns into her faceless street to enter her dingy,
unfeatured hotel. Her room says, "Quite like old times. Yes? . . . No"
(p. 145), just as it did at the novel's outset. The repetition expresses
her entrapment; squalid hotel rooms have become both her refuge
and her punishment. Her downhill skid into middle age carries
danger but no excitement. "When I have had a couple of drinks I
shan't know whether it's yesterday, today, or tomorrow" (p. 145), she
says; the best way to lurch down the rocky scree of time is
unconsciously. To the fast-fading urban spinster, time is the great
enemy. Shabbier clothes, fewer friends, and smaller, draftier rooms
in worse neighborhoods stake out the limits of Sasha's faded life.

The narrative tempo picks up here. The opening of Part IV gives
the impression that all of Part III and perhaps some of the
abbreviated Part II took place in Sasha's mind within several hours.
The note she gets from the gigolo at the start of Part IV refers back to
the phone call from Rene that ended Part One; indeed, the placing of
the phone call, which Sasha never received, and the writing of the
note probably took place within hours of each other. That nasty
wraith, Sasha's next-door neighbor, the *commis*, also reappears,
calling Sasha "*sale vache*" (p. 149), or dirty cow. She passes him
quickly and, unlocking her door, finds Rene waiting for her. He has
come to take her for a last round of drinks before departing for
London; a beautiful American, it seems, is paying his way. A
specialist in getting money and other favors from women, Rene, or
the gigolo, as he is usually called, cadges a meal from Sasha. She
doesn't mind paying, saying inwardly, "This man . . . makes me . . .
feel natural and happy, just as if I were young" (p. 155). But her
euphoria does not last. Her knowledge that she cannot escape her
predicament shows in her failure to break the dreary cyclical pattern
of her life. Unchecked, Rene enters her room, which she had kept him
out of the night before; the restaurant she and Rene choose for their
farewell meal is the same one in which she was insulted by the young

Englishwoman in Part I. Has she exhausted her options? Can anybody have his way with her?

   An answer is teased out dramatically. Rene behaves predictably over dinner, asking for information about London—clubs, restaurants, tailors, places to meet rich women: what he wants most is a woman who will support him elegantly. To his pleas for information, Sasha replies with dry irony. Her conversation with the gigolo carries a heavy load of subtext. Both attracted to and repelled by each other, they will say the first thing they think of, speak with brutal directness, or indulge in subtleties. Their speech both conceals and reveals because Jean Rhys never explains underlying motives; what looks like offhand banter may be part of the verbal fencing. Thurman sees the ambiguity running through Part IV of *Midnight* as the zenith of Jean Rhys's first four novels: "*Good Morning, Midnight* ends with a series of rapidly executed reverses which are, in a sense, the climax of all four novels—the last act of a tragedy. It is a modern one, whose suffering isn't resolved in loss or death, but by the sterner moral of ambiguity."[11]

   Rising from the conversation, though, is the unambiguous impression that, still fixated on her old fur coat, Rene believes Sasha a rich woman who will pay for his sexual favors. She encourages this impression. While refusing to sleep with him, she claims that she wants him; then she whets his lust still further by alleging fears irrelevant to him: even though she might enjoy a tumble with him, she could not risk the danger to her reputation. She seems to value her reputation more than her life, which usually burdens or puzzles her. As has been seen, her yearning for sleep, drink, and the immobile stupor of movie-watching all spell out a death wish. Especially attractive when separated from moral blame, death looms as a release, even as a friend. She nearly says out loud to Rene, "If I thought you'd kill me, I'd come away with you right now and no questions asked. And what's more, you could have any money I've got with my blessing" (p. 172). Rene continues to press the sexual line. Moving his hands "like a baker kneading a loaf of bread" (p. 175), this half-baked gigolo does not know that the crust has already formed and hardened on Sasha. Too weary for love, she chose to spend time with him to begin with because his arrant self-seeking posed no sexual threat. Yet they have more in common than either suspected, her inner scars corresponding to his physical ones. "We are threatened with the oldest bittersweet cliché in the business, a moment of honesty between two self-conscious fakers,"[12] says Francis Hope of their last

encounter. Sasha's first tremor of feeling for the gigolo scares her. "If we're going to start believing each other, it's getting serious, isn't it" (p. 174), she says of the candor that has replaced their verbal stratagems. But her next statement, made inwardly, reveals her discomfort with candor: "I want to get out of this dream" (p. 174). She has lost the gift of letting herself go: sexual excitement is a dream; reality, a dingy gray waste of being alone, bracing oneself for calamity.

### III    *Outriders of the Long Night*

Like the endings of *Mackenzie* and *Voyage*, that of *Midnight* emits horror because the heroine's final overthrow could be worse; Julia, Anna, and Sasha might have easily suffered worse fates than the ones described. After saying goodnight in the street, Rene follows Sasha into the dark corridor of her hotel. But after welcoming his embraces ("I stand there hugging him, so terribly happy" [p. 177]), she turns him out. Reputation still overrides sexuality. "If there is one thing I want to avoid, it is a scene in this hotel" (p. 180), she pleads, gripping her only fixed mooring. The abundance of dialogue in Part IV, in sharp contrast to the wistful ruminations of Part III, shows a stepping-up of communication and interchange. But Sasha is too out of touch with her instincts to have sex with Rene. "This is really damned comic" (p. 181), he says, after failing to force her. Her witty reference to the two beds in the room lace the comedy with self-irony: "We're on the wrong bed. . . . And with all our clothes on, too. Just like English people" (p. 181). But comedy is all she can muster. "It hurts, when you have been dead, to come alive" (p. 182), she says of her failure to follow through on her impulses. But what about Rene's impulses? To placate him, she says that he earned the money he usually gets for servicing women. Thus she tells him to take a thousand-franc note from her coat pocket on his way out.

Ironically, an offspring results from the time the gigolo spends in Sasha's room wtih her. Despite her moral fatigue, she still holds the seeds of renewal. Jean Rhys makes the point symbolically. Once Sasha is alone, she lies foetus-like on her side, huddled "as small as possible . . . knees almost touching . . . chin" (p. 184). Signalling her rebirth is the sudden fear that the gigolo took all the money from her coat; the ability to care—if only for oneself—denotes life. Like the tears she shed minutes before, her swollen, bleeding mouth (bruised from his rough kisses) proves that being reborn hurts; one incarna-

tion of the self must die before another can spring to life. Reborn against her will, she nevertheless finds her new world friendly and welcoming: the gigolo left all her money behind. Perhaps coming to life was worth the pain, after all. Yet the last scene does not show her rejoining the gigolo amid passionate avowals, the novel's bleak mood calling for a grimmer finale. What happens in the last four pages refers back to the retribution implied by Jean Rhys's allusion to the *Eumenides*. Because Sasha has spurned a handsome young man who craves her, she must embrace a scrawny old one with contempt in his heart; no less than birth, rebirth entails sexuality, she learns. The learning comes hard. "Venus is dead; Apollo is dead; even Jesus is dead" (p. 187), she mutters to herself. Replacing love, harmony, and spirit is the machine. Perceived with a sharpness almost unique in the novel, this mechanical destroyer has a terrifying beauty. Like the drooping watches of Salvador Dali, it embodies realistic techniques of observation to create unreal effects:

All that is left in the world is an enormous machine, made of white steel. It has innumerable flexible arms, made of steel. Long, thin arms. At the end of each arm is an eye, the eyelashes stiff with mascara. . . . And the arms wave to an accompaniment of music and of song. . . . And I know the music; I can sing the song. (p. 187)

The human counterpart to this mantislike robot makes her song a lament. Though she concentrates her will, sending her spirit out to the gigolo, her trance summons her next-door neighbor. The odious *commis* must have mistaken the sound of Sasha's scuffle with Rene for sexual activity, and, having heard Rene leave, now wants *his* turn with her. "His mean eyes flickering" (p. 190), he is wearing a dressing gown which is the same color, white, as the Daliesque machine. Elgin Mellown sees Sasha's final "Yes-yes-yes" (p. 190) as an affirmation, echoing Molly Bloom's words at the end of *Ulysses*. "Out of compassion," says Mellown, "she gives herself to the man in the adjoining room whom she had previously despised."[13] Supporting his thesis is a genuine enlargement of moral vision in Sasha. Her moral awakening occurs just before she pulls the *commis* on top of her: "I look straight into his eyes and despise another poor devil of a human being for the last time" (p. 190). In addition, she had twice linked him to father figures. When he knocked on her door in Part I, wearing his clean white dressing gown, Sasha observed, "He looks like a priest" (p. 35), or church father. Then, right after the dream in which

her father is shot through the head, she meets the *commis* in the hall; his reminding her of a ghost in his white dressing gown suggests the resurrected father. Now father-figures in Freud excite lust. The number of much-older lovers and husbands in the Rhys canon reveal a Freudian strain; if the canon did not contain so many blurred or missed sexual connections, the strain would be more noticeable. The animosity building between Sasha and the older *commis* has constituted the first steps of a slow dance on the sexual killing ground. Rather than pressing a minor character into service to end her novel, Jean Rhys closes the book with a sharp note of inevitability.

Curiously, *Midnight* ends much like a conventional love story; having overcome obstacles strewn in their path both by themselves and others, the bickering couple make love; the transition from being neighbors to lovers is short and easy. Further, the lovemaking affirms a dedication to a commitment on Sasha's part. But can she communicate her feeling to a man who has taken her in loathing rather than tenderness? Her truest self may have been bared along with her body, but can she also overcome her usual defensiveness by speaking her heart? And will her heartbeat strike a friendly rhythm in the *commis*? Willing to settle for the rank pleasures of casual sex, he knows nothing of Sasha's vision; to him, she is still a *sale vache*. In order to justify Mellown's optimistic reading, he and Sasha will have to share a communion attained nowhere else in the canon.

Whether they attain this sharing matters to us. Jean Rhys put a great deal of herself into *Midnight*. Marcelle Bernstein notes the similarity between Enno and Jean Rhys's own husband, with whom, as Sasha did with Enno, the novelist lived near Paris's Galeries Lafayette before he walked out. Mary Cantwell also explains that Jean Rhys had a son who died in his infancy.[14] But the dead son and the runaway husband do not dominate *Midnight*. Maintaining proper aesthetic distance between these real-life people and their novelistic transfiguration is Jean Rhys's excellent use of the first-person narration. Mellown has shown how the technqiue suits Jean Rhys's aims in both *Voyage* and *Midnight*:

Anna Morgan and Sasha Jansen know only that they suffer and that therefore they exist; anything outside themselves exists only because it impinges upon their consciousness. . . . The aesthetic value of both *Voyage in the Dark* and *Good Morning, Midnight* is raised because the first person point of view is the technical correlative of Jean Rhys's understanding of life.[15]

The first-person technique, by controlling narrative selection, lets Jean Rhys say more and more about less and less. As her narrative purview shrinks, her view of it both sharpens and deepens. (The nameless *commis* is the only one of Sasha's fellow-boarders we meet.) Since abstractions mean nothing to Sasha, she lives very close to her physical surroundings. The piecemeal recitation of her feelings about these surroundings helps account for the novel's unforced truthfulness of observation. The sensations and events comprising her disconnected life, free from the restraints of a formal plot, reach us both as process and modern morality fable.

Unhurried and giving each scene and recollection its just weight, Jean Rhys leads us through the main landmarks of Sasha's wayward life. This life, as has been seen, is both fixed and free. Often, Jean Rhys will make this point through repetition, as with the various telescopings of French and English experience. In addition, Sasha's monthly pay at the Paris dress shop where she worked as a receptionist was 400 francs, the same sum she saw quoted on the price tag of a dress she liked at the time. The figure occurs again, as the rental of one of the rooms in her hotel some twenty years later. Small effects like this bring home both the circularity and littleness of Sasha's life. *Midnight* does not aim for grandeur, power, or graciousness. Nor does it make any tenderhearted plea for sympathy, its author accepting Sasha's predicament coolly, even blandly. The events of the novel square with the everyday reality of women like Sasha. And the novel gets much of its tense authority from Jean Rhys's respect for this reality; she will not invade Sasha's secret heart or reduce her problems to a sociological formula. This refusal to heighten the late autumnal bleakness gathering around Sasha fits well with the random structure, creating a fusion of the relaxed and the severe.

For much of the way, Jean Rhys's refusal to stylize Sasha's routine, to sentimentalize, or to use Sasha to undergird a humanistic argument makes the reader feel forgotten. Then, we see that the pointlessness of Sasha's routine provides both the novel's main point and chief value. Ironically, the ambiguous tie Jean Rhys establishes between reader and novel holds well. Fresh, unrehearsed, and unliterary both in its form and character development, *Midnight* lets Sasha be herself. This astonishing novel, boldly disregarding narrative technique in the familiar scene, not only marks a peak for Jean Rhys; it also belongs on the upper range of English novels of the 1930s.

# CHAPTER 7

# Wide Sargasso Sea

TEN years in the writing,[1] *Wide Sargaso Sea* (1966) probes Jean Rhys's personal and ancestral past more deeply than any of her earlier novels. The lonely, disoriented heroine returns, more distraught than ever, but in nineteenth-century Jamaica rather than in modern Europe between the wars. *Sargasso* fuses two traditions— that of the white slaveholder in the predominantly black West Indies and that of Victorian fiction. Antoinette Cosway, the main character of the Rhys novel, was Edward Fairfax Rochester's mad Creole wife in Charlotte Brontë's *Jane Eyre* (1847). Walter Allen prefers Jean Rhys's portrait of Antoinette to that of Brontë, who "tells us nothing about [Antoinette] presumably because she knew nothing about her."[2] Allen judges well. Jean Rhys's island girlhood both lends authority to Antoinette's madness and relates madness to the heroines of the earlier novels (Thurman calls Antoinette "the grandmother"[3] of these heroines). As a girl, Jean Rhys wanted to be black because blacks enjoyed life more than her fellow whites.[4] Antoinette, too, like Anna Morgan before her, prefers the vibrancy of the blacks to the stiffness, hypocrisy, and profiteering of the English plantation owners and their families. Whereas the other whites seek to subdue Jamaica, Antoinette glories in it—walking through its forests, swimming in its lakes, and gaining inspiration from its beautiful vistas. Her lyricism pushes into the human sphere. Reared by a black woman, she has a little black girl as her first friend.

But the times go against this intimacy. *Sargasso* opens soon after the freeing of the Jamaican slaves in 1834. Unexpectedly, emancipation has heightened the interracial tensions that prevailed under slavery, frightening whites and blacks alike. Once held in check, these tensions now threaten to flare. And nobody knows what form they will take or what can be done to quell them.

Issues like this the book meets head-on, working them into the daily lives of its characters. Though its broad time scheme entails a

rigorous selection, *Sargasso*, hewing to a clear narrative line, is Jean
Rhys's most dramatic work. The fear and hatred brewing on her
tropical island erupt with great force. Antoinette, as badly scalded
by the eruption as anybody, stems logically from her less damaged
predecessors in books like *Mackenzie* and *Midnight*, as Wyndham
says.[5] But her predicament differs. Called by Alvarez, "one of those
who are defeated as though by natural right,"[6] she leads a deprived,
diminished life formed by specific events rather than by habit; she
drifts into nothing. Yet she does not take her suffering for granted,
giving the book, in her attempt to resist the will of others, some of the
surge and inevitability of tragedy. Unlike Julia Martin, Anna
Morgan, and Sasha Jansen, she fights to keep what she loves. Her
mind darkens because of her refusal to accept alienation and
stagnation. Antoinette tries harder than any Rhys heroine before her
to shape the realities steering her life. Growing out of her moral
hopes, her failure encompasses both triumph and menace. Jean
Rhys's recounting of this brave failure shows such skill and depth that
it nearly redeems the twenty-seven-years' wait since her last novel.

## I   *Black Englishmen and White Niggers*

Antoinette does not wince alone, the opening pages of *Sargasso*
putting her squarely in a continuum of suffering that includes her
family, her social class, and her race. Although, unlike Marya Zelli
(*Quartet*), Julia, and Sasha, she does inherit a tradition, it has become
despised and burdensome. Her mother, mistress of the disused
plantation, Coulibri Estate, in Spanish Town, Jamaica, learned
privation early. As a bride, she was cut off from her female neighbors
by her youthful good looks and from her husband by a great age span.
Newly widowed, Annette Cosway is now cut off from him by death.
She has no male protector, an invitation to danger in Jean Rhys. The
clamor and upheaval that shortened her husband's life—resulting
from Emancipation—also drove her next-door neighbor to kill his
dog, totem of loyalty and trust, and then drown himself. Like the
freeing of the serfs in *The Cherry Orchard* (1904), a humane and
much-needed law ruins the privileged classes. But the tropical fever
bedeviling Jamaica in 1834 does not resemble the slow romantic
decline of Chekhov's Ranevsky family in late-century Russia. Blacks
jeer at Annette, especially when her clothing gets shabby, and they
poison her horse—an act symbolizing the loss of male strength in the
home. The only male left at Coulibri is Antoinette's brain-damaged

little brother. No rock on which to build anything in spite of his name, little Pierre, "who staggered when he walked and couldn't speak distinctly" (p. 19), cannot take care of himself. As if magnetized by him, both Annette and Coulibri droop and deteriorate for five sad years.

Giving Antoinette the mother love that Annette can no longer muster is Christophine Dubois, a black family servant from Martinique rumored to be an obeah woman. ("Obeah is the same as voodoo, but much milder,"[7] said Jean Rhys in a 1969 interview.) But even Christophine's dark power cannot save Antoinette from the pent-up anger of the freed slaves. She hears her family called white cockroaches and white niggers; she learns about the half-castes sired by the local planters, or black Englishmen; she finds the dead horse. Knowing that ideas in fiction fall flat unless individualized, Jean Rhys next gives Antoinette a little black friend. But Tia, whose mother is Christophine's best friend, steals Antoinette's clean, freshly ironed dress after the two girls swim together. The next sub-chapter introduces another dubious relationship. Annette ends five years of widowhood by marrying a Trinidadian planter from England named Mason. The snide remarks Antoinette hears at the wedding make her fear for her mother's happiness. At first, her fears look groundless; Jean Rhys usually raises her character's hopes before dashing them. With reckless optimism, Mason repairs Coulibri, buys new furniture, and hires servants. His English eyes look suspiciously at the fears of the old Jamaica hands. Underrating both the power and the malice of the local blacks, calling them "too damn lazy to be dangerous" (p. 32), he ignores Annette's pleas to sell the estate when tensions build. He fails to see the new prosperity of the ex-slaveholding Cosways rankling the blacks, who viewed their groveling and scraping as poetic justice.

Mason soon regrets ignoring Annette's wishes to leave Coulibri and Spanish Town. What he dismisses as a harmless diversion by "a handful of drunken negroes" (p. 38) turns out to be a large-scale, irreversible disaster—the firing of the estate. While Coulibri burns, little Pierre dies and Annette loses her wits—perhaps permanently. Symbol and event combine well to point poor Annette's downfall. Before the fire she had lost so much weight worrying about her children's safety that her wedding ring slipped from her finger and rolled into a corner. During the blaze that kills Pierre, her hair burns. The dead son, the scorched hair, and the wedding ring that goes astray because it no longer fits all express Annette's maimed

sexuality. This plays itself out in a rest home, where, barefoot and clad in an evening dress, she is used sexually by her black attendant. (None of the book's main characters escapes interracial sex.) As she and her fear-gripped family flee Coulibri, they are stoned by the drunken mob outside. Then Jean Rhys smuggles in a contrivance to spare her from further hurt. The shouting and the stoning end when the black raiders see the family's pet parrot all ablaze on the terrace railing; because local superstition deems it bad luck to kill a parrot, the flaming bird cools the mob's rage. The attack on the Mason/ Cosway family ends more quickly than it began.

That the bird could not fly to safety because Mason clipped its wings conveys both the destructiveness and the ignorance of natural process connected with men. That the flightless bird escaped its cage and made it to the terrace smears the effect with crude improbability. But no crudeness smears the ending of the scene. As Coulibri burns, Antoinette starts walking toward her little black friend Tia, with whom she had just eaten, slept, and bathed. Tia sees Antoinette as both a friend needing help and a vulnerable underdog. If part of her wants to befriend Antoinette during her crisis, another part seizes the chance to lash out. What happens next reaches us as a rush of impressions. The image of a jagged stone in Tia's hand blurs into the sensation that Antoinette's face is running with blood. In a mirror recognition that occurs before she blacks out, Antoinette compares her blood-streaked face with the stricken, tear-jerked one of Tia. The stone-throwing incident shakes both girls. What it costs Tia is never known. The heavy toll it exacts on Antoinette, on the other hand, begins surfacing straightaway. The next time she appears, six weeks have passed and her mind is just starting to clear.

But does it clear to a sharp focus? The question touches some of the novel's main issues. As she did with Annette, Jean Rhys roots many of Antoinette's sexual troubles in the night of the fire. The cutting of Antoinette's burned hair, the association made by her aunt between Antoinette's wedding and the scar caused by Tia's stone, and Antoinette's feverish discovery of a snake all move to the fore after she wakes up in a sick room. Time passes quickly once the worst part of her recovery is over. She visits her mother, whom she only recognizes at first as "a white woman sitting with her head bent . . . low" (p. 48) in a little house. After welcoming her daughter, Annette flings her away, literally banishing her from the maternal bosom. The bosom of the church is offered as a substitute. The next scene shows Antoinette walking to the Spanish Town convent school she will

attend for the next five years, through 1844 or so. Two children taunt her as she goes to her new school. But they are routed by her half-caste cousin, Sandi Cosway, in an act that will always warm her heart. Another source of warmth is her schoolmate, Louise. Though collapsing at the convent door from the strain caused by her two tormentors, she responds quickly to Louise's kindness. Neither sullen nor hapless, she flourishes amid love; of Louise, she notes, "She was very pretty and when she smiled at me I could scarcely believe I had ever been miserable" (p. 52). Her first day at school tells a good deal about Antoinette. She can shake off adversity; she prefers cheer to gloom; she will make friends if offered friendship. A reactive personality, she lives in a borrowed light: love her and she will glow; abuse her, she wilts and goes rank.

Over the years, Mason, her step-father, pays her little attention. On his only reported visit to the convent, he shows rare solicitude to the seventeen-year-old Antoinette—telling her to come out of hiding, asking her if she would like to live in England, and then adding nonchalantly that she can expect an English visitor: he has already arranged her marriage to Edward Fairfax Rochester. The memory of her mother's dead horse links her coming wedding to her smothered paternity. (Later, Rochester will think of *his* absent father while riding a horse.) Mason never returns to the action. Having arranged her marriage, he drops out of Antoinette's life. The loss haunts her. On the next page, she has a nightmare. She leaves the dormitory, helped by a nun, after having dreamt she was in Hell. Hell means the loss of the family. Her loss is heightened rather than redeemed. To help compose herself, she has a cup of hot chocolate, the same drink she had a year before, following her mother's funeral. The recollection saddens her. Part I, a cunning weft of recurring events, expanding symbols, and foreshadowings, ends in the shadows, as Antoinettte creeps back, unconsoled, to her hard, dark domitory bed.

Along with the new setting and subject matter, the strong declarative voice booming from the first paragraph of Part II identifies the speaker as Antoinette's bridegroom, young Rochester; for the first time in her writing career, Jean Rhys is using a man as narrator. Rochester's first words, "So it was all over" (p. 65), strike an ironic chord that will sound through the whole section, by far the longest of the book's three parts. All over? Nothing is settled for Rochester as he goes to his honeymoon cottage with Antoinette and their pretty half-caste servant, Amélie. He has not crossed the ocean by choice. A younger son of a strict believer in primogeniture, he had

no other way to secure money and property than through a dowry. The following summary, from *Jane Eyre*, shows that, to know him, the best way to the dissenter is through the father; Rochester is speaking:

He [Rochester, Sr.] could not bear the idea of dividing his estate and leaving me a fair portion: all, he resolved, should go to my brother, Rowland. Yet as little could he endure that a son of his should be a poor man. I must be provided for a wealthy marriage. He sought me a partner betimes. . . . When I left college, I was sent out to Jamaica, to espouse a bride already courted for me. . . . Her family wished to secure me because I was of a good race; and so did she.[8]

Rochester still feels sold up. Though he married Antoinette a month after arriving in Jamaica, he spent the first three weeks of his stay prostrate with fever. Did he marry unwisely? Any joy his bride could bring him is marred by a sense of powerlessness. His marriage has aggravated his pawn complex: "It has been arranged that we would leave Spanish Town immediately after the ceremony and spend some weeks . . . at a small estate which had belonged to Antoinette's mother. I agreed. As I had agreed to everything else" (p. 66).

His damaged self-respect drives him to downgrade everything connected with his marriage, and the person nearest his smoldering wrath is Antoinette. Her family has married her off without settling any money or property on her. Nor has Rochester provided a settlement, even though she has nothing of her own. Perhaps the underdog enjoys the bottomdog's dependence and insecurity. Her heart, he finds, is also vulnerable. Within the first several pages of Part II, he complains both about her "pleading expression" (p. 70) and her eyes, which he finds too big. Because she is the only one he can defy, he makes her pay for his pent-up resentments; she will suffer for having been the instrument of his father's iron will. A friendly suggestion she makes on the way to Granbois, their honeymoon cottage, shows him prepared to punish her for loving him: "She spoke hesitatingly as if she expected me to refuse, so it was easy to do so" (p. 67), he notes. His negativity persists. Finally reaching Granbois, a place full of happy childhood memories for Antoinette, he meets the person who has loved her best, Christophine. But he dismisses her from his mind as negligible. He also dismisses Granbois as an awkward colonial imitation of an English summer home, and, once inside, tramples a frangipani wreath left by the servants as a wedding gift.

This mulishness creates the need for some freshening. Both to avoid miring the novel in Rochester's sulkiness and to balance her moral perspective, Jean Rhys flashes back to the time of the wedding. Antoinette also had misgivings about the marriage. These were amply justified by the selfishness of the marriage's promoters. Her feelings and needs could not compete with the luster of a £30,000 dowry on the one hand and an English establishment on the other. Foremost in the mind of her puling stepbrother, Richard Mason, is Rochester's father (the absentee father rides hero and heroine alike in *Sargasso*). Rochester's chief worry is saving face; he does not want to slink home as the rejected suitor of a Creole girl. Yet he accepts her negative decision cooly enough: "If she won't, she won't" (p. 78), he says with uncharacteristic calm, stemming perhaps from relief at seeing his father defied without his, Rochester's, having had to lift a finger. He does not try to change her decision, asking only that she explain it. Her recalcitrance, meanwhile, following weeks of compliance, attracts him to her more than ever. As in *Jane Eyre*, he is no nugatory lover, his sexual arousal inciting powerful conviction. His promises of peace, happiness, and safety, mingled with fervent kisses, convince Antoinette to marry him, as planned. But they do not drown her misgivings. His last question before leaving her, "Can I tell poor Richard that it was a mistake?" (p. 79), shows her that, rather than considering her, he has his mind on family politics.

Her having cold hands at the wedding, despite a hot sun overhead, conveys the persistence of her misgivings (or cold feet). Keeping her forebodings afloat are problems in communication. The streets and buildings of the great northern city, London, make as little sense to her as Jamaica's mountains and rivers do to him. Yet of the two, she works harder to bridge the cultural gap. And she uses the right methods. During their first night at Granbois, she suggests dousing the candles, in order to let the moon and stars do their romantic work; next, she tells Rochester about an experience of childhood terror she had never even mentioned to Christophine. The intimate disclosure, the moonglow, and the heavy floral scents of the starry night touch his heart. Rocking her in his arms, he sings a childhood song and toasts their happiness.

Unfortunately, this happiness lacks staying power. Although bride and groom have quieted many of their pre-nuptial doubts, they have not healed the split caused by their differences in background. The first rent in their idyll comes from this cultural rift. Behavior that she accepts cheerfully, he grumbles about. Christophine brings the honeymooners their breakfast in bed—inopportunely, at the very

moment Rochester is planning to make love to Antoinette. Christophine's gamy language and her long dress, which trails along the bedroom floor, both pique Rochester, even after being told that trailing dresses denote respect rather than slovenliness in the West Indies. Bilked of his early morning sex, the fuming bridegroom of one-and-twenty has no ears for explanations. He chides Antoinette for hugging and kissing Christophine. Then, in a brilliant stroke of anticipatory irony, all the more brilliant for fitting into the cross-cultural matrix of their talk, he says that he would never kiss a black. His peevishness sends his island bride, Antoinette, into gales of laughter. Though she explains nothing, she knows that, if Rochester stays in Jamaica for any time, he will crave black flesh as much as the other English settlers she has known, including her father.

As it did in *Jane Eyre*, sex rankles the self-doubting Rochester. He lacks the self-esteem to see that he and Antoinette, having already hurdled many of the obstacles caused by their families' scheming, enjoy excellent prospects for happiness. Self-doubt robs his heart of stability. Antoinette's beauty intoxicates him; at other times, he tries to convince himself of his great good luck to have married a beautiful girl with a big dowry; then, afraid of being a local mockery, he claims that she means nothing to him. Unfairly, he also resents her for not wanting to marry him, despite his own strong reservations during their courtship. This resentment asserts itself sexually. No sooner does she begin enjoying sex with him than he withdraws his heart. What he feels for her now, he claims, is lust, not love: "I did not love her. I was thirsty for her, but that is not love. I felt very little tenderness for her, she was a stranger to me" (p. 93). Then his confusion chills his lust. So anxious is he to discredit Antoinette that anything he hears, or thinks he hears, against her virtue or her sanity weakens his faith in her. Yet he also derides himself for his unfairness; his wavering faith, he sees, comes largely from being a younger son, taught early in life to scale down his hopes. Why should Antoinette pay for his repression?

Two answers have already been suggested: because she is the most convenient target for his anger and because, as his wife by a brokered marriage, she is standing in for the father he never had the nerve to defy. His marriage tailspins when he gets a letter from a local mulatto calling himself Daniel Cosway and claiming to be Antoinette's half-brother. Strengthening the argument that letters in Jean Rhys's fiction always spell trouble, Daniel has written to malign the Cosways: these wicked ex-slaveholders, who also have a family

tradition of sexual looseness and insanity, have wronged him. He claims not to want Rochester wronged by them, too. Will Rochester accept his help? Help? Rochester's suspicions over Daniel's so-called Christian motives make sense. If Daniel did not want to stir as much trouble as possible, he would have sent his letter before the wedding. Thin on evidence, he uses phrases like "and worse besides" (pp. 98, 99) to beguile Rochester. Rochester should have seen through this cheap appeal to the power of suggestion. Though Daniel writes with a sweaty urgency, he also indulges pseudogeneralities, like "the madness that is . . . in all these white Creoles" (p. 96) and transparent self-pity: "They [the Cosways] are rich, I am poor" (p. 97). But Rochester does not dismiss this casuistry. He has been fretting over Antoinette since leaving England. Daniel can relieve this anxiety. Thus he folds the letter carefully before pocketing it and carelessly trampling a spray of flowers on his way to the cottage. These acts and the mentality they reflect carry into his marriage immediately. Outside the cottage, he overhears Amélie taunting Antoinette: "Your husban' he outside the door and he look like he see zombi. Must be he tired of the sweet honeymoon too" (p. 100). When Antoinette slaps Amélie's face, as the girl deserves, she is called a white cockroach and nearly bitten. But rather than defending his wife, Rochester chides her and sends Amélie away with a kind word. Reentering the room some minutes later on an errand, Amélie smiles at him sideways. That she insults her mistress and then flirts with her husband gauges the disrepair of the marriage. Amélie has dared nothing she could not get away with. Still worse, Christophine has decided to go away, leaving Antoinette with nobody to turn to.

Rochester has wandered too far off course to help her. Jean Rhys conveys his distraction with skill. Though he leaves Granbois to escape women, he goes to a nearby forest, powerful symbol of female sexuality. The leafy tunnels and glades baffle the city man, setting him adrift. He, in turn, frightens a young child, who believes him a zombie. Mistakenly? The child's terror recalls Amélie's comparing him to a zombie five pages before. He has indeed joined the walking dead. The darkest voodoo could not hurt Antoinette more than he does. The cruellest father and elder brother in the world could not hurt him more than he hurts himself. He speaks his heart when he says, later in the novel, "Do you think that I wanted all this? I would give my life to undo it. I would give my eyes never to have seen this abominable place" (p. 161). (Ironically, his marriage *will* cost him his eyes, as is revealed in Chapter 36 of *Jane Eyre*.) Lost, frightened, and

feverish, he needs the help of a manservant who had followed him into the forest to get back home to Granbois.

## II  *Slow Fires of the Soul*

Jean Rhys chooses this anguished time to turn Part Two over to Antoinette. She chooses well. If Antoinette's voice breaks narrative consistency, it has the offsetting virtue of describing her at a time of crisis—when she reveals her true worth. Besides touching in information that Rochester omitted, like his recent practice of sleeping alone, the interruption also shows the purity of Antoinette's motives; love, rather than vengeance or spite, spurs her to act. She takes her problems to Christophine, who, besides loving her as a daughter, embodies both the folk wisdom and dark mystery connected with the black islanders. Speaking simply, Christophine prescribes bitter medicine for Antoinette's plight: "You ask me a hard thing, I tell you a hard thing, pack up and go" (p. 109). Her reasoning, couched in the same West Indian cadences that trilled through "Let Them Call It Jazz" (1962), shows both soundness and clarity: "When man don't love you, more you try, more he hate you, man like that" (p. 109). But Antoinette has strayed beyond the purviews of reason. She wants Christophine to prepare a love potion that will win back Rochester's love. Again speaking good sense, Christophine balks: "You talk foolishness. Even if I can make him come to your bed, I cannot make him love you. Afterward he hate you" (p. 113). Yet sense gives way to feeling. Christophine cannot deny Antoinette in her throes. The details ending the tipped-in narration show Christophine to have been won over against her better judgment. Antoinette notices a pile of chicken feathers in the corner of Christophine's hut as she carries a leaf-wrapped bundle into the morning air.

The restoration of Rochester's point of view in the next unit sustains the excitement. Having learned of his coldness toward Antoinette, Daniel Cosway sends Rochester another letter in which he threatens to come to Granbois unless Rochester visits *him*. This appeal to the English fear of scandal wins the day for Daniel. What follows parodies the epic hero's descent into hell. Two pages after he receives the threatening letter, Rochester is sitting in Daniel's hot, airless room in the lower village, looking at a framed legend bearing the words, "Vengeance is Mine." Like the other important figures in the book, Daniel feels wronged. And he will not wait for God to settle the score. Actuated by primitive justice, sweaty, spindly Daniel un-

loads a heavy charge of malice. "I tell you this so you know what sort of people you mix up with" (p. 122), he begins, telling of a visit he made at age sixteen to Antoinette's—and, he insists, his—father at Coulibri. The rich white planter chased him off his land, denying any blood tie. The money he sent afterward fell far short of the sum he gave his acknowledged half-caste son, Alexander, who now owns several thriving stores and whose handsome son, Sandi, Antoinette's protector her first day at the convent school, may have also been her lover. (Amélie, Daniel's spy at Granbois, had already told Rochester that Sandi and Antoinette were once said to have been engaged.) Daniel has saved most of his heavy fire for Antoinette: "They say she worse than her mother, and she hardly more than a child. Must be you deaf you don't hear people laughing when you marry her" (p. 125). Rochester listens to this attack passively. Is Daniel telling him what he wants to hear? He does not protest till asked to buy Daniel's silence with £500.

The visit to Daniel has by-products. Although Rochester pays out no money, he does identify Antoinette with her alleged half-brother at the worst possible time—when she is preparing the love potion. The rage and disgust he feels for yellow, wet-faced Daniel he transfers to his wife. While sharing their dinner, Antoinette and Rochester both harbor secrets touching the other. Her secret, the potion, begins taking effect right away. In the same paragraph where he notices a decanter of rum, he feels the enchantment of the night. Also buoying him up is his moral decision to believe Daniel. Objective truth no longer concerns him; to believe in Antoinette's corruption is to soothe his frayed nerves. His nerves are no longer frayed. When asked why he has been ignoring her, he replies coolly that he has just left Daniel. Antoinette, who knows Daniel and his claim to the family name, repeats much of what he told her husband that afternoon:

You saw him. . . . I know what he told you. That my mother was mad and an infamous woman and that my little brother who died was born a cretin, an idiot, and that I am a mad girl too. That is what he told you, isn't it? (p. 128)

But her point-by-point rebuttal of Daniel's argument does not move Rochester. Without a scrap of supporting evidence, he has already decided against her; he cannot afford to open his mind, let alone his heart.

Antoinette speaks out, anyway. Brushing the doctored rum with her lips, she explains in rich, dramatic language the loneliness and

stagnation that rode her family for the five years between her father's death and her mother's marriage to Mason; she, her mother, and her brother would have died, she adds, but for Christophine, who fed them, washed their clothes, and helped clean their derelict estate. Antoinette's poignant speech brings back many of the events of Part I—the poisoning of the horse, the burning of Coulibri, and the long delirium following Tia's stone—in order to show their long-range impact on her. The recitation touches Rochester, as it would anybody with a jot of sympathy: "I said, 'Antoinette, your nights are not spoiled, or your days, put the sad things away. Don't think about them and nothing will be spoiled, I promise you'" (p. 133). But his unspoken thought following these reassurances, "My heart was heavy as lead" (p. 133), refutes them. He lacks the candor, compassion, and courage to make a happy life with her. And, hopelessly committed to the lies that press on his heart, he knows it.

Meanwhile, Christophine's aphrodisiac has roused his lust. Intellectually repelled by the thought of sleeping with his wife, he calls her Bertha, her mother's real name. Because he cannot make love to her as Antoinette, the cause of his woes, he must remake her—as clear a demonstration of obeah as the love potion; innocence vanishes quickly in this blasted tropical paradise. The name, Bertha, not only screens him from her; it also identifies her with the mother of an idiot son who spent her last years as a demented sexual plaything. How can Antoinette enjoy sex with her mother's sorrow weighing on her? How can she escape the incest craving connected with identifying with Annette, or Bertha?

The next scene widens the gulf between her and Rochester, making good Christophine's forecast that he will hate her after the effect of the potion wears off. Feeling cold, sick, and breathless, Rochester fears that she has poisoned him. Looking at a blanket, which is the same color, yellow, as Daniel, whom he has taken as her alter-ego, he vomits. The screen provided by another woman's name has not cut him off from his carouse with her; sterner measures must be taken to rub out the love-making. And along with it, the lover: covering Antoinette with a sheet, "as if I covered a dead girl" (p. 138), he leaves the house. Greeting him at his dazed return several hours later is not Antoinette but the coquettish Amélie, who feeds him "as if I were a child" (p. 139). His transvaluation of values is nearly complete. He consummated his sexual reunion with his wife by covering her with a shroud; the woman he had earlier called a child now babies *him*. Her ministrations soon hoist him out of his symbolic infancy. The proper

English gentleman who cringed at the thought of touching black flesh now craves it. But Amélie rouses other motives in him, as well. In order to hurt Antoinette, he tumbles Amélie in the room next to the master bedroom. He spends the night with her in a deep sleep, glad to have betrayed his wife within her range of hearing. Like money, interracial sex has cut across his marriage, leaving it in ragged strips.

Just when Rochester thinks his world is stable, it is most disordered. At this point, he has lost control of his purposes and methods, perhaps even his mind; the civilized English spirit cannot cope with the tropics. The next morning, the cook resigns; the overseer does not call Rochester sir; the other servants keep away from him. Looking darker-skinned and thicker-lipped than before, Amélie now repels him. But her moral conscience has expanded, making him look cheap and vain. Rather than gloating over her sexual victory, she pities her enemy. That enemy, who has spent the day drinking and crying, evokes pity. Having exerted all her powers to heal her marriage, Antoinette has not only lost her husband and the esteem of her servants but also her self-esteem. Sleeping with Amélie in clear view of the other servants is the greatest insult Rochester could have perpetrated. More grisly offspring crawls from the mad night. He has also polluted Granbois, one of the few places in the world Antoinette loves, and, along with it, Antoinette herself. The Antoinette Rochester first talks to after leaving Amélie resembles the raging attic dweller of *Jane Eyre*: "When I saw her I was too shocked to speak. Her hair hung uncombed and dull into her eyes which were inflamed and staring, her face was very flushed and looked swollen" (pp. 145–46). Her soul reflects her wild looks; had Christophine not stepped in, she might have slashed Rochester with a jagged bottle.

Having moved to center-stage, Christophine stays there for one of the book's most exciting, deeply imagined scenes. Rochester turns on her, even though she has tried to save this marriage, his wife's sanity, and his life. Less of a witch than a vessel of good sense, with special insights into the psychology of sex, she confronts him with his darkest sins:

Everybody knows that you marry her for her money and you take it all. And then you want to break her up, because you jealous of her. She is more better than you, she have better blood in her and she don't care for money. (p. 152)

You bring that worthless girl to play with next door and you talk and laugh and love so that she hear everything. You meant her to hear. (p. 154)

She has mentioned these sins in order to give him a chance to redeem them; lowering his English rectitude will also lower his bargaining power. Insisting that Antoinette still loves him, she tells him either to go back to her or give back half her dowry and leave Jamaica so she can remarry. Her words booming in his head, he admits the fairness of Christophine's demand—but only inwardly. Aloud, he blames her for wrecking his marriage. He does not want Antoinette, and he does not want anyone else to have her, either. Her unhappiness has become his ruling purpose. Christophine, the only person who loves her and wants to help her, he threatens with arrest. The threat works. Already jailed once for practicing obeah, she cannot afford to run afoul of white man's justice again. But the betrayal symbolized by the crowing cock after her dignified departure also applies to him. Rochester has defeated his best hopes by driving Christophine away. Only she could have helped Antoinette become the wife he, in his innermost heart, wants her to be.

It is a false dawn, not the warming, healing sunshine that the crowing cock ushers in. The rest of the novel is muffled in moral darkness. The need to crush Antoinette—oddly, both for consenting to and then protesting against the wedding—has maddened Rochester. Whereas Christophine called her a child of the sun, he vows that she will never laugh in the sun again. The last section of Part II, describing the departure from Granbois, draws darkness tightly around the couple. Associations between impressions and ideas blur; Rochester's sentences move sluggishly or leak into silence; torn by conflicting emotions, he stops thinking consecutively. But his last look at Granbois saddens him enough to make him ask Antoinette's forgiveness. This contrition glows but briefly, though, her hate-filled eyes invoking a colder, bleaker hatred in him. A terrifying portrait of cruelty, he magnifies her slightest infractions and rejects her most gentle appeals. His reason serves his madness. She embodies for him a female mystery he can never again know. Admitting to himself that rejecting her means denying this soft magic, he resents her all the more. She must pay for all his setbacks as well as his misdeeds and mental conflicts. "I'd sell the place for what it would fetch," he says of Granbois. "I had meant to give it back to her. Now—what's the use?" (p. 173). Months of dawdling have brought him to the point where he can use her madness as an excuse to defraud her. But he denies this deviousness. Having conspired to buy him and thus enforce his feelings of inferiority, he reasons, she has gotten just what she deserves. His last word, "Nothing" (p. 173), describes him as

a moral wilderness. Bled of love, he has narrowed to a knife-edge of hatred and denial. He gives nothing, shares nothing, and, because his stand against Antoinette entails a closed, calcified heart, aspires to nothing.

Thus he does not appear in Part III. Though the last section of *Sargasso* belongs to Antoinette, it starts with a one-sided talk between Grace Poole, Antoinette's keeper at Thornfield Hall in England, and another servant. The talk, while preparing for the entrance of Antoinette, brings in data that could not plausibly come from a madwoman. Ironically, the deaths of Rochester's father and brother during his Caribbean voyage removed the need for him to have married Antoinette to begin with; as the inheritor of Thornfield, he no longer needed her dowry. The prologue to Part III, spoken by Grace Poole, makes him a victim; "His stay in the West Indies has changed him out of all knowledge," says Grace. "He has gray in his hair and misery in his eyes" (p. 178). He is now away from the Hall, relieved to be separated from his torment, Antoinette. At first glance, Antoinette does not look capable of tormenting anybody. She appears shivering at early dawn and warming herself by the fire that Grace has built in their cold attic apartment. She is usually out of touch, even with herself: her window is too high to see out of; she has no mirror; loss of appetite has wasted her body; she does not even know where she is: "They have taken everything away. What am I doing in this place and who am I?" (p. 180) she asks. Above all, she refuses to believe that her cold, dark prison is in England, the sum of her romantic hopes since childhood: "They tell me I am in England but I don't believe them. We lost our way to England. . . . This cardboard house where I walk at night is not England" (p. 181).

One dovetailing of materials from *Sargasso* and *Jane Eyre* (Chapter 20) comes in Antoinette's discussion of her step-brother, Richard Mason's, visit to Thornfield with Grace. Although she savaged Richard the night before, she only remembers his not recognizing her as he walked into her room. Nor does she recognize herself in the mirror as she prowls the Hall later that night, having unlocked her door with a sleeping Grace's key. "The woman with the streaming hair" (p. 188) who looks out at her from the downstairs mirror she takes as the ghost said to haunt the Hall. But her following deeds suggest an unconscious self-recognition. Memories and impressions from different times of her life throng her mind, including her rejection of Sandi's offer to stay with him in Jamaica instead of leaving with Rochester. She becomes confused. Accidentally, she sets

a tablecloth and a set of curtains on fire. The blossoming, zig-zag
flames ignite more pieces of her past. Then she wakes up. Her
accidental firing of Thornfield has been a dream. But now she will
taste the passion symbolized both by the flames and the red dress she
wore during her last tryst with Sandi. Her madness takes on a weird
clarity: "Now at last I know why I was brought here and what I have
to do" (p. 190), she announces inwardly. The book's closing sentence
shows her slipping out of her garret-prison in her drab gray wrapper,
her candle lighting the cold, dark corridor. In her deranged way,
perhaps her only available way, she has triumphed over her surroundings.

### III    *Winter's Darkening*

Both *Sargasso* and *Jane Eyre* (published forty-seven years to the
day before Jean Rhys's birthday, 24 August 1894) fuse poetic and
realistic details. Both also lean heavily on religion. Barbara Hardy
calls *Jane Eyre* "a religious novel" in which prayers are answered, the
good are rewarded, and evil is punished.[9] Starting with Charlotte
Brontë's £30,000 dowry figure, Jean Rhys stresses betrayal in her
religious symbolism. The crowing cock, the yellow-eyed Judas-figure
of Daniel, and the banished savior, Christophine, all limn a world in
which prayers are ignored and where obeah outpaces Christianity.
Yet similarities between the early years of Jane and Antoinette
suggest triumph in the later book. Both girls overcome a childhood
trauma, Jane's being locked in a dark room at Gateshead Hall
correponding to the burning of Coulibri. Orphaned and displaced,
both girls attend boarding schools for the same amount of time,
about eight years. Both marry Edward Rochester. Why does the one
woman prosper while the other loses all?

What happens to Antoinette in *Sargasso* justifies Brontë's portrait
of her as a hag with dark, swollen lips and rolling red eyes:

A figure ran backwards and forwards [notes Jane of Antoinette the first time
she sees her]. What it was, whether beast or human being, one could not, at
first sight, tell: it grovelled, seemingly, on all fours; it snatched and growled
like some wild animal: but it was covered with clothing; and a quantity of
dark, grizzled hair, wild as a mane, hid its head and face.[10]

Betrayal, bloodshed, and domestic crises during Antoinette's girlhood damaged a psyche left weak by heredity. Colin MacInnes says

of her, "Antoinette is the child of a ruined and desperate Creole family, and the greed and lust of her dead father and the anguish of her unstable mother, are in her blood."[11] As if this legacy were not hobbling enough, she loses everything she prizes—family, childhood home, and the home she had the wit and courage to make for herself in convent school—by age seventeen. The main event of her life—her marriage—is decided without any thought given to her feelings or financial security. Yet, here too, she shows resiliency and grit, coming to love the husband she married grudgingly; although more attention is given them, Rochester's reservations did not exceed hers. This strength vanishes piecemeal. The firing of Coulibri, Tia's sharp stone, Annette's mental decline, and her own marital strife all weaken Antoinette's self-grip. Finally, Rochester's carouse with Amélie in an adjoining room pushes Antoinette into the madness he had fabricated, first, to gain power over her and, next, to rob her. Though he only sets out to defeat her, he soon finds the way to destroy her. Her womanly tendency to reflect her male surroundings makes his obsessiveness the iron bars of her cage.

This obsessiveness forges a link with *Jane Eyre*. Though Brontë compares Antoinette to a bird of prey, a snarling dog, and a tigress, she also uncovers wildness in Rochester, Victorian fiction's exemplar of male passion. The merits of Jean Rhys's portrait of him go beyond maintaining consistency with the earlier version. Besides uncovering the roots of his volatile temper, the Rochester of *Sargasso* calls into question posterity's attitude toward him. Jean Rhys asks us, first, to ponder his sexual maturity. Coming under suspicion straightaway are passages in Chapters 26 and 27 of *Jane Eyre*, where he attacks his wife with all the malice of Daniel Cosway:

Bertha Mason is mad; and she came of a mad family;—idiots and maniacs through three generations! Her mother, the Creole, was both a mad woman and a drunkard!—as I found out after I had wed the daughter: for they were silent on family secrets before.

These were vile discoveries; but, except for the treachery of concealment, I should have made them no subject of reproach to my wife: even when I found her nature wholly alien to mine; her tastes obnoxious to me; her cast of mind common, low, narrow. . . . No servant would bear the continued outbreaks of her violent and unreasonable temper or the vexations of her absurd, contradictory, exacting orders.

Within fifteen pages, he calls Antoinette "that fearful hag," "a pigmy

intellect," "the lunatic," and "the maniac,"[12] and he charges her with
nearly every vice imaginable—intemperance, stupidity, looseness,
violence, and depravity. Yet how convincing are these charges,
coming from one so easily misled by sex; Barbara Hardy has said,
"His mistresses are all handsome but either mercenary, unprincipled,
unfaithful, or mindless."[13] His attacks against both Antoinette and
the Parisian mother of Adela, his daughter or ward, show him either
choosing women badly or bringing out their worst. Even Jane he
mistreats—trying to involve her in bigamy and then blaming her
*beforehand* for the life of vice he intends to live if she spurns him. This
stern, heavy-browed man of wild moods will sacrifice anybody to get
his way. Yet he also knows that his way is not always the best. Though
he takes pride in his maleness, he distrusts it. His self-doubt expresses
itself as a denial of natural process. Now flora traditionally denote joy
and fulfillment; their absence, barrenness and hunger. After having
lived right up against teeming nature in the tropics, this anguished
sensualist who tramples flowers thrives on the grimness of Thornfield. "I like that sky of steel; I like the sternness and stillness of the
world under this frost. I like Thornfield; its antiquity; its retirement;
its old crowtrees and thorn-trees; its gray facade, and lines of dark
windows,"[14] he tells Jane in Chapter 15. Not accidentally, the estate
of this enemy of green growing things burns during harvest time.

All this fits Jean Rhys's portrait of him. With delicate fingers, he
can pick up and then free a moth that blunders into a candle. He
admits that his doubts about his marriage may be groundless: "It was
the first time I had seen her smile simply and naturally," he says of
Antoinette on their way to Granbois. "Or perhaps it was the first time
I had felt simple and natural with her" (p. 71). He praises her beauty,
drinking it in for minutes at a time: "I wonder why I had never
realized how beautiful she was. Her hair . . . fell smoothly far below
her waist. I could see the red and gold lights in it" (p. 80). But his
father has taught him not to expect the shining and the beautiful: in
an imaginary letter to him, Rochester mentions "the furtive shabby
maneuvers of a younger son" (p. 70). How can this underdog rate his
errand to Jamaica as anything but punishment? How can he have
faith in any close personal tie? No wonder he spends his first three
weeks in Spanish Town in a sick bed. There is nothing familiar or
friendly nearby to raise his spirits. The blazing sun, the clamoring
green hills, and the heavy, floral-scented air perturb him. Then Amélie
and Daniel perturb him anew, the one claiming his body while the
other corrupts his mind. His well-shored inferiority complex stops

him from coping with Antoinette's beauty, let alone enjoying it. He becomes a casualty of psychological warfare. The person who believes he deserves the worst gets the worst, even if he has to inflict it upon himself.

Rochester's evil stems more from weakness than from depravity. Because he controls Antoinette's money along with her heart, he can end the bitterness infecting his marriage. But he lacks the inner strength to resist the power of psychological suggestion. His sense of unworthiness, his being on alien turf, and his resentment toward his father and brother all aggravate the negation rather than end it. His moral confusion is best summarized by Christophine, the book's wisest character: "The man not a bad man, even if he love money, but he hear so many different stories he don't know what to believe" (p. 114). Like the "caged eagle"[15] of *Jane Eyre*, he acts both cowardly and dishonestly in most of his dramatic encounters. He lets Daniel call Antoinette a liar and a lecher. He lies and then changes the subject when Antoinette tries to discuss these charges. He also wriggles out of justifying his conduct to Christophine, nodding mechanically as she speaks her wisdom and then threatening her with jail when the wisdom comes too close to home. Easily cowed, he lets each of his interlocutors, Daniel, Antoinette, and Christophine, set and then hold the style of their conversations with him. Yet anything they say that goes against his needs, he disregards. He prefers certainty to doubt, even if certainty means sacrificing another person. But the peace of mind he pays so much for comes only years later, after he has lost his sight, his arm, and his property.

But how *many* years later? He tells Jane that he spent four years with Antoinette in the West Indies before bringing her to Thornfield ten or eleven years ago. Yet *Jane Eyre* came out in 1847, and Antoinette attended convent school in Spanish Town from 1839–44, through age seventeen or eighteen. Jean Rhys does not change Brontë's chronology to impugn Rochester's honesty: *Sargasso* stresses his youth as often as *Jane Eyre* does his moody middle age. Her motive is more thematic. In order to weld Antoinette's downfall to that of her unlucky family, Jean Rhys seats her heroine's first great setback in the burning of Coulibri; Antoinette cannot escape her past any more than Rochester can escape his. Other changes are less thematic. Jean Rhys gains sympathy for Antoinette by making her thin rather than outsize and younger than Rochester rather than his senior. The author's making feeble Richard Mason Antoinette's stepbrother, rather than full brother, also strengthens Antoinette's

case, casting doubt on Rochester's charge that Antoinette and Richard are victims of the same hereditary madness. But at a cost to the novel's plausibility: if Rochester, Sr., leaves his younger son nothing, why should Mason, no paragon of virtue or enlightenment, will half his fortune to a stepdaughter he had stowed in a convent and then all but forgotten? The placing of his wife's death during Antoinette's convent days, as opposed to Brontë's allowing Annette to survive her daughter's wedding as an inmate in a lunatic asylum, works better as fictional art: Rochester's moral breakup is meant to come from hearsay and innuendo rather than from tangible proofs. Finally, Antoinette's wild attack on Richard Mason, reported in Chapter 20 of *Jane Eyre*, occurs while Rochester is away from Thornfield in *Sargasso* in order to avoid showing him and Antoinette together: the division between the couple at the end of Part I, enforced by Rochester's last word, "Nothing" (p. 173), *should* remain total.

The novel's title clinches this estrangement. The Sargasso Sea, which Antoinette and Rochester sailed through en route to England, lies north of the Canary Islands and west of the Azores. John and Mildred Teal's *Sargasso Sea* tells us, "At times the Sargasso seems devoid of life."[16] Accounting for its low fish population, they add, is a low food supply with few nutrients. Appealing to Jean Rhys just as strongly as the idea of a desert sea is the Sargasso's isolation: its encircling currents have cut the Sargasso off from the tidal flow of the rest of the Atlantic. Tradition has compared the alleged menace of these swirls to that of Homer's Sirens. Donn Byrne (1889–1928) conveys the dark mystery and fascination generated by their heavy, plowing rhythm in his story, "Sargasso Sea": this "port of missing ships" looks like "a newborn continent, or an old forgotten one, so far does it stretch and so lonely is it. . . . 'A barren place. . .' the folk stories say, 'without music and mellow ale; a prison of lost souls.'"[17] Isolated, sluggish, and trapped in a barren place, Antoinette qualifies as a Sargasso on her own. Just as legend claims the sea to be choked with algae and kelp, so is her mind clogged with bitter regrets. (The green substance that clogs minds and numbs hearts in the novel is money.) The swirling currents of the Sargasso join her privation to that of Julia Martin and Sasha Jansen. The down-pulling tides that hem her in shut out life as inexorably for her as encroaching middle age does for women who live off men; the powerless have always had to go around in dizzy circles. The fires at either end of the novel, both of which burn life out of Antoinette, and the well-meaning English

husbands who destroy both Antoinette and her mother extend the argument. Within marriage as well as without, woman has always been a victim. Annette's final sorrow is to become a sexual object. Antoinette's is to be scorned for a nymphomaniac, perhaps with some justice; the many red apparitions in Part III show her to be fixated on sex. In any case, neither she nor Annette escaped sexual classification or sexual punishment.

The three-part structure supports this grim inference. In Part III Antoinette's mind has become a small, dark place and Annette is long dead. Howard Moss attacks this part of the book for faults Jean Rhys has sidestepped through careful narrative selection. Moss finds *Sargasso* "the least telling" work in the Rhys canon "precisely because the heroine *does* go mad, and because she commits a final demonic *act*—the burning of Thornfield Hall. Miss Rhys's specialty is neither action nor madness but the precipitants that precede them."[18] Moss has flubbed his facts. The novel ends with Antoinette leaving her garret-prison, candle in hand; she is never seen firing the Hall. Why should she be? Instead of describing an event whose consequences have already been discussed (in *Jane Eyre*), Jean Rhys treats it as both an act of natural justice and a logical offshoot of Antoinette's methodical madness. This finale is carefully pointed. Part One of *Sargasso* is ruminative, tracing memories, sifting feelings, and making important disclosures, like Annette's death, off-handedly. The action begins during Antoinette's childhood, shortly after 1834, the date Negro slavery ended in the British West Indies, and it ends with Antoinette reaching the end of her stay in the convent some ten years later. Not thoroughly in charge of her materials, Antoinette half dreams and half remembers her childhood. Recorded slantwise, in scraps, or through a haze, Part I sets into motion the disaster that will later speed through several lives.

Part II gives the disaster its urgency. Besides offering another view of Antoinette—that of a dazed, resentful husband who barely knows her—it also shows the sudden breakup of that husband's peace and hopes. Part II has a glowing, sometimes white-hot intimacy of observation. Rochester's fraught response to the strange, frightening landscape pressing on him with its hard colors and heavy smells creates scenes of great power. No mere backdrop or relief, these descriptions sustain the excitement touched off by Rochester's emotion-charged interviews with Daniel, Antoinette, and Christophine. The plangent masculine prose of this section attains both the suddenness and resonance of tragedy. What is more, Mellown has

shown Rochester's voice working antiphonally with that of Antoinette to give the tragedy an ironic frame:

The whole story is known to Antoinette as she writes. . . . Rochester's narration, however, takes place at the moment that events occur, and consequently we share with him his revelations and growing horror. Thus the two voices tell us one story, giving us not merely the contrast of their attitudes, but more important for the effects of horror which it produces, the contrast of the victim who knows his fate with that of the victim who must gradually learn his. Antoinette knows from the start that she is doomed . . . while Rochester imagines that he is a free agent.[19]

Citing the novel's nightmare ambience, Walter Allen rightly terms *Sargasso* "Caribbean Gothic":[20] the private grudges, racial anger, and tropical heat, all compressed inside a setting where obeah overrides Christianity, make fear a major condition of the book. The voices of the sick, dazed narrators mingle dread and bewilderment. But this frenzy is controlled by shrewd technique. Scenes like Annette's funeral and Christophine's preparation of the love potion go unreported for the purpose of maintaining a sharp focus on Rochester's relationship with Antoinette. Causing no distractions from the book's main subject, these scenes work better as imaginative presences than they would as documented actions. This selectivity helps Jean Rhys get the most from her materials. Depth and drive fuse powerfully in *Wide Sargasso Sea*. Each scene has a purpose—to move the story forward or to throw new light on what happened before. The strongest of Jean Rhys's novels exudes golden atmospheres, dramatizes human stress, and invites moral subtleties. A sign of its merit is its ability to defy invidious comparisons with *Jane Eyre*. Based on Brontë's classic novel, it has enough originality to stand as a sequel, a criticism, or a free-standing work of art.

## IV  *Jean Rhys Today*

The fiction portrays few middle-class citizens and no socialites, cultists, technocrats, or members of the industrial working class. Extrusive rather than stripped, the novels dwell on a special breed of underdog, or have-not, and realize her in both time and space. A substructure of order and rationality undergirds the lives of women like Anna Morgan, Sasha Jansen, and Antoinette Cosway Rochester. Under the disordered surface of their daily routines, an irresistible current of reason drives them to greater self-awareness.

But not to greater self-command: lacking power, they set their sights low. Jean Rhys's contribution to modern fiction inheres in having turned their powerlessness into narrative art. Beyond freedom and dignity, these women are everybody's family; they belong to all of us. Even though we try to push them away, they remain a publicly owned product of the urban West.

Jean Rhys speaks for them, bringing their frustrations and hopes to life. The novels do not usually offer the surface excitement of sexual love, strong central situations, and happy endings. Instead, they free their heroines from the constraints of a plot, but only to deny them any room in which to grow. Options are shut off quietly. Though well-planned, the novels do not look preconceived or rehearsed. Avoiding literary postures and moral nudges, they observe, with deadly accuracy, the exact surfaces of their heroines' lives—*Sargasso* also delving far below the surface. Their sparse, suggestive prose achieves a new concentration of character. Rather than documenting a public world, Jean Rhys creates, in a reserved, softspoken way, a coherent world of her own. Inwardly realized, her books are so graceful and unforced that they invite dismissal by impatient eyes for alleged randomness.

Though small scale, they hit most of their targets. Jean Rhys does not overrate fertility, subordinating inventiveness to warmth and directness of observation. In this regard, she invites comparison with two other English writers who, like her, only produced a handful of restrained novels—Jane Austen and E. M. Forster. Full of atmosphere and essence, her played-down, irrelevant-seeming novels uncover more truths about women than any number of works by rationalists, fantasists, and social reformers. Her refusal to shout, shock, or trumpet an ideology carries the added benefit of making us better readers. Masterpieces, we are often reminded, sometimes pretend to look like failures. Reading Jean Rhys carefully shows that there are more ways of stating a case than we might have believed.

Any judgment of her worth must include her sly power to provoke nonliterary judgments. Her heroines all share a special situation and exert a special claim. This claim refuses to be shrugged off or discredited; it is as central to modern life as speed and violence. The threats it poses could even surpass those posed by runaway change. But how to cope with this special claim? In vain, we invoke Supreme Court decisions and other public policies; in vain, we give our counterparts uneasy side glances. We still feel uneasy. Rather than making us look askance at those around us in buses, post offices, and supermarkets, the Rhys heroine makes us look askance at ourselves.

CHAPTER 8

# Conclusion

THE Rhys archetype resembles other heroines in modern British fiction. Like Katherine Mansfield's Miss Brill, Dorothy Richardson's Miriam Henderson of the thirteen-part sequence novel *Pilgrimage*, and Doris Lessing's Martha Quest, she beats back loneliness. Antoinette Cosway Rochester speaks for her whole deprived sisterhood when she tells her bridegroom, in *Sargasso*, "I am not used to happiness. . . . It makes me afraid" (p. 92). She and her counterparts have never learned the self-esteem to feel that they deserve happiness. Through them, Jean Rhys rejects both the idea of female subservience and the male-determined formulations it rests on. Both sexual and political, these formulations merit her scorn; for women, as she sees them, have no creative or even independent role in the prevailing masculine order. Antoinette personifies this plight. Stripped of her name, her money, and her property, she subsists as a prisoner in a small attic, denied the fresh air and sunlight enjoyed by other living creatures.

Jean Rhys is a major figure in the development of English fiction by women, particularly that branch dealing with female masochism and rootlessness. Her women are persecuted because of their sex. Demanding, insensitive men use them physically and then discard them without trying to know them. "He never used to talk to me much," says Julia Martin of an ex-lover in *Mackenzie*, adding, "I was for sleeping with—not for talking to" (pp. 172–73). Such exploitation is accepted by men as routine and normal. Because of it, women depend on men, waiting passively for overtures while their good looks and material means both wane. This exploitation also blocks the formation of an honest, loving relationship around sex. Jean Rhys is not the only female novelist of the century to argue that many men dislike women, reducing sex with them to the exercise of power and control. Just as Marya Zelli's lover in *Quartet*, H. J. Heidler, fails her sexually, so does Dorothy Richardson's Miriam complain about

the lack of imagination and tenderness in her first lover, Hypo G. Wilson. Doris Lessing's women find sex with men just as bleak. Most of Martha Quest's lovers in *Children of Violence* leave her uninvolved, and Anna Freeman Wulf of *The Golden Notebook* discuss differences between clitoral and vaginal orgasms instead of experiencing these thrills directly.

Anna's intellectualizing wouldn't occur in a work by Jean Rhys. Both in her short stories and in her novels, Jean Rhys underplays her protests against the patriarchy and capitalism that punish women. Instead of launching attacks, she will use a small but revealing detail to define woman's reduced place. Not one male character appears in the 1963 story of London during the Luftwaffe air-raids, "A Solid House." Yet male domination exerts force; a woman who has run out of cigarettes notes mentally that her local tobacconist won't sell cigarettes to women when they are in short supply. Jean Rhys also joins the one-sided battle of the sexes to war between nations in *Voyage in the Dark* and "Petronella," both works identifying their heroines' grief with the collapse of Europe by mentioning the date, 1914. Jean Rhys's argument is clear: to deny women is to deny the process by which societies become civilizations. As is shown in the tyranny Rochester exerts over Antoinette, the political effects of male domination compel our attention. Heterosexual relations rob women of will, making them want to put their necks beneath a male heel. "I would like to put my throat under your feet" (p. 28), writes Mackenzie to Julia. Sexual cruelty lives in his mind; so does the knowledge that he controls his relationship with Julia. Whatever masochist fantasies he conjures up will not hurt him. His words to the contrary, Julia is debased, not he. Losing him as a protector lowers her self-esteem. Although she survives the loss, there is less of her than before. The jilting conveys, however subtly, European fascism in miniature. Converted to female terms, it also conveys the chief crisis in Kafka—that of the victim stripped of all will. The crisis recurs in "Let Them Call It Jazz" (1962), whose heroine, it bears repeating, is a black West Indian living in London, which makes her an underdog on the basis of her race as well as her sex. A Mr. Sims she meets in a café offers her shelter after her eviction from her Notting Hill flat. Some trouble with neighbors soon results in her being jailed and fined. After serving her sentence, she learns that she is free; her fine has been paid. But the judge will not name her benefactor. She has no control over her life, even when it goes well. Although Sims probably paid her fine, he has not asked for any services in return. His silence

vexes her; an unstated obligation can fray the nerves more than one that is spelled out. No wonder the pressures bred by passive waiting drove her predecessor to smash all the drinking glasses at Sims's flat. The sound of glass shattering rings through all Jean Rhys's fiction.


## I   *Two Islanders*

A woman writer who understands the pressures exerted by being beholden to a man is the New Zealander Katherine Mansfield. Not surprisingly Mansfield shares many of the values distinguishing Jean Rhys—a suspicion of middle-class values, a distrust in the ability of men to make women happy, and the fear of being dismissed by the English as a crude colonial. Besides being nettled by having come from a remote country with no history, Mansfield also labored under burdens imposed by poor health and the death of her brother in World War I. These burdens help explain why she puts forth a vision sometimes as painful as that of Jean Rhys. Her stories swarm with victims; close relationships crack; revelations usually bring more sorrow than uplift. Like those of Jean Rhys, many of her characters feel trapped or excluded, predicaments sadly familiar to their authors, both of whom write as aliens. Yet alienation hasn't upset all. Both authors write, as well, from a female standpoint, i.e., a civilizing one. Their feline sensibilities move to the fore in their touches of humor, their psychological accuracy, and their interest in improving the man-woman relationship. If such concerns are alien, as opposed to rare, then humanity is foundering badly.

How to maintain balance? A common wish to tell the truth rules out a reliance on intellectual systems for Jean Rhys and Katherine Mansfield. Instead of leaning on formulas, these writers listen carefully to the noises of silence, those tremors of the spirit which reveal the hidden life of a person. The lively sense of incongruity the writers share endows these glimpses with both fun and gloom. Furthermore, both writers rate the natural and the spontaneous over affectation and pretense. Mansfield's artists ooze self-importance. The narcissistic Raoul Duquette, of "Je ne parle pas français," sees himself as a creative writer. Yet he is more show than substance. Mansfield need not criticize him in her own voice. Duquette dwarfs himself. The artistic poses he strikes reveal the difference between what he is and what he claims to be: "I confess, without my clothes I am rather charming. Plump, almost like a girl, with smooth

shoulders, and I wear a thin gold bracelet above my left elbow."¹ Jean
Rhys gives the lie to his breed of precious elites somewhat differently.
The English Miss Bruce and the Flemish Verhausen of *Left Bank*
have come to Paris, center of artistic activity for the Western world in
the 1920s. But they have come to work at their art, not to affect
artistic airs. Solid and sensible, they can't afford *hauteur*. Their art is
too demanding.

In keeping with their scorn for affectation is the candor with which
Jean Rhys and Katherine Mansfield discuss their native island
colonies. New Zealand's strange, wild back country and the lush West
Indian tropics aren't edited to please European sensibilities. Though
infiltrated with European values, both places respond to them
weakly. Thus both places suffer from the loss of European law.
Situated thousands of miles away from England, seat of their cultural
heritage, the Caribbean islands and New Zealand, lacking an
indwelling system of legal controls, abound in brutality. This
primitive terror is presented without apologies. The clawlike roots,
tough stalk, and serrated leaves of the aloe, central symbol of
Mansfield's "Prelude," put forth the same primordial menace that
dogs Rochester in the Jamaican jungle. The tropics corrode mainland
codes of conduct elsewhere, English people and their home-grown
values coming to grief in the late Rhys tales, "Pioneers, Oh Pioneers,"
"Goodbye Marcus, Goodbye Rose," and "Fishy Waters." Mansfield's "The Woman at the Store" and "Ole Underwood" describe
other by-products of the loss of mainland law. The New Zealand of
these stories is hot and dusty, lonely and lawless, with vast tracts of
silence and space dividing people. This raw, dowdy place, with its
makeshift frontier ethics, thwarts the imagination; the title character
of "The Woman at the Store" beats her daughter for drawing
pictures. Her fellow New Zealander, Ole Underwood, enacts an
uglier truth. Some thirty years before the time of his story, Ole killed
his wife for deceiving him with another man. The shockwaves pulsing
from his crime of passion still race through him. His heart pumping
madly, he kills his cat, the only creature who loves him in the windy
prison town where he lives as an outcast.

Ole's wife's infidelity raises the subject of marriage in Mansfield's
New Zealand. As her many portraits of marital stress indicate,
Mansfield offers little comfort on this score. Bertha Young, a
member of the rising middle class in "Bliss," finds that her husband
has been deceiving her with somebody to whom she, Bertha, felt
mystically attuned. The story, written in the vein of Chekhov and

Joyce, ends on a chord of helplessness and isolation. Bertha shares more with Pearl Fulton than is good for her. Linda Burnell's extroverted husband, Stanley, in "Prelude" does not commit adultery. But his male heartiness beats Linda down. She cannot relax until he leaves the house in the morning for work. What weighs on her most heavily is his sexuality. She dislikes having sex with him; above all, she dreads the prospect of pregnancy. Her consuming fear gains voice in her referring to her children as "lumps," or tumors. For all its horror, she envies the aloe tree, or century plant, growing near her home because it only buds once every hundred years. Would that she could remain fruitless for so long, Linda muses. Her marriage has wrecked this hope. But the realities that darken her heart help Stanley thrive. He looks forward to sex with her so much that she imagines him as a Newfoundland dog forever jumping at her. Oblivious of the pain he has been causing her, large, meaty Stanley takes pride in moving the family to a larger home (to house more children?) in a better district. Nor is Linda the only female Burnell hurt by his pluming maleness. "Prelude" focuses on his and Linda's nine-year-old daughter Kezia, who sees the family's move as an unfortunate exchange of childhood warmth and security for adult stress. As the family sets out for its new home, Kezia learns that she can't squeeze into the buggy carrying the others. Her tidy girlhood world has cracked; being excluded from the buggy has killed the sense of adventure with which she had hoped to join her family in its new home.

Like many other Mansfield stories, "Prelude" ends with the collapse of the heroine's romantic illusions. Young Kezia suffers from the same moral desolation gripping Bertha Young in "Bliss," the title characters of "The Little Governess" and "Miss Brill," and the middle-aged Pinner sistsers of "The Daughters of the Late Colonel." These women must all face emotional crisis unaided, particularly by men. If men cause a great deal of female woe in Mansfield, they do little to relieve it. Like those in Jean Rhys, Mansfield's men are strong, selfish, and evasive. They want power without responsibility. The reality they dodge most often, once again, is that of women. They don't like women because they haven't tried to know them. Women must be kept at bay or on a chain. Retreating into wounded self-righteousness, a man in *Voyage* refuses to discuss his daughter with his mistress. Although Anna Morgan, the mistress, pleases him sexually, her talking about Carl Redman's daughter with Redman would smirch the daughter's purity. No doubt Redman's idealizing of her blinds him to her reality as effectively as his moral typecasting of

Anna keeps him from seeing Anna clearly. He also faces problems originating in his psyche. To discuss his daughter with Anna, who is probably only a few years older than the daughter, might force Redman to face his incest craving. Men like him and Bertha Young's husband in "Bliss" prize the middle-class conventions of security, ownership, and respectability. They don't want their neat routines upset by a prying or an hysterical woman: Mackenzie will give Julia Martin the money she asks for rather than risking a scene. In "Night Out 1925," a man whose date has tipped some nightclub entertainers extravagantly frets that the entertainers will laugh at him. He punishes his date for exposing him to ridicule by dropping her off at a bus stop rather than driving her home.

Though small, the world that shatters at the end of "1925" matters. The masculine need to control women saps the vitality of male-female ties in both Mansfield and Jean Rhys. Married couples can be estranged, even when living together. In Mansfield's "The Stranger," Jane Hammond believes that her husband's proprietary view of her has put more distance between them than can be bridged. The climax of Jean Rhys's "Fishy Waters" shows Maggie Penrice morally convinced that her husband battered a West Indian child and then shifted the blame to another man. Her conviction brings the "overwhelming certainty" that her husband is "a complete stranger." Men like Matt Penrice alienate themselves from women because they hide their hearts. Had Penrice let himself go emotionally with his wife, he would have released the bottled-up tensions that led him to batter the little black girl. But Anglo-Saxon men are taught to suppress feeling, any emotional display being frowned upon as both undignified and unmanly. Thus their bluff, hearty fronts; thus their innocence and vulnerability. Mackenzie had the sensitivity to publish a book of poems; no clod, Heidler suffered a nervous breakdown a year before the time-setting of *Quartet*; a crisis of conscience stemming from his unfairness to Antoinette turns Rochester's hair gray, lines his face, and troubles his sleep. Emotional insecurity also betrays that tender tyrant Stanley Burnell of "Prelude" and "At the Bay" into plaguing his wife. The moral and psychological harm he inflicts on Linda in the name of love always recoils. Like him, the cruel boss in Mansfield's "The Fly" also helped, heartened, but finally destroyed a loved one, his son; despite his tender motives, the boss treats the son as sadistically as he dispatches a fly trapped in his inkwell. His juddering revelation consists of identifying both himself and his son with the fly he tortured before killing. Similarly,

Rochester crushes his own heart while preventing Antoinette from becoming the wife he both wants and needs. Male arrogance defeats itself in its vain gestures of self-perpetuation.

Female impulsiveness can also wring hearts. The title figure of the early Mansfield story "The Tiredness of Rosabel" goes to bed hungry because she spent her last money on flowers rather than food. Another side of Anna Morgan, possibly Jean Rhys's most impulsive person, surfaces in "Pictures," a Mansfield story whose heroine has sex with a man to coax a dinner out of him. Such sexual bartering occurs less often in Mansfield than in Jean Rhys. As stories like "The Little Governess," "The Daughters of the Late Colonel," and "Miss Brill" show, the Mansfield heroine usually shrinks from self-assertion. Brittle, spinsterish Miss Brill partakes of the glamour and excitement of Paris vicariously. Yet even her secondhand pleasure is snatched from her when she overhears a young couple on a park bench deriding the fur piece she is wearing. Their derision smashes her self-esteem. Immediately she leaves the park, goes home, and packs away the fur piece. Heretofore worn with pride, the mousy fur now spells out her shabbiness and defeat. Miss Brill is no actress in a vibrant life drama, as she had believed, but a discard. Her sad self-knowledge both jars and isolates her. Unlike a Rhys heroine, though, she will not ease the strain by getting drunk or by taking money from strange men. Yet her plight resembles that of a Rhys heroine, who, no mere wanton, can impress us with her pluck and restraint. Though desperate, Sasha Jansen of *Midnight* refuses both to sell her body and to buy the body of a gigolo. Women in both Mansfield and Jean Rhys want to join humanity, not dramatize differences or invent a new separatism.

Their humanizing purposes are served by similar narrative techniques. Like most of the works in *Left Bank*, Mansfield's two most personal tales, the autobiographical "Prelude" and "At the Bay," extend atmospheres rather than build stories out of tight sequences of events, moral issues, and coherent characterization. The ability to evoke mood in the Chekhovian vein came later to Mansfield than to Jean Rhys, the early Mansfield works suffering often from editorial intrusions. This blanket moralizing shows a lack of authorial faith in the stories' ability to make their own point. Mansfield learned craftsmanship slowly. The moral caricatures found in apprentice pieces like "The Tiredness of Rosabel" and "The Sister of the Baroness," together with the clumsy satire smudging "Germans at Meat," have no counterpart in *Left Bank*. Later, though, both writers

developed the craft and the artistry to write from the point of view of unsympathetic characters—Mansfield in "Je ne parle pas français" and Jean Rhys in "La Grosse Fifi" and the second part of *Sargasso*.

As these works show, both writers know how to fuse technique and purpose. Mansfield portrays the rugged frontier people and the new bourgeoisie of New Zealand. But she ignores the Maoris, her country's original black settlers. No Maori in the Mansfield canon enjoys the prominence of Christophine, the maternal obeah woman of *Sargasso*, let alone that of Selina Davis, the black West Indian who meets grief in "Let Them Call It Jazz." Yet Mansfield's world can sparkle with a freshness and a clarity absent from Jean Rhys, especially her Europe-based work. Laura Sheridan of "The Garden Party" learns that life thrums with meaning—some sad, some exhilarating, all rich and vibrant. The real and the ideal fuse triumphantly for her. This triumph induces a mood light years away from that created by the blank walls, worn furniture, and featureless fitments the Rhys heroine stares at every day in her lonely bedsitter. By toning down poetic effects, like imagery, Jean Rhys conveys her heroines' fear of being swallowed up by drabness. The technique reaps solid gains. The wide gulf between their unspoken longings and the shabbiness of their surroundings defines these women as sharply as the techniques Mansfield uses to define characters as different as Laura, Ole Underwood, and Raoul Duquette. In both writers, technique develops and criticizes character. The vision and craft identified with Katherine Mansfield and Jean Rhys have enriched modern British fiction.

## II  *Selection and Saturation*

An English novelist whose discontent with her male-dominated society matches that of Katherine Mansfield and Jean Rhys is Dorothy Richardson, author of the thirteen-volume work *Pilgrimage* (1915–67). Women in *Pilgrimage* are ill-used by both lovers and employers; so deeply ingrained in society is the principle of male dominance that it robs women of the power to better their lot on the job as well as at leisure. Richardson's main character, Miriam Henderson, protests against the male image of God put forth by the Victorian clergy. Her anger moves her to action, most of it futile. Miriam tests her social conscience in tense, teeming London, where she works on various social and economic questions. Later she will

give up public crusading for the private sphere of religious faith. What she learns from these challenges has both a saddening and separating effect. She becomes as hostile to organized religion as she was to Victorian society and business. *Dimple Hill*, the twelfth work, or "chapter," in the sequence, occurs in a Quaker community, whose remoteness from London provides the distance she needs to assess British life.

In contrast to the Rhys heroine, who tires quickly, Miriam assesses and acts with a Victorian zeal. Feeling alienated and useless, she seeks to better herself by working as a teacher, a governess, a journalist, a translator, and a dental assistant (jobs also held by Dorothy Richardson, who identifies nearly completely with Miriam). This earnestness hasn't dulled her impulses. Reflective and sensitive, warm and outgoing, she responds vividly to natural scenery in Germany (*Pointed Roofs*), England (*Honeycomb*), and Switzerland (*Oberland*). No such lyricism marks the responses of Marya Zelli, Julia Martin, or Sasha Jansen. But why should Jean Rhys's passive urbanites feel uplifted? They live their dreary lives either indoors or on monotonous gray streets. Other differences between them and Miriam come to mind. Anna Morgan and Miriam both go to foreign countries in their late teens. Anna sails from the West Indies to England for fun. In sharp contrast, financial pressures at home send Miriam to Hanover, Germany, to teach English in a boarding school. What she accomplishes with her students gives Miriam a sense of achievement and self-worth. This, she proudly explains to her family. At the end of *Pointed Roofs*, a welcoming family greets her return to England. Anna enjoys no such homecoming. Because she has squandered all on clothing and drink, she has no money to book passage home. Nobody would greet her dockside in any case. Dodging responsibility, her stepmother tries to shame her into leaving England. But she refuses to pay the price of being rid of her. Anna's uncle in Jamaica plays the same double game. Though he has invited Anna to live with him, his insistence that her stepmother pay her passage home insures him that his invitation can never be accepted.

Anna's life is thus a dead end. Miriam moves more freely because her author's reading in John Bunyan and Quaker mysticism has made the journey, or pilgrimage, a metaphor for life (whence the collective title given the long autobiographical novel). To Miriam, life consists of process and change. Lacking this sense of purpose, the Rhys heroine either feels trapped or wheels in dizzy circles. Scenic contrast

defines the difference between the two women. In *Backwater*, the second "chapter" of *Pilgrimage*, Miriam has a mystical insight while walking up a flight of stairs. Her illumination recalls Julia Martin's wild outburst on the staircase of her London rooming house in *Mackenzie*. That Julia is going up the stairs with her lover calls forth a Freudian reading that helps explain Miriam as well as Julia herself. The Freudian equation of stairs with the sexual act calls to mind the fact that Miriam mostly uses the stairs either in daylight or while carrying a light; she can see where she is going. The revelation and truth symbolized by her lighted passage bypass Julia, who keeps stumbling from one dark space to another. Characteristically, she climbs the steps of her lodging with George Horsfield in the dark, and, owing to her outburst, sees her prospects darken immediately. She is evicted on the spot, and, in shocking the cautious, evasive Horsfield, she throws away her chance to win a benefactor. Darkness is her special domain. At the novel's outset, she is sitting in a somber room of a cheap hotel; at the end, alone again, she is sipping a drink while the dusk gathers and thickens around her.

The difference in outlook between Miriam and the Rhys heroine is matched by one just as startling in their creators' techniques. As her later forays into mysticism show, Richardson's mind was no more analytical or theoretical than Jean Rhys's. Dripping feminine sensibility, *Pilgrimage* tries to capture through Miriam the whole of the female consciousness. As often happens in Henry James, the outer world only fosters self-awareness; Miriam reads external reality in order to read herself. She undertakes the task of introspection with the same yeomanlike courage practiced by her spiritual forebear, John Bunyan. This diligence helps make her inner growth an extended act of moral exploration. Thomas F. Staley has shown how Dorothy Richardson's stream of consciousness technique invests Miriam's pilgrimage with discovery and self-understanding: "Events take place, but . . . the importance of them is only in their relationship to Miriam and what she chooses to make of them. The structural unity of the entire novel is dependent, therefore, upon the single character and the journey. . . . Miriam is the center of conscience, the sensitive character through whom all the novel's considerations are filtered."[2]

Jean Rhys aims at other effects. Only in the first part of *Sargasso*, where memories blur and merge, does she use the free association that defines interior monologue. And only in *Midnight* does she abandon plot in favor of the open narrative form so central to *Pilgrimage*.

Though the technique works well, the innovations in *Midnight* do not make Jean Rhys an avant-garde novelist. Extending under 200 pages, her 1939 novel is less than a tenth as long as *Pilgrimage*, and it represents no conscious rejection of traditional narrative norms. Most of her departures from established storytelling traditions stem from the impressionism she learned from Ford Madox Ford in the 1920s. In their individual ways, both she and Richardson created a feminine counterpart to realism, a natural product of the male secularism ruling Victorian England. Richardson abandoned plot, linear chronology, and the omniscient narrator. More aware of the interplay between time and female beauty, Jean Rhys describes women differently, exploring changes in their financial and sexual dependence upon men over the years.

Are her descriptions more readable, more honest? They certainly give a truer picture of the sort of woman that interests Jean Rhys. This woman acts in keeping with motives we can believe in. The same cannot always be said of Miriam. For instance, Miriam's love affair with the Russian Jew Michael Shatov, in *Deadlock*, consists of discussing ideas; at no point does Miriam want to have sex with Shatov, even though she claims to love him. On the other hand, the archetypal Rhys figure does have a sex life. Four of Jean Rhys's five novelistic heroines have been married; two have had children; four have been kept by lovers; all five reject sexual overtures. Neither promiscuous nor prudish, they depict collectively a believable spectrum of sexual response. They also touch us more deeply than the spinsterish Miriam, whose sexual innocence strains belief as much as her sometimes bland, tedious, 2,000-page personal record strains our attention. Only posterity can say if Jean Rhys offers a better description of woman's subservience than Dorothy Richardson. The Rhys heroine differs in both background and outlook from Miriam; she has different goals, and she associates with different kinds of men. But the streets and boardinghouses of our cities contain more women like her than like Miriam. Her case deserves to be stated. That Jean Rhys states it smoothly and insightfully has won her a forum that Richardson still awaits.

### III    *Rooms Noisy and Quiet*

At first look, Jean Rhys stands closer to Doris Lessing than to Dorothy Richardson. Both writers grew up in British colonies where blacks outnumbered the less vibrant whites and where the shaky

myth of white supremacy ruled all interracial relations. Both writers, for the most part, use two geographical settings in their work— Europe and the distant colonies where they grew up. The literary corpus of each features a five-novel sequence held together by the same heroine or a heroine seen at different ages and given different names. The fifth and last novel in each sequence, finally, veers sharply from its four predecessors in both method and purpose. Just as *Sargasso* begins in the 1830s with a brutal fire, *The Four-Gated City* ends in 1997 with the annihilation of mankind. Mental disorder also throngs the two novels. Martha Quest's memory keeps failing her. And at one point she deliberately calls herself by a false name. This alienating behavior raises questions about female identity as large as those inferred by Antoinette's predicament of being caged in a foreign country and known by a name, i.e., Bertha, supplied by a husband she never sees.

More revealing, though, than the similarities between Jean Rhys and Doris Lessing are the glaring differences. Jean Rhys's father was a physician. Lessing grew up on her father's Southern Rhodesia farm, the model, incidentally, for the unproductive, mismanaged farm of *The Grass Is Singing* (1950). Like her autobiographical fictional heroine, Martha Quest, linchpin of the five-part *Children of Violence* (1952–69), she left Africa for England in 1949 at age thirty. Martha has the same moral seriousness as Richardson's Miriam Henderson, and, also like Miriam, she seeks self-identity with great moral energy. Her determination pushes to the fore immediately. The first novel in the sequence, *Martha Quest,* finds her at age fifteen chafing to leave her rural nest. By turns, she moves to the city of Zambesia (i.e., Salisbury), works as a typist in a law office, and marries a civil servant with leftist leanings. Security means more, though, to the suburban Douglas Knowell than do politics. Pressures rising from his conventional job make him ask Martha to stop her radical activities. His demands do not move her. While continuing her leftist work in public, Martha has also taken a lover, who helps her join a secret Communist cell. But all this protest goes for naught. Her rebellion from the suburban traps of marriage and family proves empty. She learns in Southern Rhodesia and later in London that communism promotes neither racial justice nor equality for women. (Leftists in Lessing's *Golden Notebook* also deny the effectiveness of communism.) This failure is contagious. Despite the freedom her second husband, the Communist Anton Hesse, gives her, marriage again stifles Martha. In fact, the party workers in her Communist cell bore

her as much as did the suburban housewives she met in her first marriage. Her fellow leftists keep plaguing her. In England, nobody in her political set knows the difference between a Stalinist and a Trotskyite. The jargon-ridden quarrels she hears undermine radicalism more than they hurt capitalism or the middle class. This quarreling finally drives her from organized politics altogether.

But it does not lower her commitment to personal freedom. Her urge to satisfy the deeper demands of self by helping the common cause still glows brightly in *The Four-Gated City,* where, as a woman in her fifties, Martha serves as secretary-lover to a British social reformer. For purposes of contrast, both Martha and Anna Freeman Wulf seem to outshine the Rhys heroine. Both are active, committed, and attuned to the realities of their consumer-industrialist society. The close detailing of contemporary politics in *Four-Gated City,* borne out in references to the Korean war, McCarthyism, Stalin's death, and the Hungarian revolt, would be out of place in a Jean Rhys novel. One could, in fact, argue that the Rhys heroine's political ignorance reinforces the male dominance that breaks her. Conversely, Lessing's women use politics, writing, and sexual love to make sense of a chaotic, unjust universe. Martha fights for racial equality, stumps for the Communist party, writes with a sense of mission, and uses sexual love as a means of self-fulfillment. Anna Wulf is a novelist, political activist, psychological outpatient, friend, and mother. So busy is she that she has trouble squeezing in everything on her schedule. So multi-faceted is her life that she must devote a separate notebook to each of her activities to bring order to them. Her black notebook discusses her days in Africa; in the red notebook she deals with communism; the yellow notebook gives a fictionalized account of the main tensions in her personal life; by contrast, the blue notebook sets forth her comings and goings with little or no editorializing.

As has been made clear, the Rhys heroine lacks this resolve. She has great tracts of time to fill in. To pass her idle hours, she may count the knobs on a chest of drawers; she sits by her lonely window, half expecting the answer to her problems to come walking down the street; she leaves important matters to chance: "If a taxi hoots before I count three, I'll go to London. If not, I won't" (p. 57), says Julia Martin one morning in Paris. Through Julia and her counterparts, Jean Rhys explodes the myth of the whore with a heart of gold. Problems Julia has. But she does not try to solve them, either privately or collectively. The most she can hope for is to delay the

moment of defeat. Her delaying game can create more pressure than it relieves. Drinking and drifting in and out of relationships are psychological shadow games. Like a prostitute, she gets help from nobody. Men use her sexually and then cast her off; women mock and slander her. Thus she cannot afford the introspection practiced so doggedly by Martha, Anna, and Miriam Henderson of *Pilgrimage*. Self-knowledge means displacement, sorrow, and even danger.

But what of the threats facing Lessing's women? These are many. Their writing does not satisfy them; the causes they work for all go smash; their sexual relationships all frustrate. Perhaps the freedom they pursue does not exist. Perhaps having no ideas about social justice is better than burning energy on lost causes. Lacking ideas certainly beats being idea-ridden. Enmeshed in the cotton wool of ideas, most of Martha Quest's coping mechanisms fail her. In spite of her intellectual honesty, she usually ends up in defeat and isolation. Her high idealism has the same separating effect as the Rhys heroine's amoral passiveness.

Martha's sex life brings more self-avoidance than self-enactment, regardless of her talk about commitment. From the age of fifteen, when she first appears, she takes sex very seriously. In fact, she first materializes in *Martha Quest* reading a study of sexuality by Havelock Ellis. Later in the novel, she strips naked and examines herself in a full-length mirror. Still acting like a D. H. Lawrence heroine, she makes the quick and lyrical surrender of her virginity a moral necessity. This idealism collides with reality. Her first sexual experience repels her, and neither of her two husbands fulfills her sexually. Her love partners keep letting her down, both in and out of marriage. The legacy of Puritanism inherited by her first husband blunts his enjoyment of sex; another man suffers premature orgasm; a third can only become aroused if Martha has just made love to another man. These problems may have been worsened by Martha's practice of intellectualizing sex; all of her men pose mental challenges she seems to invite. Anna Wulf approaches sex even more analytically and self-consciously. The parallel with Martha is clear. If sex made either woman happy, it would not exist as an object of thought. The physical sensation would be enough.

Despite its self-conscious theoretical frame, sex in Doris Lessing's work says no more about the female psyche than in Jean Rhys. Sex provides little beyond physical sensation in either writer. But it is not trivialized. One great merit of Lessing and Jean Rhys is their ability to involve us in the sexual problems of their heroines. In spite of huge

differences in personality and attitude, these heroines face many of the same woes. Martha gives her virginity to one Adolph King, a Jew and therefore an outcast in Southern Rhodesia. Many of her friends and her lovers both in Africa and England are also Jewish. A similar pattern takes shape in Jean Rhys. The husbands of Marya Zelli, Sasha Jansen, and the narrator of "Vienne" are all fidgety, undersized, petty crooks. Regardless of her schooling and humanistic principles, Martha can claim no moral superiority over them. Nor does either of her marriages work better than theirs. Like them, she falls in love with men who will reinforce her feelings of being a victim. Her marriages run the reefs of nervous impatience. She has numerous lovers while married to both Knowell and Hesse. Although she and Anton live together, they have separate commitments. On the other hand, no evidence shows that either Julia Martin or Sasha deceived their husbands during their married years; Jean Rhys's other married novelistic heroines, Marya and Antoinette, only committed adultery after their neglectful husbands stopped paying attention.

But the main issue stemming from a comparison of Jean Rhys and Doris Lessing is not one of self-avoidance or self-confrontation. The main issue goes beyond the heroines of the novels. That women as different as Martha Quest and the Rhys archetype should both suffer defeat and isolation describes modern woman's entrapment. To be just, any public policies enacted in the future will have to include persons as dissimilar as Martha and Sasha Jansen. The one woman deserves attention as much as the other. Every writer perceives the truth in fragments. But these fragments can refract light. They can also cohere in a strong, sweeping vision. For presenting the rich variety of femininity, Jean Rhys and Doris Lessing both deserve to be thanked by future legislators as well as by readers.

## IV    *Envoi*

Neither the complexity and robustness of Martha's mind nor the mystical bent of Miriam Henderson's finds a mirror image in the Rhys archetype. Miriam holds jobs that require skill and training; the secular-humanist Martha commits herself politically and aesthetically. The Rhys heroine doesn't test herself so deeply. The jobs she has held—model, actress, manicurist, chorus girl—require chiefly that she be pretty and smile a good deal, so that men will enjoy looking at her. Some of these men she sleeps with, unlike the chaste Miriam. Yet she brings to sex none of the romantic idealism of

Martha or Bertha Young of "Bliss." She would no more use sexual love to put meaning into her life than she would become a Quaker, like Miriam. Such commitments transcend her powers. When faced by the truth that success as a singer or dancer depends on hours of hard practice, she quits the stage altogether.

But she does manage a life for herself. Miriam's introspectiveness cannot fend off a spiritual crisis; nor does psychotherapy, mother-hood, or politics save Anna Wulf from a nervous breakdown. The policy of asking little from life spares the Rhys heroine these torments. Ignoring stress whenever possible, she fantasizes about buying new clothes and getting a new hairdo when most sorely tried. The political solutions sought in vain by the Communists Anna and Martha she does not waste her time exploring. Yet she survives so marginally that she has few comforts and hopes; as with Mansfield's Miss Brill, a stranger's careless remark can rattle her for hours.

Her discomfort is not a literary vibration. By avoiding a linear narrative structure, Jean Rhys puts her characters' past and present, their memories and feelings, on a par. The characters exist for themselves, not to serve a plot. They are more like somebody you know in real life than like figures from a book. Free of literary flourishes, Jean Rhys's fiction presents women in a moving present where they have no pilgrimages, causes, or close relationships from which to take meaning. They are alone, and in their aloneness they reveal themselves to us with appalling clarity. Only a writer of rare gifts can create characters who, by doing nothing, can appall us and make us wince. Chekhov is one such writer. Jean Rhys is another.

# Notes and References

The dates, titles, and pagination referred to in the text correspond with one exception to the editions of Jean Rhys's books published by Andre Deutsch in London. The exception: for stories from *The Left Bank* not included in *Tigers Are Better-looking*, I have used the pagination from the 1927 London (Jonathan Cape) edition.

### Chapter One

1. Paul Theroux, "Novels," *Book World*, 13 February 1972, p. 6; Francis Wyndham, "A Stark Reserve," *Sunday Times*, 17 December 1967, p. 26; Shirley Hazzard, "Marya knew her fate and couldn't avoid it," *New York Times Book Review*, 11 April 1971, p. 6.

2. Pierre Leyris, *La Nouvelle Revue Française*, 202 (October 1969): 481–507, esp. 481–83.

3. Stella Bowen, *Drawn from Life: Reminiscences* (London: Collins, 1940), p. 166.

4. Hannah Carter, "Fated to Be Sad: Jean Rhys Talks to Hannah Carter," *Guardian*, 8 August 1968, p. 5.

5. Ibid.

6. Rosalind Miles, *The Fiction of Sex: Themes and Functions of Sex Differences in the Modern Novel* (London, 1974), p. 99.

7. A. Alvarez, "The Best English Novelist Alive," *New York Times Book Review*, 17 March 1974, p. 7.

8. Ibid; Robert Nye, "What Man Has Made of Woman," *Guardian*, 15 May 1969, p. 9; see also Ralph Tyler, "Luckless Heroines, Swinish Men," *Atlantic*, January 1975, p. 82.

9. Hazzard, p. 6.

10. Elgin W. Mellown, "Character and Themes in the Novels of Jean Rhys," *Contemporary Literature*, 13 (Autumn 1972): 463.

11. Ibid.

12. Alvarez, p. 7; V. S. Naipaul, "Without a Dog's Chance," *New York Review of Books*, 18 May 1972, p. 29.

13. Miles, p. 98.

14. Howard Moss, "Going to Pieces," *New Yorker*, 16 December 1974, p. 161.

15. Mellown, p. 464.

16. Mary Cantwell, "A Conversation with Jean Rhys," *Mademoiselle*, October 1974, p. 210.

17. Alvarez, p. 7; John Hall, "Jean Rhys," *Guardian*, 10 January 1972, p. 8.

18. Mellown, pp. 463–64.

19. Cantwell, p. 208; Miles, p. 104; Judith Thurman, "The Mistress and the Mask: Jean Rhys's Fiction," *Ms.*, January 1976, p. 52.

20. Ford Madox Ford, "Rive Gauche," in Jean Rhys, *The Left Bank and Other Stories* (London, 1927), p. 24.

21. Mellown, p. 465.

22. Thurman, p. 50.

23. Jean Rhys, "Whatever Became of Old Mrs. Pearce?" *Times*, 21 May 1975, p. 16.

24. Thurman, p. 81.

### Chapter Two

1. "Latest Works of Fiction," *New York Times Book Review*, 11 December 1927, p. 28.

2. Miles, p. 97.

3. Moss, p. 166.

4. "Latest Works of Fiction," pp. 28, 30.

5. "Jean Rhys," *Current Biography 1972* (New York, 1972), p. 365; Hall, p. 8.

6. Tyler, p. 82.

7. Mellown explains (p. 461n) that Ford published a poem, "Petronella at Sea," in 1927 which pays tribute to an old affair.

8. Thurman, p. 51.

9. Moss, p. 166.

10. Jean Rhys, "I Spy a Stranger," *Art and Literature*, 8 (Spring 1966): 41; Marcelle Bernstein, "The Inscrutable Miss Jean Rhys," *Observer Magazine* (London), 1 June 1969, p. 42.

11. Rhys, "I Spy a Stranger," p. 43.

12. Ibid., p. 44.

13. Ibid., p. 45.

14. Ibid., p. 50.

15. Ibid., p. 46.

16. Ibid., p. 50.

17. Ibid., p. 51.

18. Ibid., p. 52.

19. Ibid.

20. Jean Rhys, "Temps Perdi," *Art and Literature*, 12 (Spring 1967): 122; cf. Jean Rhys, "Vienne," in *Tigers Are Better-looking* (London, 1968), p. 204.

21. Rhys, "Temps Perdi," p. 121.

22. Ibid., p. 127.

23. Ibid., p. 132.
24. Ibid., p. 137ff.
25. Jean Rhys, "Sleep It Off Lady," *New Review*, 1 (June 1974): 45.
26. Ibid.
27. Ibid.
28. Ibid., p. 49.
29. Ibid., p. 45.

### Chapter Three

1. Mellown, p. 468.
2. Ibid., p. 463.
3. Hazzard, p. 6.
4. Miles, p. 98.
5. Moss, p. 161.
6. Alvarez, p. 7.
7. Ford Madox Ford, *The Good Soldier: A Tale of Passion* (New York, 1951), p. 25.
8. [Ford Madox Ford,] *Letters of Ford Madox Ford*, ed. Richard M. Ludwig (Princeton, N.J., 1965), p. 178n.
9. Arthur Mizener, *The Saddest Story: A Biography of Ford Madox Ford* (New York and Cleveland, 1971), p. 178; see also pp. 345–50.
10. Thurman, p. 52.

### Chapter Four

1. Francis Wyndham, "Introduction," Jean Rhys, *Wide Sargasso Sea* (London, 1966), p. 7.
2. Thurman, p. 52.
3. Naipaul, p. 30.
4. Ibid.
5. Thurman, p. 51.
6. Ibid.
7. Mellown, p. 470.
8. In "Jean Rhys," *Current Biography*, p. 364.
9. Naipaul, p. 30.

### Chapter Five

1. In a letter to the present writer, 12 July 1974, Miss Rhys named *Voyage in the Dark* her favorite novel in the canon.
2. Martin Shuttleworth, "Mrs. Micawber," *Punch*, 16 August 1967, p. 253.
3. Bernstein, p. 40.
4. "Jean Rhys," *Current Biography*, p. 365.

5. Francis Hope, "Women Beware Everyone," *Observer Review*, 11 June 1967, p. 24.
6. Ibid.
7. Alvarez, p. 7.
8. Bernstein, p. 49.

## Chapter Six

1. Tyler, p. 88.
2. Sara Blackburn, "Novels: Women's Lot," *Book World*, 5 April 1970 p. 6.
3. Hall, p. 8.
4. Naipaul, p. 30.
5. Wyndham, p. 10.
6. Ibid.
7. Mellown, p. 467.
8. Thurman, p. 52.
9. Alvarez, p. 7.
10. Ibid.
11. Thurman, p. 81.
12. Hope, p. 24.
13. Mellown, pp. 467, 462.
14. Bernstein, p. 49; Cantwell, p. 208.
15. Mellown, p. 470.

## Chapter Seven

1. Hall, p. 8.
2. Walter Allen, "Bertha the Doomed," *New York Times Book Review*, 18 June 1967, p. 5.
3. Thurman, p. 81.
4. Bernstein, p. 42.
5. Wyndham, p. 12.
6. Alvarez, p. 7.
7. Bernstein, p. 42.
8. Charlotte Brontë, *Jane Eyre* (Boston, 1959), p. 289.
9. Barbara Hardy, *Jane Eyre (Charlotte Brontë)* (New York, n.d.), p. 28.
10. Brontë, p. 278.
11. Colin MacInnes, "Nightmare in Paradise," *Observer Weekend Review*, 30 October 1966, p. 28.
12. Brontë, pp. 277, 285, 290, 291, 294–95, 300.
13. Hardy, p. 45.
14. Brontë, p. 136.
15. Ibid., p. 409.
16. John and Mildred Teal, *The Sargasso Sea*, illustrated by Leslie Morrill (Boston, 1975), p. 10.

17. Donn Byrne, "Sargasso Sea," in *Sargasso Sea and Other Stories* (London, n.d.), p. 1.
18. Moss, p. 165.
19. Mellown, p. 471.
20. Allen, p. 5.

## Chapter Eight

1. Katherine Mansfield, *Stories by Katherine Mansfield* (New York, 1956), p. 167.
2. Thomas F. Staley, *Dorothy Richardson* (Boston, 1976), p. 44.

# Selected Bibliography

PRIMARY SOURCES

1. Novels

*Postures*. London: Chatto and Windus, 1928; American title, *Quartet*. New
   York: Simon and Schuster, 1929. Rpt. London: Andre Deutsch, 1969,
   as *Quartet*.
*After Leaving Mr. Mackenzie*. London: Jonathan Cape, 1931; New York:
   Knopf, 1931. Rpt. London: Andre Deutsch, 1969.
*Voyage in the Dark*. London: Constable, 1934; New York: William Morrow,
   1935. Rpt. London: Andre Deutsch, 1967.
*Good Morning, Midnight*. London: Constable, 1939; New York: Harper &
   Row, c. 1967. Rpt. London: Andre Deutsch, 1967.
*Wide Sargasso Sea*. London: Andre Deutsch, 1966; New York: Harper &
   Row, 1967.

2. Short Stories

*The Left Bank and Other Stories*. Preface by Ford Madox Ford. London:
   Jonathan Cape, 1927.
*Tigers Are Better-looking, with a selection from The Left Bank*. London:
   Andre Deutsch, 1968; New York: Harper & Row, 1974.
*Sleep It Off Lady*. London: Andre Deutsch, 1976; New York: Harper & Row,
   1976.

SECONDARY SOURCES

ALVAREZ, A. "The Best English Novelist Alive," *New York Times Book
   Review*, 17 March 1974, p. 7. Surveys Jean Rhys's themes and praises
   them for "emotional penetration . . . formal artistry" and "unemphatic,
   unblinking truthfulness."
BERNSTEIN, MARCELLE. "The Inscrutable Miss Jean Rhys," *London Observer Magazine*, 1 June 1969, pp. 40–42, 49–50. Discusses the impact
   of real-life forces on the writer's art.
CANTWELL, MARY. "A Conversation with Jean Rhys," *Mademoiselle*,
   October 1974, pp. 169, 171, 206, 208, 210, 213. A popular survey of the
   writer's career.

CARTER, HANNAH. "Fated to be Sad: Jean Rhys Talks to Hannah Carter," *Guardian*, 8 August 1968, p. 5. The writer discusses some of the ideas underlying her work.

HALL, JOHN, "Jean Rhys," *Guardian*, 10 January 1972, p. 8. Gives a sketch of the writer's career, mostly biographical.

"Jean Rhys," *Current Biography*. New York: H. W. Wilson, 1972, pp. 364–67. Summarizes the life and literary career of the writer.

MELLOWN, ELGIN W. "Character and Themes in the Novels of Jean Rhys," *Contemporary Literature* 13 (Autumn 1972): 458–75. Gives an excellent systematic introduction to the writer's work with perceptive readings of individual novels.

MILES, ROSALIND. *The Fiction of Sex: Themes and Functions of Sex Difference in the Modern Novel*. London: Vision, 1974, esp. pp. 96–106. Explains the writer as the enemy of the established middle-class male sexist society; supplies a reading of "I Spy a Stranger" (1966).

NAIPAUL, V. S. "Without a Dog's Chance," *New York Review of Books*, 18 May 1972, pp. 29–31. Reviews *After Leaving Mr. Mackenzie* and discusses the theme of exile in the writer's work in general.

THURMAN, JUDITH. "The Mistress and the Mask: Jean Rhys's Fiction," *Ms.*, January 1976, pp. 50–53, 81. Discusses the writer's portrayal of women as underdogs.

"The Times Diary," [London] *Times*, 14 December 1967, p. 10. Announces the writer's winning of the W. H. Smith Literary Award for 1967.

TURNER, ALICE K. "Jean Rhys Rediscovered: How It Happened," *Publishers Weekly*, 1 July 1974, pp. 56, 58. Discusses the impact of the Jean Rhys revival on the American book industry.

# Index

Agee, James, *A Death in the Family*, 254
Allen, Walter, on *Sargasso*, 137, 158
Alvarez, A., 16, 19, 21, 26; on *Midnight*, 123; on *Sargasso*, 138
Austen, Jane, 31, 159

Baudelaire, Charles, 30
Bernstein, Marcelle, on the Rhys heroine, 103; on *Midnight*, 135
Blackburn, Sara, on *Midnight*, 121
Bowen, Elizabeth, 31
Bowen, Stella, 79-81; on Rhys's personal character, 17
Brecht, Bertolt, 37
Brontë, Charlotte, *Jane Eyre*, 17, 27, 137, 142-45, 149, 151-57
Bunyan, John, 169
Byrne, Donn, "Sargasso Sea," 156

Cantwell, Mary, 135
Carter, Hannah, interview with Rhys, 18
Chekhov, Anton, 44, 53, 163, 175; *The Cherry Orchard*, 138

Dickinson, Emily, 121
Durrell, Lawrence, *The Alexandria Quartet*, 67; *Justine*, 67

Eliot, T. S., 30
Ellis, Havelock, 173
*Eumenides, The* (Aeschylus), 134

Ford, Ford Madox, 17, 30, 43, 80, 81, 170; *The Good Soldier*, 79; *Provence*, 80; on *The Left Bank*, 29, 33, 34
Ford, Stella, see Stella Bowen
Forster, E. M., 24, 159; *Howards End*, 84

Greene, Graham, 100

Hall, John, 26, 41, 42; on *Midnight*, 121

Hamer, Max, 17
Hardy, Barbara, on *Jane Eyre*, 154
Hazzard, Shirley, 15, 16, 19
Hemingway, Ernest, 33, 94
Hope, Francis, on *Midnight*, 132; on *Voyage*, 109, 111

Ibsen, Henrik, *A Doll's House*, 90

James, Henry, 19, 31, 80, 89, 169
Joyce, James, 19, 100; *Ulysses*, 41, 93, 134
"Just One More Chance" (popular song), 51

Kafka, Franz, 161
Kaplan, Sydney Janet, *Feminine Consciousness in the Modern British Novel*, 15
Kipling, Rudyard, *Kim*, 45

Langlet, Jean, 16
Lawrence, D. H., 173; contrasted with Rhys, 29
Lessing, Doris, 25, 160, 170, 174; *Children of Violence*, 161, 171; *The Four-Gated City*, 171, 172; *The Grass is Singing*, 171; *The Golden Notebook*, 161, 171; *Martha Quest*, 171

MacInnes, Colin, on *Sargasso*, 152-53
Mansfield, Katherine, 160; "At the Bay," 165, 166; "Bliss," 163-65, 175; "The Daughters of the Late Colonel," 164, 166; "The Fly," 165; "The Garden Party," 167; "Germans at Meat," 166; "In a German Pension," 32; "Je ne parle pas français," 161-62, 167; "The Little Governess," 164, 166; "Miss Brill," 164, 166; "Ole Underwood," 163; "Pictures," 166; "Prelude," 163-